C0-AWX-262

DISCARDED

Towards a Labour Market in China

Studies on Contemporary China

The Contemporary China Institute at the School of Oriental and African Studies (University of London) has, since its establishment in 1968, been an international centre for research and publications on China. *Studies on Contemporary China*, which is edited at the Institute, seeks to maintain and extend that tradition by making available the best work of scholars and China specialists throughout the world. It embraces a wide variety of subjects relating to Nationalist and Communist China, including social, political, and economic change, intellectual and cultural developments, foreign relations, and national security.

Series Editor

Dr Frank Dikötter, Director of the Contemporary China Institute

Editorial Advisory Board

Dr Robert F. Ash

Professor Hugh D. R. Baker

Professor Elisabeth J. Croll

Dr Richard Louis Edmonds

Mr Brain G. Hook

Professor Christopher B. Howe

Professor Bonnie S. McDougall

Professor David Shambaugh

Dr Julia C. Strauss

Dr Jonathan Unger

Professor Lynn T. White III

Towards a Labour Market in China

JOHN KNIGHT
and
LINA SONG

OXFORD
UNIVERSITY PRESS

OXFORD
UNIVERSITY PRESS

Great Clarendon Street, Oxford OX2 6DP

Oxford University Press is a department of the University of Oxford.
It furthers the University's objective of excellence in research, scholarship,
and education by publishing worldwide in

Oxford New York

Auckland Cape Town Dar es Salaam Hong Kong Karachi
Kuala Lumpur Madrid Melbourne Mexico City Nairobi
New Delhi Shanghai Taipei Toronto

With offices in

Argentina Austria Brazil Chile Czech Republic France Greece
Guatemala Hungary Italy Japan South Korea Poland Portugal
Singapore Switzerland Thailand Turkey Ukraine Vietnam

Published in the United States
by Oxford University Press Inc., New York

© J. Knight and L. Song, 2005

The moral rights of the authors have been asserted

Database right Oxford University Press (maker)

First published 2005

All rights reserved. No part of this publication may be reproduced,
stored in a retrieval system, or transmitted, in any form or by any means,
without the prior permission in writing of Oxford University Press,
or as expressly permitted by law, or under terms agreed with the appropriate
reprographics rights organization. Enquiries concerning reproduction
outside the scope of the above should be sent to the Rights Department,
Oxford University Press, at the address above

You must not circulate this book in any other binding or cover
and you must impose the same condition on any acquirer

British Library Cataloguing in Publication Data

Data available

Library of Congress Cataloging in Publication Data

Data available

ISBN 0-19-924527-4 9780 1992 452 77

3 5 7 9 10 8 6 4 2

Typeset by Newgen Imaging Systems (P) Ltd., Chennai, India
Printed in Great Britain
on acid-free paper by
Biddles Ltd., King's Lynn, Norfolk

Preface

Our research interest in the subject of this book began in the early 1990s, when—in many respects—China did not possess a labour market. The old administered labour system remained largely intact in urban China, and restrictions on labour remained pervasive in rural China. Over the last twelve years we have witnessed, and studied, China's movement towards the creation of a labour market. We have published or completed more than twelve research papers, written jointly or separately. As we explain in the book, China still does not possess a well-functioning labour market—that is for the future. Nevertheless, the changes which have already taken place present us with the opportunity to tell a fascinating story. We decided to collect our research studies together, to join them up and to generalize from them. That is how *Towards a Labour Market in China* was born.

Our motives for studying this subject are twofold. First, it is a phenomenon of utmost importance. With its labour force of 700 million, China is a labour-surplus economy *par excellence*. This highlights the questions: To ensure the efficient and equitable use of that labour, how should a society and economy be organized; in particular, what role should a labour market play? The remarkable transformation and growth of the Chinese economy—involving the development of many product and factor markets and the greatest migration in human history—has necessitated vast and rapid change in the allocation, the use, and the remuneration of labour. The accompanying labour market reforms have affected the quality of life of hundreds of millions of people.

Secondly, the subject presents an intellectual challenge which has not yet been comprehensively addressed. The growing availability of microeconomic household and worker sample surveys in China—some of which we were not only able to analyse but also to design with hypotheses in mind—offered the exhilaration of exploring virgin territory. Economists very rarely have the opportunity to examine the process by which a poor country moves step-by-step along the path of replacing a rigid labour system with a labour market. Such a study raises many issues of interest not only to labour economists but also to development economists and transition economists. We attempt to place the Chinese case within the broad theoretical framework needed to examine the efficiency and equity of the operation of the labour market. We hope that specialists in the Chinese economy will find much that is new to them but we are primarily writing for a broader readership of economists interested in labour, development, or transition issues.

Our general approach is in line with the detailed empirical methodology, involving specific hypothesis testing, that is conventional in economic research today. We write a series of chapters, each chapter examining particular questions and sufficiently self-contained to be read on its own. A number of the chapters first appeared—in a different, usually narrower, form—as papers in refereed journals. However, we attempt to draw out the common themes—encapsulated in the phrase 'the imperfect labour market'—throughout, but particularly in the concluding chapter. Our hope is that the whole adds up to more than the sum of the parts.

Since economic reform commenced, the amount of rigorous economic analysis of the Chinese labour market has grown exponentially, from small beginnings. We do not attempt to provide a survey of the research findings of other scholars. Rather, we make our own contribution to the literature. We choose to draw on other research only where it is directly relevant—in a distinctive or complementary way—to our arguments.

The research was made possible by the financial support of the Leverhulme Trust, the UK Economic and Social Research Council, the UK Department for International Development, the British Council, and the Ford Foundation. The Leverhulme Trust provided a grant (reference number F519/C) for our research project entitled 'Towards a labour market in China'. The ESRC funded our project 'Income distribution and the labour market in China' (reference number R000236846), and DFID our project 'The new urban poverty in China: efficiency versus equity?' (reference number 7526). The British Council arranged our 'Academic Link' with the Ministry of Labour in China, and supported our research collaboration with the ministry. The Ford Foundation in Beijing funded the two labour force surveys which were the subject of that collaboration (linking into the Leverhulme-funded research), as well as the surveys which formed the basis of the ESRC- and DFID-funded research projects. We are grateful to these bodies for the confidence they showed in us.

Our many contacts in China played a vital role in the research. We owe a great deal to our friend and collaborator, Li Shi, who contributed much to the success of the project by helping to plan and conduct the surveys, and in their analysis during several visits to Oxford. The Institute of Economics of the Chinese Academy of Social Sciences provided support and cooperation, in particular by enabling Zhao Renwei and Li Shi to visit Oxford and collaborate with us. We are extremely grateful to the officials and researchers in the Ministry of Labour and Social Security with whom we collaborated, including Zhang Xiaojian (now Vice Minister), Liu Danhua, Chai Haishan, Jia Huaibin, Mo Rong, and Huang Huabo. We were fortunate to be invited to several international conferences on related topics, mainly in China but also elsewhere, which enabled us to present our ideas and findings to assembled experts and receive feedback.

We wish to thank a number of our co-authors for allowing us to make use of research reported in our joint papers with them. These include Li Shi (Chapters 4, 7, 9), Zhao Renwei (Chapter 4), Simon Appleton and Qingie Xia (Chapter 6), Linda Yueh (Chapters 7, 10), Xue Jinjun (Chapter 2), and Jia Huaibin (Chapter 5). In no case is this joint work simply reproduced, and in each case further acknowledgement is made at the relevant point in the text. Linda Yueh (Oxford) and Qingjie Xia (Nottingham) also provided excellent research support.

Thanks are due to the editors and copyright holders of the following journals and books for permission to use material which we, alone or with co-authors, first published in them: *China Economic Review* © Elsevier Science Inc., *Economics of Transition* © The European Bank for Reconstruction and Development, *Journal of Chinese Economic and Business Studies* © The Chinese Economic Association-UK, *Journal of Comparative Economics* © Association of Comparative Economic Studies, *Journal of Development Studies* © Frank Cass and Co. Ltd., *Oxford Development Studies* © International Development Centre, Oxford, and Carl Riskin, Zhao Renwei, and Li Shi (eds), *China's Retreat from Equality. Income Distribution and Economic Transition* © Carl Riskin. Specific references are given in each chapter that contains such material.

We are grateful to the small but global and growing band of researchers on the Chinese labour market with whom we have had helpful discussions or from whom we have received comments. In addition to those mentioned above, there are our colleagues on the various international research projects to which our research has been affiliated (including Björn Gustafsson, Azizur Khan, Xin Meng, Carl Riskin, and Hiroshi Sato) and others with whom we share interests (including Bai Nansheng, Arne Bigsten, Loren Brandt, Cai Fang, Sarah Cook, Dong Xiaoyuan, Belton Fleisher, John Giles, Ted Groves, Denise Hare, the late D. Gale Johnson, Luo Xiaopeng, Margaret Maurer-Fazio, Katsuji Nakagane, Barry Naughton, Albert Park, Tom Rawski, Scott Rozelle, Terry Sicular, Wei Zhong, Zhao Yaohui, Yao Yang, Yue Ximing, and Zhou Qiren). At the Department of Economics (formerly the Institute of Economics and Statistics) in the University of Oxford, which provided outstanding support, we wish to thank Gillian Coates, who administered our grants, Giuseppe Mazzarino for his computing advice, and Ann Gibson for all her secretarial support. Laura Wu created the index.

Contents

List of Figures

List of Tables

PART I

INTRODUCTION

1

Setting the Stage

For many years, under the planned economy, China had no labour market. Instead, from the 1950s to the 1980s, it had a system of wage administration and labour allocation. This system gave the state—essentially the Chinese Communist Party (CCP)—great powers to pursue its various objectives, including egalitarianism and party control.

With the death of Mao the new Chinese leadership changed objectives in favour of economic improvement. A process of economic reform began, from the late 1970s in rural areas and from the mid-1980s in urban areas. Among the reforms was a move towards the creation of a labour market in China—slow and faltering at first but quickening and becoming cumulative in recent years. Even today, however, China does not possess a free labour market—one which involves market responses to supply and demand, potential for labour mobility, and economic incentives for efficiency—of the sort that characterizes most other developing countries. It is a market in transition, a market in formation. In this book we shall explore the move towards a labour market in China—what came before it, where it has got to, and how it might, and should, develop.

The legacy of central planning under old-style communism has inevitably moulded the nature of the new labour market. Crucial to its evolution is the rural–urban divide, an institutionally imposed 'invisible Great Wall'. This phenomenon was the subject of our previous book *The Rural–Urban Divide. Economic Disparities and Interactions in China* (Knight and Song 1999). A powerful urban bias in state institutions and government policies shielded urban people from the labour market competition of rural people, and for the most part continues to do so.

In this and other ways the Chinese urban labour market remains segmented. Perhaps the main division now is between those urban workers—largely in the state sector—who continue to enjoy government favours, on the one hand, and rural–urban migrants and urban short-term contract and private-sector workers, on the other. The former group has disproportionate political power, albeit latent. The rapid growth in importance of the latter group—although relatively powerless—has enlarged the scope of the labour market and put competitive pressure on the labour system as a whole. We shall explore the various institutional and political constraints on the operation of the labour market, and their evolution over time.

Although the gradualism of China's economic reforms—'crossing the river by feeling the stones'—has been contrasted with the 'big bang' approach of some former socialist countries, the pace of reform is rapid, and the river we cross today is not the one we waded in yesterday. This presents a challenge to economists, who are better equipped to analyse marginal and specific changes than dramatic evolution in which many variables are changing simultaneously in non-marginal ways. As we shall see, labour market reform is closely interrelated with other economic reforms, with causation running in both directions. For instance, increased product and capital market competition creates pressures for the reform of the labour market, and increased labour market competition requires the reform of housing and pensions. Reform of the labour market cannot be understood in isolation from the changing economy and economic reform in general. We shall adopt a systemic approach.

Much of the book takes the form of positive analysis—explaining what has happened, for what reasons, and with what consequences. Underlying this descriptive and explanatory approach, however, are issues which require ethical judgements. For instance, there are these positive questions: Have the labour market reforms improved incentives for both workers and employers to use labour resources more productively; and have they increased income inequalities? Behind them lies the normative question: What labour market policies should be pursued in order to achieve the right balance between efficiency and equity objectives? We hope that the book will be helpful to policy-makers without doing their job for them.

1.2 THEORETICAL FRAMEWORK

A labour market is a mechanism for matching the supply of and the demand for the factor of production labour by means of contracts between buyers and sellers of labour (Horton, Kanbur, and Mazumdar 1994: 2). There are many different types of labour, differentiated by location, skill, and other characteristics, and thus there are many different labour markets. These labour markets are interdependent because the conditions in one influence the workings of another. This system of interlinked labour markets in a country can be called *the* labour market.

By what criteria can it be judged whether a country's labour market is 'working well'? Economists normally appeal to the tenets of welfare economics. In theory, under the assumptions of private property, full information, perfect competition in product and factor markets, and in the absence of externalities, market clearing would allocate labour efficiently both in a static and in a dynamic sense. On the demand side of the labour market, with the marginal product of labour the same in all activities and equal to the wage, it would be impossible to increase current production by reallocating labour among locations, sectors, employers, and occupations. On the supply-side of the labour market, with the marginal rate of substitution between work and leisure equal to the wage and the same for all identical workers, it would be impossible to increase economic welfare by varying employment. Again on the supply side, the competitive market equilibrium could provide the right incentives for workers to apply effort, for mobility among locations, sectors, employers, and occupations, and for investment in human capital—in each case the marginal social benefit would equal the marginal social cost.

The stringent conditions required for the achievement of economic efficiency are never met in real economies. In practice many product and factor markets are characterized by market imperfections, there are informational imperfections and asymmetries, and there are market externalities. In the labour market, for instance, the wage may itself determine labour productivity, or the existence of firm-specific skills may generate negative externalities. These complications—incorporated in the 'efficiency–wage' and 'labour turnover' wage theories, respectively—provide reasons why a wage set at the competitive level can give rise to economic inefficiency.

Despite these reservations, the practical test that is often applied in evaluating labour market performance is coloured by the competitive labour market model, that is, are wages and employment sufficiently flexible to ensure that the supply of and demand for labour are equated in a timely way? A move towards labour market equilibrium is commonly assumed to improve efficiency. However, even in assessing a move towards greater competition we should be mindful of the problems associated with 'the theory of the second best'. We should guard against presuming too readily that a more competitive labour market is a more efficient one.

In any case, the labour market in any actual economy is likely to diverge far from the free market model. The efficiency–wage and labour turnover theories provide explanations of why—even in economies characterized by competition and profit-maximization—the wage can exceed the competitive level. It is common to find long-term employment relationships that are insensitive to the forces of labour supply and demand. They are sometimes embodied in 'internal labour markets', characterized by administrative wage determination within the firm, seniority wage payments, security of employment, promotion from within, and little reference to external labour markets (Doeringer and Piore 1971). Institutional arrangements of this sort can be efficient in that they help to promote human capital formation and retention and to maintain employee cooperation when information is imperfect, there is a danger of moral hazard, and firm-specific skills are important. The United States is sometimes regarded as having a competitive labour market, to be contrasted with the 'Eurosclerosis' of western European labour markets and the internal labour markets of Japan. However, even parts of the US labour market are characterized by long tenures and negotiated wages.

The labour market is by nature a very special kind of market which is likely to contain social as well as economic aspects (Hicks 1963: 317; Solow 1990: ch. 1, p. 43). Labour markets are institutions which evolve to produce rules and customs that provide the incentives and information required for their smooth operation (McMillan 1995). Labour market actors are embodied in systems of personal relations and social networks that help to generate information, trust, and cooperation (Granovetter 1985). Moreover, workers are not just a factor of production: They are also people, concerned about their welfare, and citizens, whose government is concerned about their welfare. Workers' and citizens' desires for, and pursuit of, such objectives as fairness, security, solidarity, and autonomy, and their acceptance of social norms, are liable to mould the market and its institutions. For instance, if a free market generates great wage inequality among workers, we may expect workers, or trade unions, or government, to press for a non-market outcome involving less inequality; or the desire for job security may lead to forms of employment protection. These social aspects are another source of departure from continuous market clearing of labour supply and demand. For instance, even in the relatively competitive labour market of the United States, forms of labour market discrimination are to be found despite the theoretical prediction that they would be competed away in long-run equilibrium.

The transition from an administered labour system to a competitive labour market should have the following benefits. Market prices should provide better signals for the efficient allocation of labour. For instance, the likely rise in the reward to education should encourage workers to invest in education and employers to economize in their use of educated labour. Wage differences across regions, industries, or employers should induce movement of labour so as to equate marginal products. Rewards for effort should improve incentives for effort. Relaxation of the constraints on workers—such as permitting occupational and geographical choice—should enable them to pursue their own best interests, and—through the 'invisible hand' of the market—should be beneficial to society.

However, not all the changes involved in the transition need be individually or socially beneficial. The marketization of labour can have negative as well as positive effects. Urban workers in China have enjoyed guaranteed employment and income security. Labour market reform involves unemployment—at least of a transitional nature—and increased personal insecurity. It also has potentially powerful distributional consequences, from which there are losers as well as gainers. Those with human capital or enterprise stand to gain, and those thrown into competition with the underemployed peasantry stand to lose. The degree of inequality of labour income is likely to rise sharply.

If in some respects it is inappropriate to assess the Chinese labour market against the competitive ideal, it might instead be assessed against the performance of comparable economies. One potentially helpful comparison is with other transition economies. They differ from China in that there is generally a clear starting point for the transition, associated with sharp political change, and an initial shock to the labour market. In the countries of east and central Europe (ECE), the provision of non-employment benefits meant that the shock took the form of a fall in employment rather than a fall in real wages, whereas in the countries of the former Soviet Union (FSU), the protection of employment meant that real wages collapsed (Boeri and Terrell 2002; Svejnar 2002).

Unemployment, unknown before transition, emerged rapidly in ECE, but social safety nets prevented income inequality from rising dramatically. In FSU, by contrast, the divergence of wages meant that the Gini coefficient increased by some 20 percentage points over a decade. The Russian case was said to resemble the neoclassical model, and to provide an extreme example of a flexible labour market (Layard and Richter 1995). Yet the protection of employment in the state sector and the low wages in the private sector retarded labour reallocation—dependent, as it was, on voluntary quits. The greater influence of the market generally raised the returns to a year of education in the transition economies—from the range 2–5 per cent before transition to 5–9 per cent in the mid-1990s. However, the returns to employment experience—well rewarded under Communism—actually declined in most transition economies as market forces took hold (Boeri and Terrell 2002: 61–2).

A further potentially helpful comparison is with similar developing countries. The more a labour market is created and developed, the more do the remaining problems, and the policy issues, resemble those faced by other countries at a similar level of development (Gelb 1999). Labour market imperfections can be large in developing countries, often taking the forms of segmentation and discrimination among workers. Rural–urban migration is an important phenomenon, and one which can give rise to serious economic and social problems. A large disparity between the urban formal sector wage and the supply price of rural labour gives rise to an inflow of migrants from the countryside to the cities. Given wage rigidity in the urban formal sector, the equilibrating device is not the wage but the level of urban unemployment or informal sector employment (Harris and Todaro 1970). Depending on their economic institutions, many developing countries have high urban unemployment or huge urban informal sectors which act as pools to absorb the inflow of migrants. In these various respects the Chinese labour market is best assessed by comparison with economies at a similar level of development.

The so-called 'Lewis model' of economic development (Lewis 1954) envisages a transfer of labour from the agricultural (or rural) sector to the industrial (or urban) sector as the economy industrializes and the urban sector expands. The real wage is assumed to be determined by market forces. It is governed by the rural supply price and is held constant by an unlimited supply of labour from the rural sector. Only if and when rural labour becomes scarce does the rural supply price, and hence the urban real wage, begin to rise. This is brought about by an improvement in agriculture's terms of trade as industry expands, and by an improvement in agriculture's land/labour ratio as labour migrates—both raising the marginal product of labour on the land. In practice, however, in many developing countries the growth of the labour force has exceeded the growth of urban employment, and the land/labour ratio in peasant agriculture has worsened: A market-determined real wage would decline. China's labour market performance needs to be assessed—both absolutely and comparatively—against the backdrop of the Lewis model.

1.3 SOURCES OF EVIDENCE

Until the mid-1980s there was very little hard evidence available on the Chinese labour market. The statistical situation has improved considerably over the period of economic reform. Fairly reliable aggregate data on labour, employment, unemployment, and wages have become available from such official sources as the *Census of Population*, the *China Statistical Yearbook*, and the *China Labour Statistical Yearbook*. The official national household survey has been published on an annual basis over many years but only at a fairly aggregative level and without emphasis on labour issues. We shall draw on these official sources at various points in order to obtain a national picture, especially of trends over time.

We ourselves have participated in survey-based research, involving at least five data sets, which will be used intensively in this book. These are the 1988 and 1995 national household surveys of the Institute of Economics, Chinese Academy of Social Sciences (IE, CASS), the 1994 national rural labour force survey of the Ministry of Labour, the 1995 four-city survey of rural migrants employed in urban enterprises, again conducted by the Ministry of Labour, and the 1999 urban household survey of the IE, CASS. Indeed, apart from the 1988 survey, we were able to participate in the design of each survey and its questionnaires, bearing research issues and hypotheses in mind. We refer to the surveys as IE, CASS 1988; IE, CASS 1995; MOL 1994; MOL 1995; and IE, CASS 1999, respectively. Table 1.1 presents their salient features. Consider each in turn.

The IE, CASS 1988 survey was the first nationally representative household survey to be available at the microeconomic (household and individual) level. Its main research results were published in the volume edited by Griffin and Zhao (1993), the Annex to which describes the survey. Separate rural and urban samples were drawn, respectively covering twenty-eight and ten of China's

TABLE 1.1 *The sample surveys*

	IE, CASS 1988		IE, CASS 1995		IE, CASS 1999	MOL 1994	MOL 1995
	Urban	Rural	Urban	Rural	Urban	Rural	Urban
Number of provinces	10	28	11	19	6	8	4
Number of cities	60	n.a.	68	n.a.	13	n.a.	4
Number of counties	n.a.	112	n.a.	103	n.a.	24	n.a.
Number of households	9,000	10,300	7,000	8,000	4,500	4,000	n.a.
Number of persons	31,800	51,400	21,700	34,700	13,600	16,600	n.a.
Number of workers	18,100	30,700	12,400	21,000	8,600	10,400	2,900

n.a. = not applicable.

thirty-one provinces. Each survey used a scientifically selected subsample of the sample used by the State Statistical Bureau (as it was then known) for its (annual) household income and expenditure survey in 1988. However, the questionnaires were designed to investigate income distribution in China with research hypotheses in mind, and were more detailed than the official ones, so permitting the analysis of causes and consequences.

The IE, CASS 1995 survey was designed by the same research team (of which we were members) to be comparable with the IE, CASS 1988 survey. The rural survey covered nineteen of the twenty-eight provinces included in 1988 and the urban survey was conducted in eleven provinces, including all ten surveyed in 1988. Many of the same questions were asked, although the 1995 questionnaire also reflected the move away from central planning and towards a market economy. The main results of the IE, CASS 1995 survey were published in the volume edited by Riskin, Zhao, and Li (2001). The two snapshots enable us to make comparisons of 1988 and 1995 and to analyse changes that occurred over this seven-year period.

The MOL 1994 rural labour force survey was the product of our collaboration with the Ministry of Labour (as it was then known). The survey covered eight provinces chosen to be typical of different parts of China, and 500 households in each province were drawn from the three counties representing its 25th, 50th, and 75th percentile of income per capita. The survey was designed to investigate the phenomenon of rural–urban migration from a rural perspective. It enables us to examine the economic activities of rural people and in particular their choices among farming, local non-farming, and migration.

MOL 1995 was planned as a complementary survey, exploring rural–urban migration at the urban end. It was based on a stratified random sample containing 118 enterprises (each employing at least ten rural–urban migrants) in four cities (Beijing, Shenzhen, Wuhan, and Suzhou). There were two parts to the questionnaire, one relating to individual migrants and the other to their employers. The survey enables us to investigate migrants employed in urban enterprises, and to view them from three perspectives: That of the migrants themselves, that of their employers, and that of governments at different levels.

Because China is still moving towards a labour market, it was difficult to choose an end-year for our coverage of this process. Our initial intention was to set a cut-off date in the mid-1990s, so stopping with the analysis of the three surveys conducted at that time. However, this was precisely when the Chinese Government embarked on its policy of reforming the state-owned enterprise (SOE) sector, which involved the laying-off of millions of urban workers and high urban unemployment. Any account of the formation of a labour market would be deficient without analysis of this new development. We decided to extend our period and to end our story, somewhat raggedly, in the year 2000.

IE, CASS 1999 was an urban survey, conducted in the year 2000, covering thirteen cities in six carefully selected provinces. It was intended to address the new urban poverty in China, much of it associated with labour retrenchment and unemployment. Unlike official surveys and the previous two IE, CASS surveys, it contained a subsample of urban migrant households. This made possible the comparison of migrants and urban workers, both those who had been retrenched and the unretrenched.

1.4 PLAN OF THE STUDY

In Chapter 2, we begin with a brief account of the Chinese labour and wage system under central planning. We then describe and explain the labour market reforms, their evolution, and their general consequences, set against the backdrop of the evolving political economy. Underlying the interaction between policy and economy are the questions: Did labour-abundant China move towards a tighter labour market? How was labour reallocated so as to meet the needs of the rapidly growing and changing economy? This chapter provides a bird's-eye view of the emerging labour market that is self-contained and can be read on its own. Each of the more detailed, subsequent, chapters is written so as to be fairly self-contained.

Part II is concerned with various aspects of the urban labour market. We start, in Chapter 3, by analysing the changes in the structure of wages over the period 1988–95 (using IE, CASS 1988 and IE, CASS 1995). We pose the questions: With labour market reform, did the wage structure become economically more rational? Was there an increase in the returns to productive characteristics, and a decrease in the extent of institutionally imposed wage segmentation? We find that the spatial segmentation of wages increased, reflecting the low mobility of urban labour. Accordingly, we examine this phenomenon in Chapter 4 in order to understand the forces making for wage divergence across China.

Another source of labour market segmentation is the institutionally imposed divide between urban residents and rural–urban migrants. Chapter 5 analyses the employment of migrants in urban enterprises using MOL 1995: Their wages both absolutely and relative to those of urban employees in the same enterprises, the extent to which they substitute for or complement urban workers, and the policy restrictions on their employment. Chapter 6 examines the dramatic redundancy programme of the late 1990s and the labour market consequences for those made redundant. What sort of labour market were they summarily thrust into?

Apart from those recently made redundant, the mobility of urban residents from one employer to another is extremely low. This presents an obstacle to the formation of competitive market wages. In Chapter 7 we again make use of IE, CASS 1999 to explore this immobility and its labour market implications. One implication is the likelihood of wage segmentation among employers. We go on to analyse the powerful relationship that exists between the profitability and the wages of enterprises: A further indication that the labour market still remains incomplete and imperfect in urban China. IE, CASS 1999 also makes it possible for us to compare the wages of migrants, retrenched and re-employed urban workers, and never-retrenched urban workers in order to assess the extent of labour market competition and segmentation among these groups.

In Part III we turn to the rural labour market. Chapter 8 uses MOL 1994 to investigate the allocation of rural labour. Peasants have a choice of three economic activities: Farm work, local non-farm employment, and (temporary) employment elsewhere, mainly in the urban areas. The latter two activities have both grown remarkably in recent years, and they provide higher incomes than does farming. We examine how activity choices are made, and the extent to which people are constrained in their choices, so giving rise to the rationing of non-farm jobs.

Part IV is our attempt to generalize about the imperfect labour market. Chapter 9 is concerned with the ways in which this still incomplete market operates. We examine the roles that information and social networks play in securing employment and determining wages, the former by means of a small but detailed survey of migrants that we conducted in Handan in 1993, and the latter by using measures of *guanxi* (social connections) in the IE, CASS 1999 survey. The concluding chapter (Chapter 10) brings the evidence together and presents it systematically, considers the policy implications of the analysis and examines the political economy of the labour market reform in China, both past and future. For readers wanting an overview of our research and its conclusions, it can be read on its own.

REFERENCES

Boeri, Tito and Katherine Terrell (2002). 'Institutional determinants of labour allocation in transition', *Journal of Economic Perspectives*, 16, 1 (Winter): 51–76.

Doeringer, Peter and Michael Piore (1971). *Internal Labor Markets and Manpower Analysis*, Lexington, MA: D.C. Heath.

Gelb, Alan (1999). 'The end of transition?', in Annette Brown (ed), *When is Transition Over?*, Kalamazoo: Upjohn Institute for Employment Research.

Granovetter, Mark (1985). 'Economic action and social structure: The problem of embeddedness', *American Journal of Sociology*, 9, 3: 481–510.

Griffin, Keith and Zhao Renwei (eds) (1993). *The Distribution of Income in China*, London: Macmillan.

Harris, John and Michael Todaro (1970). 'Migration, unemployment and development: a two-sector analysis', *American Economic Review*, 60: 126–41.

Hicks, J.R. (1963). *The Theory of Wages*, 2nd edn, London: Macmillan.

Horton, Susan, Ravi Kanbur, and Dipak Mazumdar (1994). 'Labor markets in an era of adjustment: an overview', in Susan Horton, Ravi Kanbur, and Dipak Mazumdar (eds) *Labor Markets in an Era of Adjustment*, Vol. 1, Washington DC: The World Bank.

Knight, John and Lina Song (1999). *The Rural–Urban Divide. Economic Disparities and Interactions in China*, Oxford: Oxford University Press.

Layard, Richard and Andrea Richter (1995). 'How much unemployment is needed for restructuring? The Russian experience', *Economics of Transition*, 3, 1: 39–58.

Lewis, Arthur W. (1954). 'Economic development with unlimited supplies of labour', *The Manchester School*, 22: 139–92.

McMillan, John (1995). 'Markets in transition', Research Report 95-06, Graduate School of International Relations and Pacific Studies, University of California, San Diego.

Riskin, Carl, Zhao Renwei and Li Shi (eds) (2001). *China's Retreat from Equality. Income Distribution and Economic Transition*, Armonk, NY: M.E. Sharpe.

Solow, Robert M. (1990). *The Labor Market as a Social Institution*, Cambridge, MA: Basil Blackwell.

Svejnar, Jan (2002). 'Transition economies: performance and challenges', *Journal of Economic Perspectives*, 16, 1 (Winter): 3–28.

2

Labour Policy and Progress: Overview

2.1 INTRODUCTION

Our purpose in this chapter is to provide an overview of the Chinese labour market and its evolution. We are concerned both with the evolution of policy and with developments in the market. The chapter provides the historical, institutional, and policy framework that is needed for understanding both the more detailed analysis to come and the current problems of labour market reform.

In a sense, it is a misnomer to talk of 'the labour market' in China. The Chinese labour system, set up in the 1950s and based on the Soviet model, involved state direction of labour and administration of wages. On the one hand, it was characterized by immobility, lack of incentives, overstaffing, and inefficiency. On the other hand, it avoided open unemployment and serious urbanization problems, it provided employees with security, and it achieved egalitarian objectives. In the era of economic reform the Chinese Government began a process of reform designed to improve the mobility, flexibility, incentives, and efficiency of labour. By comparison with other market reforms in China, however, labour market reform was tardy and limited.

The Chinese labour market has been characterized by surplus labour in both the rural and the urban sectors. It is a surplus labour economy *par excellence* and the institutions of the labour market have to be viewed in that light. Until very recently, it differed from most developing countries also in the invariably disguised nature of unemployment. Open unemployment, normally associated with landlessness, is absent from rural China. The policy of allocating village land leasehold to all households of the village, usually on a per-capita basis, and the prohibition on the buying and selling of land have curbed landlessness. In urban China open unemployment has until recently been generally avoided in two ways. One is the control of migration from the rural areas and the severe restrictions on urban settlement. The other is through employment policies which result in disguised unemployment and surplus labour in the public sector.

The labour situation can be depicted very simply in a two-sector model (Figure 2.1). The horizontal axis, OO', shows the amount of labour in the economy, assumed to be fixed. Rural sector labour is measured rightwards from the origin O. The curve MPL_a shows the marginal product of labour in the agricultural (here equated with the rural) sector. Industrial (urban) employment is measured leftwards from O'. In a competitive labour market in which the rural supply curve

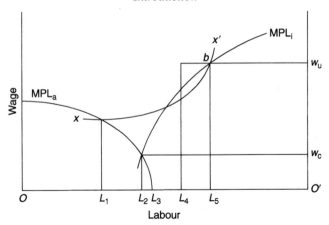

F I G. 2.1 *A model of the Chinese labour market*

to the urban sector is given by MPL_a and the urban demand curve by MPL_i, the competitive wage would be w_c and labour allocation OL_2 in the rural and L_2O' in the urban sector.

However, the urban wage is set higher than the competitive wage, at w_u. In a market economy this would imply urban employment L_5O'. In a Harris–Todaro framework the 'expected wage'—w_u multiplied by the probability of obtaining it—equals the rural supply price. With the probability equal to the ratio of urban employment to urban labour force, rural–urban migration occurs until this condition is satisfied. Given that the curve xx', passing through the point b, is a rectangular hyperbola, urban open unemployment equal to L_1L_5 is created.

This simple story would fit various developing countries with a substantial urban–rural income differential. In China, however, the outcome is different. Government has prevented open unemployment by controlling rural–urban migration and by creating surplus jobs, L_4L_5, in the urban state sector. Thus the labour force is divided into OL_4 (rural employment) and L_4O' (urban employment). The extent of rural disguised unemployment is indicated by the zero marginal product of labour in agriculture beyond point L_3.

Table 2.1 presents a summary view of the Chinese labour force over almost fifty years. The labour force grew on average by 2.6 per cent per annum: 2.1 per cent in rural areas and 4.2 per cent in urban areas. Urban formal employees, known as 'staff and workers', increased by 4.2 per cent per annum, from being 8 per cent of the labour force in 1952 to 25 per cent in 1982. However, because private enterprises and self-employed individuals are excluded from the definition, staff and workers as a proportion of the labour force and of urban employment fell over the reform period, being 16 per cent of the former and 49 per cent of the latter in 2000. Despite the rapid industrialization and urbanization, rural labour more than doubled over the half-century, whereas land was already fully occupied in 1952 and

TABLE 2.1 *The labour force and its distribution, China, 1952–2000, millions and percentage of total*

		Labour force			Urban 'staff and workers'
		Total	Rural	Urban	
1952	Million	207	182	25	16
	Per cent	100	88	12	8
1962	Million	259	214	45	43
	Per cent	100	83	17	17
1972	Million	359	287	72	71
	Per cent	100	80	20	20
1982	Million	453	339	114	113
	Per cent	100	75	25	25
1992	Million	662	483	179	148
	Per cent	100	73	27	22
2000	Million	721	489	232	113
	Per cent	100	68	32	16

Source: PRC, SSB (1993: 75; 2002: 117).

its use could not be expanded significantly. It was only in the 1990s that the growth of the labour force decelerated and—given continued rapid expansion of urban employment—the number employed in rural China remained roughly constant. By 2000 there were no fewer than 721 million workers in China, 489 million in the rural and 232 million in the urban areas.

2.2 THE PRE-REFORM LABOUR SYSTEM

The process of reforming the labour market cannot be made sense of without an understanding of the labour system that was in place before reform began. China's labour policies have been much influenced by the so-called 'Soviet model', and they have evolved from the Soviet model, despite the obstacles to reform which it embodied. Its legacy is still to be observed in the Chinese labour market today. In this section we describe the labour system which was created in the 1950s, and in the next section we attempt to explain it. We have found it necessary to examine original documents and official papers in order to identify the reasons for various policies and their evolution, both in the pre-reform and the reform periods.

2.2.1 A sketch of the labour system

After 1949 the Chinese Government adopted a bureaucratic system of administering wages and allocating labour.[1] It also compressed the wage structure: The span of incomes within enterprises was reduced from 40–50 fold, reflecting scarcity and abundance in the market economy prior to 1949, to 4–7 fold in the central planned economy of the mid-1950s (Howe 1973: 35–8). The wage reform of 1956, which applied to the state sector generally and involved a formal system of standardized wage scales, was much influenced by the Soviet model. The Soviet wage system remained largely in place throughout the pre-reform period. Administrative personnel ('staff') were put into twenty salary grades, technicians (also 'staff') into seventeen grades, and manual employees ('workers') into eight grades. Wage tables laid down the wage payments in each grade. There were only slight regional (cost of living) and industrial variations. Workers were divided into broad occupations, and each occupation spanned a number of grades. The pay specified for an occupation varied somewhat according to the size and importance of the employing organization. More importantly, inter-enterprise differences could arise on account of piece-rates, bonuses, and subsidies, dependent on the profits or resources of each employer. Within the employing unit, training and educational qualifications were relevant but seniority was the dominant criterion. Wages were more attached to individuals than to the precise jobs they performed.

The wage system nevertheless adjusted to the twists and turns of ideological and power struggle. During the Cultural Revolution wage policy was strongly egalitarian. Political activists exploited dissatisfactions created by income differentials and preferred social to technical criteria in wage setting. The need for material incentives was played down, and payments based on work performance were abolished. When rural economic reform commenced in 1978, urban wage policy also changed. Real wages were increased somewhat after years of stagnation, minor performance-related payments were reinstated, and differentials were slightly widened.

After 1957 the state exercised a virtual monopoly over the allocation of urban labour. It was the plan, and not market wages, that governed labour supply and demand. The labour 'requirements' of each enterprise were based on the plan, which was adjusted to avoid urban unemployment. Job assignments were normally made without reference to the wishes of either the employer or the employee. The system of allocation produced much mismatch and waste of human capital. The initial assignment to a job was very important: the first job was often the last. Although workers received promotions in wage grades, these rarely involved reassignments to different jobs. Nor were transfers from one employing unit to another common: Without official consent—rarely granted—such transfers were practically impossible. There was little or no private sector to which workers could move from their official assignments. The spatial mobility of labour was severely controlled and restricted by means of the residential registration (*hukou*) system.

Job rights have until very recently been firmly entrenched in urban China. The security and human dignity afforded by employment are regarded as valuable ends in themselves. State-owned units have also supplied extensive welfare benefits, including housing, medical services, pensions, childcare, and jobs for children (*ding ti*). The provision of welfare services at enterprise level has served as a deterrent to workers from quitting and to employers from firing, even in the absence of official restrictions. Almost all state employees, and many in the larger collectives, have thus enjoyed an 'iron rice bowl' (*tie fan wan*)—lifetime tenure of their job and a relatively high wage in the enterprise representing a 'mini welfare state'.

During the period of central planning there was strict control over the movement of population. In the mid-1950s the state became alarmed at the tide of migrants from the rural areas, and made attempts to stem it, including the enactment of various laws to restrict movement. Under a law of 1958 every Chinese was registered as being resident in a particular place. Any change of registration required official approval. Residence registration (*hukou*) conferred legal rights to be a resident in a locality and to share the resources of that community. In the case of a village, this involved rights to land for farming and housing. In the case of a city, it involved rights to a package of benefits, including state-subsidized food and housing and access to a permanent job. The *hukou* system functioned as a de facto internal passport system. It provided the state with the means of preventing permanent change of residence, and in particular of curbing permanent rural–urban migration. Even temporary migration was made extremely difficult by the urban rationing of grain, housing, and other necessities.

In summary, in the period prior to urban economic reform China had an administered labour system but no labour market. There was bureaucratic allocation of labour and determination of wages. Labour mobility, whether between jobs or between localities, was strictly controlled and severely restricted. The centralized control of enterprises provided no inducement for the efficient use of labour, and indeed surplus labour was imposed on enterprises. Workers had few material incentives to acquire human capital, to work efficiently, or to improve work methods. The system enabled the state to pursue its egalitarian objectives.

2.2.2 Explaining the labour system

The Chinese labour system that existed under central planning possessed two outstanding features: entrenched egalitarianism and the bureaucratic allocation of labour and determination of wages. Both posed a problem for labour market reform: Would they cause resistance if workers were faced by new competitive market forces? Would either of these characteristics survive the loss of the other? Such questions are relevant to the reform process. To answer them we must understand why the Communist Party, when it came to power, adopted these policies.

Some aspects of the pre-reform labour system had their roots in the arrangements which prevailed prior to 1949. There was a feudalistic agrarian system and a colonial-style industrial sector. The small urban labour market was very fragmented: There was considerable variation in wages, according to industry, region, occupation, and employer (Li 1992). The wages of hired workers in agriculture were normally paid in-kind. This form of payment was used by some industrial employers—reflecting not only the traditional practice but also the high inflation and the restricted location and time limits of local currencies (Li 1992). The Communist Party adopted the payment-in-kind system, both within the party before taking power and more generally thereafter. An artificially created Chinese character, combining food and clothing, was used as the unit of payment (*yi*).

The other influence on the labour system was the USSR. China followed the Soviet Union not only in its labour system but more generally in its national development strategy. Even before the foundation of the People's Republic of China on 1st October 1949, Mao Zedong stressed the need for 'leaning to one side' (Mao Zedong 1969: 1362, 1364). Moreover, 'the earlier we choose this [policy], the more advantage we will take later on because it was our own choice...' (Deng Xiaoping 1983: 135). The imposition of sanctions by the United States and the United Kingdom and the onset of the Cold War isolated China economically and politically: China had to rely on its communist neighbour, and modelled its economy on that of the Soviet Union.

The first conference on wage policy was held in 1950, and involved Soviet advice. It proposed a nationally unified wage scale at a level which would gain the general support of workers. An official document 'Wage Regulation (Draft)' became the benchmark for wage policy. It led to regional wage reforms and to the designation of eight grades of industrial worker. Wage points were converted into goods: payments were made mainly in-kind. The wage reform of 1956 created a national wage scale and set wages in terms of money. Nevertheless, enterprises continued to provide various facilities, goods, and services to their employees.

In 1957 a dispute over leadership of the communist world and ideological issues broke relations between the two countries and ended Soviet aid to China. Chinese economic policies then became based on the principle of self-reliance. China did not abandon the Soviet model but adapted the model to its own characteristics. The differences are interesting because they reflect the Chinese situation. The Chinese government exercised tighter and more centralized control, not only over labour but also more generally, than did the government of the Soviet Union.

China was more an agrarian economy and society, and its new government inherited a very small industrial sector, which employed only 3 million workers in 1949. Arable land was already fully cultivated in the 1950s, and labour was abundant in relation to land. The government adopted a development strategy of urban industrialization. This had to be achieved without the benefit of international trade and foreign investment. The government decided on a policy of central planning to raise saving and investment and thus to accelerate industrialization. All decisions relating to saving, investment, production, and resource allocation were planned and administered by the central government and its extended hierarchical structure (Naughton 1995).

The method of accumulation was by means of the 'price-scissors' policy, adopted from the Soviet Union. The prices of industrial goods were raised and those of agricultural goods were held down. The low price of food depressed peasant incomes and reduced the nominal wages of urban workers, while the high price of manufactures permitted centrally planned re-investment of the profits of the state-owned enterprises (SOEs). In this way the peasants effectively paid for industrialization (Knight and Song 1999: ch. 7).

A characteristic that distinguished China from the Soviet Union and other countries was the sharpness of the rural–urban divide. The ratio of urban to rural average household income and consumption per capita exceeded 2 to 1 and was sometimes as high as 3 to 1 throughout the period of central planning. The underlying reason for this disparity was a version of the 'efficiency wage' explanation for wages above the competitive market level: The need for social stability and worker compliance in the cities. What made the disparity possible was the restriction of rural–urban migration (Knight and Song 1999: chs 2, 8).

The overwhelming economic problem facing the incoming Communist Party government was shortage of food. Food supply was to be the main issue in the formative years. Although food production increased rapidly in the early 1950s, peasant consumption increased even more rapidly, creating a deficit in the food available to the urban sector (Bo Yibo 1991: 255–79). Given the policy of price-scissors, the price mechanism could not be invoked to elicit marketed food. It was necessary for the government to procure food compulsorily from rural-dwellers, and to ration food to urban-dwellers. A unified procurement system (*tonggou tongxiao*) was introduced, with sales and purchases of staples being permitted only through state agents. Compulsory quotas for the sale of grain, cotton, and oil-bearing crops were imposed on the peasants. Unlike the Soviet Union, which collected food purely through the price-scissors mechanism (Bo Yibo 1991: 276–7), the Chinese Government also used agricultural and land taxation. It is arguable that rural collectivization—the People's Communes—was introduced, in 1958, in order to make the procurement system more effective (Knight and Song 1999: 30–4).

The economic development strategy that we have described in turn moulded the labour system. To expand the supply of, and restrict the demand for, marketed food, it was necessary strictly to control and to curb rural–urban migration. Similarly, the policy of maintaining an urban–rural income disparity required that the peasants be kept on the land. This was done through the system of household registration (*hukou*), the commune system, and the system of urban food rationing. Because food ration coupons were issued and managed locally, urban–urban labour mobility was also restricted.

The central administration and control of urban job allocation may partly have served a political purpose, but it had the effect of reducing mobility among jobs. In this non-market economy there was a logic, afforced by the payment-in-kind tradition, in giving the employer the functions of providing pensions, housing, and healthcare. In this way the system of lifetime employment became entrenched, with the enterprise forming a mini welfare state and its employees enjoying their iron rice bowls. The absence of competition among producers meant that employment was as secure as government wished it to be.

The wage egalitarianism in China under central planning was similar to that in the Soviet Union. The underlying reason may well have been ideological.

However, this would have been bolstered by the Chinese tradition of egalitarianism and by the sense of community in the enterprise, normally based on shared residence and shared welfare services as well as shared workplace. Moreover, the extremely low mobility of labour among employers meant that there was no scope for labour market forces to operate. It was possible in China, more so than in the Soviet Union, to enforce the policy of wage equality.

A characteristic that has sharply distinguished China from market economies is the Chinese 'work-unit', known as the *danwei*. The *danwei* was not an employer in the Western sense, but rather a social institution. It imposed a mindset on managers, workers, and policy-makers which is far removed from that of labour economists. Labour market reform would require a dramatic change in the objectives and functions of Chinese employers. It would involve a difficult transition for workers, from being *danwei* people with a culture of dependency to being citizens with a culture of individualism. As we argue below, the *danwei* has proved to be an obstacle to the creation of a labour market in urban China. The sense of community, and the welfare services, provided by the *danwei* have been valued by its members. The economic gains from labour market reform are less well, or less personally, perceived than the losses in terms of social support and economic security.

2.3 THE POLITICAL ECONOMY OF ECONOMIC REFORM

In the Third Plenum, December 1978, the reformers Deng Xiaoping and his colleagues seized control; so began a remarkable process of economic reform. The basic reason for the initial policy-switch was a reordering of priorities from the political to the economic. The reforming coalition interpreted the state's predicament in the following way. It was now necessary to promote development and welfare in order to provide a new form of legitimacy for the regime: Failure to reform would mean economic stagnation, social tension, and political decline.

The sector most in need of reform was the farm sector, which had stagnated for many years. The rural reforms rapidly outstripped the intended measures, for two reasons. First, the peasants interpreted them as a signal that change was possible, and took the initiative as unorganized individuals but in overwhelming numbers. The rural reforms were that rare economic event, a Pareto improvement, benefiting almost all rural people. Secondly, a process of cumulative causation was set in motion. When one aspect of economic life was privatized or marketized, gains were impeded unless other aspects of economic life were allowed to follow. Once the household became the production unit, it was inevitable that capital and labour markets would ensue. The newly incentivized peasants required longer leases in order to invest in their farms. The need for farm credit and off-farm employment opportunities caused peasants to lease land, rent it, hire labour to work it, and use it as security for loans. When the restraints on non-agricultural activities were relaxed, many profitable opportunities were there to be seized. A new rural entrepreneurial class began to form, with which the state aligned itself.

In summary, the reformist coalition gave first priority to rural reform. This proved to be relatively easy. Processes of atomistic peasant behaviour and of cumulative causation galvanized the rural economy and pulled the leadership along behind (Knight and Song 1999: ch. 2). Can the same type of analysis be applied to the urban economic reform process? Only in the mid-1980s, when the major rural reforms had been achieved, did government turn seriously to urban reform. This was to prove more difficult. It is a story of the gradual diminution of state control of the urban economy, flowing from the decentralization of decision-taking to state enterprises and the growth of the non-state sector. In 1978 the state sector accounted for 78 per cent of urban employment, and the private sector for 9 per cent. In 2000, the corresponding figures were 54 and 36 per cent, respectively.

The underlying motivation for reform was to improve the efficiency of the, then ubiquitous, state sector. This was done by encouraging product markets to operate, permitting competition among state firms and with the non-state sector, and granting greater managerial autonomy in many spheres, including labour. The labour reforms included abandoning the system of labour allocation, requiring or permitting real wages to rise, and introducing performance-related wage incentives.

Nevertheless, urban economic reform was tardy and gradualist—well described by the saying 'crossing the river by feeling the stones'. One reason for this was ideological: Resistance from among the leadership to the creation of a labour market, stemming from the tenet that labour is not a commodity (Lee 1997). However, there were two main obstacles to progress: The difficulty of reforming the entrenched state sector and the resistance of urban workers to the erosion of their privileged position. Change was impeded by the systemic nature of the problem. Reform of one aspect required consistent reform of other aspects. Unlike the case of rural China, coordinated action on various fronts was required, involving system-wide reform by various tiers and segments of government.

This was particularly true of the labour market. In the late 1980s, it was arguable that, of all aspects of planning in China, 'the allocation of labour resources is by far the furthest from the market mechanism' (White 1988: 14). An urban labour market was not swept into being by a process of cumulative causation. Labour market reform inevitably connects with other urban reforms, for instance, with regard to public finance, enterprise management, enterprise ownership, bankruptcy, housing, social services, pension, unemployment, training, and migration policies. A worker leaving a job had to give up much more than a job. Until late in the reform process, he lost his iron rice bowl and the mini welfare state provided by his work-unit. This made workers reluctant to quit, and employers reluctant to dismiss them. Attempts to achieve a more flexible labour market would involve severe hardships and accordingly meet resistance from urban workers unless these interrelated problems were solved together.

The pace of urban economic reform accelerated in the mid-1990s. The new determination to reform the SOEs was forced on the government by the declining profitability and the rising incidence of loss-making in the state-owned sector. This had adverse implications for government revenue, the prospects of continued rapid economic growth, and China's entry to the World Trade Organization. Faced with this threat to the achievement of its main objectives, the government was willing to risk a degree of political threat inherent in the erosion of urban-dwellers' privileges. It embarked on a draconian policy of labour-shedding, transferring unemployment from the state sector (where it was disguised) to the streets (where it was open and visible) in the hope that the non-state sector would with time expand sufficiently to absorb the redundant workers.

Before the start of rural economic reform, rural–urban migration of any sort was tightly restricted and indeed, with only minor restrictions, prohibited. The introduction of the 'household responsibility' system in farming meant that surplus labour, previously disguised by commune work rules, became available for new farm and non-farm activities. The growth of rural industry in response to market disequilibrium was the outstanding rural phenomenon of the 1980s, but this slowed down in the subsequent decade as equilibrium was established and competition from the reforming urban sector intensified. Instead, rural–urban migration was the outstanding rural phenomenon of the 1990s.

This redirection of rural labour absorption was assisted by the abolition of urban food rationing, the acceleration of the urban reforms that had commenced in the mid-1980s, and—as the one-child family policy took lagged effect—a deceleration of urban labour force growth. The rapid growth of the urban economy compared with the slow growth of the urban-born labour force meant that there was an increasing need for rural migrants in the urban areas. Growth-minded governments at various levels permitted temporary migration to expand to meet that need.

Different levels of government have different objectives. Central government is most concerned to ensure that flows of migrants are orderly and do not threaten social stability. It has favoured temporary rather than permanent migration, and has maintained the household registration (*hukou*) system in order to prevent the permanent urban settlement of rural people. Governments of sending areas—at the province or county level—encourage out-migration and operate recruitment agencies to assist it. As rural–urban migration began to burgeon in the 1990s, city governments, concerned to protect their citizens against the influx of migrants, introduced systems of control over in-migration. Their objectives were to allow temporary migrants into jobs unfilled by urban residents but to protect their residents against undercutting competition. In the late 1990s city governments responded to the widespread redundancies of urban employees by restricting the recruitment and re-employment of rural migrants, and urban job centres gave priority to unemployed urban-*hukou* residents. In this way, unemployment could to some extent be transferred to the rural areas, where it posed a lesser threat to social and political stability.

The government led by Deng reacted against the situation that had prevailed under Mao. In adopting its reform policies, the leadership espoused output objectives above all else. Where there was a conflict between efficiency objectives and equality objectives, egalitarianism was played down. With marketization and privatization, the Gini coefficient of household income per capita rose rapidly, for instance by 7 percentage points, from 38 to 45 per cent, over the seven years 1988–95 (Knight and Song 2001: 84). Over the same period the Gini coefficient of earnings per worker in urban China rose by 8 percentage points, from 23 to 31 per cent (Knight and Song 2001: 107). As economic reform proceeded, the changes in the economy created new interest groups and a shifting balance of political power. The government's objective function was itself influenced and moulded by the reform process. Egalitarianism was increasingly eschewed in favour of allowing some areas and some people to prosper, with the expectation that their prosperity would assist others and spread: 'Prosperity to some, to most, then to all' (Du 1989: 92).

2.4 THE EVOLUTION OF LABOUR REFORM POLICIES

Reform of the centrally planned economic system commenced in 1978, largely in the rural sector, but urban wages were affected by the reinstatement of minor performance-related payments—bonuses and piece rates—and a slight widening of differentials. Reform of the urban labour system began in 1980, when the state monopoly of labour allocation was replaced by a somewhat more decentralized one.[2] Central and local labour authorities continued to plan the labour requirements of state and large collective enterprises, and remained responsible for the placement of college graduates. Under the reform, however, labour exchanges were set up for the registration of job vacancies, most job placements, and training. 'Labour service companies' were established to create new enterprises for the absorption of the surplus labour of existing enterprises. In the 1990s the planning quota for recruitment by state enterprises was abolished, and enterprises were allowed to choose their own employees. The state no longer took responsibility for matching the supply and demand for labour. In 1999 there were 30,000 labour exchanges or 'employment-service' offices, 22,000 being affiliated to the Ministry of Labour and 8,000 being labour service companies (PRC, MOL 2000: 90). In principle, they should have made the labour market more flexible.

Enterprise reform gained pace in the mid-1980s. It took the form of decentralization of decision-taking and greater managerial autonomy within the state sector. There was managerial leasing of some small enterprises, managerial contracting of some large enterprises, and shareholder participation in some other cases. With managerial pay now partly dependent on profits, managers became a pressure group for more independence in labour and other matters. The 'optimal labour reorganization scheme', designed to reduce surplus labour in the SOEs, was extended nationwide in 1989. The selected enterprises were subjected to reorganization, redeployment, and retraining of labour. In the 1990s, the government finally decided to push state enterprises into the market, holding them responsible for their losses even to the point of bankruptcy. The pressure on them increased. In 1985, profits of state-owned industries were 19 per cent of the net value of fixed assets, and the losses of the loss-making enterprises (LMEs) represented 4 per cent of the profits of the profit-making enterprises (PMEs); in 1995 (the worst year) the corresponding figures were 4 and 49 per cent, respectively (PRC, SSB 1998: 461). Up to the mid-1990s, a combination of retraining and attrition managed to keep open unemployment low in urban China. Bankruptcies and redundancies then began to escalate, turning previously disguised unemployment into a more open form.

In the 1990s, an unemployment insurance system was gradually introduced. By 2000, 103 million employees were covered, with pooling mostly at city level (PRC, MOL 2001: 442). This institutional development should have enhanced urban labour mobility, although there is little evidence that mobility did rise. In 1985, a system of labour contracts of limited duration for new recruits was introduced on a national scale. In 1988, only 9 per cent of urban employees were covered. The Labour Law of 1994 required all employees to have such contracts, and they were thus extended to permanent workers. The proportion of urban employees on contracts had risen to 41 per cent in 1995 (PRC, MOL 1996: 35). However, contract workers were generally treated much as though they were permanent. It was only after 1995, when redundancies in the state sector began to escalate, that the distinction between contract and permanent workers became important. Young workers bore the brunt of the reforms in another way as well. The relative expansion of the non-state sector weakened the state's control of the labour market. There was never any placement of labour in private enterprises and in the smaller collectives, nor was there any attempt to determine their wages. It was at the entry point to the labour market that this structural change was sharpest. In 1988 the state-owned sector absorbed 58 per cent of new urban employees; by 1997 the figure was down to 32 per cent (PRC, MOL 1998: 8).

From the start of the reform process the SOEs were given more authority to determine the bonus and thus the total wage. In 1983 state enterprises were allowed to redistribute after-tax profits for various purposes—including employee welfare and bonuses, subject to maximum percentages. In 1984 the bonus ceiling was repealed and replaced by a stiff bonus tax (effectively ruling out an annual bonus of more than three months' pay). An alternative experiment was introduced in 1985 to link a state enterprise's total wage bill to its tax and profit remittances, again subject to a tax on the increase in the wage bill (Li 1989). By 1988 the wage of each employee had three main components: the basic wage (derived from standardized wage scales), the functional wage (relating to status and seniority), and the floating wage (including the bonus, determined at the enterprise level). However, Walder (1987) presented a gloomy assessment of performance incentives: A web of factory interests gave rise to a fairly equal distribution of bonuses, aimed at minimizing contention. If bonuses acted as incentives, therefore, they did so at the level more of the enterprise than of the individual during the early stage of the labour market reform.

In 1992, SOEs were given more autonomy while having their budget constraints hardened. Henceforth, the growth in the wage bill was to be set according to the enterprise's economic performance, measured by the growth of realized pre-tax profits and of labour productivity, and the enterprise would have the freedom to determine how, and in what form, the wage bill was distributed. The radical bank reform of 1994, commercializing the state banks, cut the tie between the state and SOEs. Loss-making firms could no longer borrow from the banks to pay their workers: Wages became more dependent on the profitability of the enterprise.

The Labour Law of 1994, which became effective in 1995, was an important landmark in that it attempted to provide a framework within which a labour market could operate. Among its provisions were freedom to participate in and organize trade unions (Art. 7), arrangements for the settlements of disputes (Arts. 77–84), the promotion of labour exchanges (Art. 11), of enforceable labour contracts (Arts. 16–35), and of vocational training (Art. 48), the outlawing of discrimination (Arts. 12–3), the introduction of guaranteed minimum wages (Art. 48), and the development of social insurance, for instance, for unemployment and retirement (Arts. 70–6).

Although the 1994 Labour Law set up a labour relations framework and there were in 2000, 104 million official (ACFTU) trade union members, labour relations remained poorly developed. The Communist Party continued to appoint union officials and to organize the workers' congresses that are intended to assist worker participation. At plant level the workers' congresses met infrequently and the trade unions were expected to cooperate with management. They did not bargain freely over wages and other matters; at best they channelled workers' grievances. Workers often turned instead to the Communist Party, for instance, if they were dissatisfied about bonuses or discipline. It is arguable that urban workers have possessed more power, albeit latent, than this description suggests. Workers' power stems basically from their control of effort: Managers need the support of their employees. At least until the profit motive and product market competition became compelling, management identified with labour and responded to social pressures to share profits with their employees. Also, even tame trade unions had some influence because of their need to head-off more militant, unofficial unions.

The *hukou* system was preserved throughout the reform period but its effectiveness declined. Without the need to provide subsidized food, city governments were somewhat less concerned to restrict *hukou* registration. It became possible in the 1990s to buy an urban *hukou* in most of the towns and small cities at a high, revenue-raising price. From 2001, a person with stable work and residence could normally obtain local *hukou* registration in towns and small cities. However, restrictions on the transfer of residential registration continued to be rigidly enforced in the case of permanent movement from the rural areas to the big cities.

Prior to economic reform, urban rationing made even temporary migration extremely difficult. During the first stage of the reform, when the 'dual track' system operated, rationed food was distributed at low prices, as before, and higher prices prevailed in the free food markets. The ration coupon system was largely abolished in 1993: it became easier for migrants to live in the city without a city *hukou*. Moreover, with free markets for food, peasants could buy grain to meet their production quotas, that is, to pay their taxes in the form of compulsory grain sales to state agencies, so that they could more easily leave their farms.

The institutions have been designed to ensure that rural migrants are allowed into the cities to meet residual needs for labour, filling the jobs that urban residents do not want. Many rural-dwellers have an economic incentive to migrate to the urban areas, and many urban employers have a profit incentive to hire them, often in preference to more expensive and less-willing urban-dwellers. The burgeoning inflow of rural–urban migrants in the 1990s threatened urban residents with economic competition and with social problems, such as disorder and crime. City governments have therefore pursued policies to regulate the inflow of migrants.

Enterprises carried the administrative and financial burden of urban social security, and these arrangements tied workers to their employers. Labour market reform therefore required that other, related reforms be in place which would permit labour mobility. What was to replace the *danwei* as the provider of iron rice bowls for its members? The new principles of social protection were that the employer, the employee, and the state should share financial responsibility, that the funds should be pooled and administered at provincial, prefectural, or city level, and that the system should be extendable to all urban employees and not just *danwei* members. The process of transition to the new principles began in the late 1990s and is ongoing—with the reforms proceeding at a different pace in different aspects, areas, and enterprises.

A new system of urban healthcare was introduced according to these principles. Whereas healthcare was previously often free for state workers, in 1999 user fees were introduced and only the insured could claim reimbursement. By 2001, 50 million urban workers were paying for healthcare insurance (OECD 2002: 555).

Unemployment insurance has existed in China since the mid-1980s but until recently it covered only SOE workers, and not even all of them. Whereas 80 million workers were members of the scheme in 1994, the figure was 103 million—80 per cent of urban formal sector employees—in 2000. The system is financed by employer and employee contributions: Provided that the employer and employee are participants, benefits are paid for up to two years and replace 60–75 per cent of the wage up to a ceiling (OECD 2002: 566). There is a network of employment-service offices for the administration of unemployment insurance as well as to provide labour market information and to facilitate job placements.

Urban-born workers entering the labour market after 1997 were required to join a reformed retirement pension scheme, combining a (traditional) defined benefit scheme and state-guaranteed individual accounts. Employers, employees, and provincial governments all contributed to the scheme, and its management was transferred from the *danwei* to the provincial or local government. However, there were transitional arrangements to protect pension rights earned under the previous system. The reforms remained incomplete in other ways. In 2000, 134 million urban workers—representing 63 per cent of total urban employment but including very few workers outside the formal sector—were covered. Nor were all previous plans transferable between provinces, cities, and employers (PRC, NBS 2001: 13–4; OECD 2002: 562).

For many years, work-units were the main providers of urban workers' housing, so restricting their mobility among employers. The sale of public housing was sanctioned in 1994, and government encouraged residents to buy their houses by setting the purchase prices well below the levels that would be established in a housing market (Wang 2002: 191–2). In that way, the previous housing subsidy implicit in the nominal rents was capitalized. This popular development proceeded rapidly, and a national household survey in 2002 showed that 80 per cent of urban households owned their own houses. This impediment to mobility had thus been largely overcome.

2.5 CONCEPTUALIZING THE LABOUR MARKET

Chinese people show a great respect for terminology because it can carry powerful connotations. Changes in the terms used, or in the concepts they represent, may help us to understand the labour market reforms. The terminology of the old labour system implied a set of entitlements and statuses. As a labour market began to emerge, so the terms, or the concepts, also changed. We shall consider two important terms, their meaning during the period of central planning, and how that meaning changed as the labour system moved towards a labour market. These are 'the work-unit' and 'the worker'.

The work-unit (*danwei*) refers to the urban, publicly owned organizational unit in which workers are employed. It can be a factory, a school, a hospital, an administrative or party organ, and so on. *Danwei* have played a pervasive role in China's urban society, binding their employees to them in a culture of dependence. With their many functions, they are not just a workplace but a social institution. They satisfy the basic needs of their employees and their dependants, represent their interests, define their social status, accord them various rights, and control and influence their behaviour. The *danwei* is a very different concept from that of the employer in the Western sense.

Danwei are officially divided into *qiyie* and *shiyie*, the former (enterprises) providing financial support to the state and the latter (non-profit-making institutions) receiving financial support from the state through centrally controlled budgeting. The latter includes government and party functionary offices (*jiguan*) and public services (*yuan xiao*). Economic reforms have changed the nature of the *danwei* in various ways. With reform, 'extrabudgetary' revenue became increasingly important to *shiyie danwei*. Despite a prohibition on profit-making activities, many of them set up profit-making subunits, or joint ventures with *qiyie danwei*, in order to supplement inadequate 'budgetary' revenue. Moreover, many *shiyie danwei*, such as hospitals and other public services were redesignated *qiyie* when they began to charge fees and become more commercialized.

With the sale of *danwei*-owned houses to employees, the commercialization of such services as health and education, and the withdrawal of guaranteed employment, the *qiyie danwei* lost some of its many functions. Moreover, when public subsidies were withdrawn, the many LMEs were limited in the payments—in cash and kind—that they could make. The profitability of a *qiyie danwei* became an important determinant of the welfare of its workers. By contrast, new businesses in the non-state sector, more likely to hire labour on a profit-maximizing basis, would not view themselves as *qiyie danwei*.

It is helpful to understand the changing nature of *danwei* management. Under central planning, all managerial appointments were made by the Ministry of Personnel at different levels. Among the managers, the leaders were directly responsible for achieving the production targets set by the planners. However, there was also a party structure within the *danwei*. The party leaders (normally of higher rank) monitored and controlled the managerial leaders. Scope for conflict was great: The separation of powers of these two leaderships was one of the objects of enterprise reform in the 1980s. As enterprise reforms unfolded, the *danwei* leader was increasingly able to appoint and integrate his own management team. Nevertheless, the *danwei* remained a social institution with complex objectives.

Under central planning, Chinese employees were divided into two categories, cadres (*ganbu*) and workers (*gongren*). *Ganbu* included administrative, managerial, and professional staff and the normal occupations for university graduates. The Ministry of Personnel administered *ganbu*. All other employees were classified as *gongren*, and were administered by the Ministry of Labour. *Ganbu* and *gongren* had completely different wage scales, qualifications for recruitment, and criteria for promotion.

There were twenty-nine ranks for *ganbu* in the government, their pay in 1956 ranging from 26 yuan per month in the lowest rank to 405 yuan for party members and 580 yuan for non-party members in the highest cadre. Cadre salaries were determined mainly by rank but also by length of service, by the status of the *danwei*, and by locality (Takahara 1992: 171, 3). Those ranked 1–13 were superior-rank cadres (*gao-gang*). *Gao-gang* received allowances on top of their salaries and lavish benefits-in-kind, including superior housing, special hospitals, cars, and domestic servants. Before the start of the economic reform, only those who had joined the 'revolution' before certain periods could be *gao-gang*. The *gao-gang* represented political power. However, when economic reform took place, the growth of economic power and wealth outside the state sector meant that *gao-gang* were no longer the only political players. The intermediate rank cadres (ranks 14–18) usually worked in administrative positions, and ranks below that usually represented clerical positions. All *ganbu* had a social status well above that of *gongren*. With economic reform, the term *ganbu* came to mean 'staff' rather the 'cadre', reflecting growing managerial and professional functions in the more complex and the more marketized economy.

Gongren were classified into grades: The grade determined the wage scale of a worker, with minor variation according to locality and industry (Takahara 1992: 171–2). Grades 3–8 were high-skill workers, promoted through on-the-job skill tests. Length of service in the *danwei* was important not only for position on the wage scale but also for pension and housing. Chinese workers were employed in stereotypical 'internal labour markets'. There was a high degree of equality among them in respect of economic remuneration, social status, and legal rights. Nevertheless, there was some hierarchy of status according to the power and the ownership sector of the employer, with the state sector superior to the urban collective sector and central government superior to local government.

Economic reform brought sharper differentiation among urban workers. From 1985 newly recruited state employees were not given entitlement to life-time employment but were placed on fixed-term contracts. In 1994 the iron rice bowl was formally broken: Workers on the permanent payroll were to be re-categorized as fixed-term contract workers. The redundancy programme in the state sector, starting in the mid-1990s, became intense from 1997 onwards. The paternalistic relationships within the *danwei* that survived even after a dozen years of enterprise reform meant that the redundancies were painful for both managers and workers. Those displaced felt betrayed: It was as if they had been kicked out of the family home.

Many of the smaller SOEs declared bankruptcy. Their workers, and those made redundant by surviving *danwei*, were treated differently according to their circumstances. Redundant workers who had joined the state sector before 1985 became *xia gang* employees. This meant that, for three years, if their *danwei* could afford to pay them, they received a low wage and some welfare benefits but did not attend the workplace. Those displaced workers whose employers had contributed to an unemployment insurance fund on their behalf were entitled to register as unemployed and to receive unemployment benefits. Everyone else becoming unemployed was not even recorded in the administratively collected statistics and had to rely of their savings and on family support. All three groups had an incentive to find jobs in the non-state sector or to become self-employed. Workers who retained their state-sector jobs benefited from the greater profitability and job security of their reformed *danwei*.

Economic reform has divided the previously fairly homogenous urban proletariat into separate groups categorized by income, security, and status. Furthermore, it has brought urban workers into potential competition with rural–urban migrant workers. Although migrants remain at a relative disadvantage in obtaining and holding jobs, in pay, welfare provision, status, and residential security, their growing presence in the cities has inevitably weakened the economic security of city residents.

2.6 *LABOUR MARKET TRENDS IN THE REFORM PERIOD*

This section sketches out the extent of economic progress that has been achieved on issues relating to labour over the period of Chinese economic reform. We are concerned here not with the reasons for the reform policies, nor with the policies themselves, but with economic outcomes—partly dependent on the policies—and their evaluation. This bird's-eye view of progress in the labour market provides perspective for the more detailed analysis of later chapters.

Our analytical framework for assessing progress in the Chinese labour market is the classical model of economic development with surplus labour (Lewis 1954). According to the Lewis model, the industrial (urban) sector expands by drawing on abundant agricultural (rural) labour in perfectly elastic supply and reinvesting industrial profits. With industrial development in a market economy, labour transfers from the agricultural to the industrial sector. The supply curve of rural labour eventually becomes inelastic owing to the rising marginal product of labour in agriculture and an improvement in the relative price of agricultural goods. In a competitive labour market, the urban wage is determined by the rural supply price. It therefore begins to rise in real terms, and accordingly the economy enters the neoclassical stage of the development process.

Two relevant criticisms of the applicability of the Lewis model concern demography and wage behaviour. First, the growth of the labour force may outpace the growth of industry's demand for labour. In that case, pressure on the land increases, so depressing rural income and the market-determined urban wage: The neoclassical stage is postponed indefinitely. Secondly, even before the rural supply price rises, the industrial wage may rise for other reasons, such as the power of workers or efficiency–wage behaviour by employers.

The following questions can be posed of the Chinese labour market over the reform period. To what extent do the sectoral assumptions of the Lewis model— equating the agricultural with the rural sector and the industrial with the urban sector—fit the Chinese case? Have rural real incomes risen, so raising the rural supply price? Has the land–labour ratio in agriculture risen or fallen? To what extent has there been rural–urban migration? Have urban real wages risen? If so, is this the result of market forces or of non-competitive wage behaviour?

2.6.1 *Labour supply and demand*

During the period of central planning, Chinese economic development corresponded closely to the classical stage of the Lewis model, with no sign of its approaching the neoclassical stage. Between 1952 and 1978 the population of China increased by 388 million. The area of cultivated land could be raised by only 6 per cent, whereas the rural labour force grew by 66 per cent (2.0 per cent per annum). Cultivated land per rural worker fell from 11.6 to 7.4 mu. There were numerous attempts to measure the extent of surplus labour in rural China.

These produced a range of estimates but the majority suggested that surplus labour represented about 30 per cent of the rural labour force (surveyed by Taylor 1988). The per-capita grain available to rural people barely rose over the twenty-six years: peasant living standards stagnated. Similarly, urban real wages remained roughly constant, rising on average by only 0.4 per cent per annum over the planning period. Economic progress mainly took the form of industrial capital accumulation and the growth of urban employment, averaging 5.3 per cent per annum (Knight and Song 1999: ch. 2).

The absorption of the growing labour force into productive activities was thus a central problem facing the reforming coalition which took over in 1978. What success did it achieve? Table 2.2 shows the size and distribution of the Chinese labour force every five years from 1980 to 2000, both in millions and as a percentage of the labour force. These macroeconomic data are based partly on the population censuses, undertaken each decade, partly on extrapolations between census years and beyond the latest one, and partly on administratively collected data. This means that the categories urban ('other employment') and rural ('household workers') are derived as residuals, and that there can be major revisions in the total labour force and in the residual categories on the basis of new census information (for instance, between 1989 and 1990, in the light of the 1990 census returns).

The rapid growth of the Chinese economy (GDP is recorded as having grown at 10 per cent per annum) outstripped that of the labour force (2.7 per cent per annum) over these twenty years. Economic growth, together with the accompanying structural transformation of the economy, resulted in a massive redistribution of labour (Table 2.2). The urban share of the labour force rose from 26 to 34 per cent. However, employment in the state sector and urban collectives combined fell from 24 to 13 per cent, with 'other employment' (private firms and self-employment) and unemployment expanding from very little to 21 per cent of the labour force. Rural non-agricultural activities occupied 7 per cent of the labour force in 1980 but 23 per cent in 2000, whereas employment in agricultural activities ('household workers') fell from 67 to 43 per cent. By the year 2000 less than half of China's labour force was primarily dependent on the land for their living.

Table 2.3 uses the same data as Table 2.2 but presents them in a different form. For each decade, it shows how the increase in the labour force was absorbed into the economy, in millions, as percentages of the increase, and as annual percentage rates of change. In the 1980s, 128 million additional workers had to be absorbed, and in the 1990s, 87 million. The annual rate of growth of the labour force in the second decade (1.3 per cent) was well below that of the first decade (2.9 per cent). This dramatic reduction was due to demographic change (a fall in the number of women of child-bearing age during the 1970s) and policy reversal (the one-child family policy, introduced in the late 1970s).

It is notable that in the 1980s, 71 per cent of the increase in the labour force were employed in rural China, with the remarkable growth of rural industry ('TVE employment') accounting for no less than 50 per cent. However, agricultural employment continued to rise, taking in 21 per cent. Urban employment,

TABLE 2.2 *The labour force and its distribution, China, urban and rural, 1980–2000*

	1980	1985	1989	1990	1995	2000
Millions						
Labour force	429.0	501.1	557.1	651.3	689.3	737.8
Urban	110.6	130.5	147.7	174.2	199.0	248.4
Unemployed	5.4	2.4	3.8	3.8	8.6	16.9
Employed	105.2	128.1	143.9	170.4	190.4	231.5
SOEs	80.2	89.9	101.1	103.5	112.6	81.0
UCEs	24.3	33.2	35.0	35.5	31.5	15.0
Other employment	0.7	5.0	7.8	31.4	46.3	135.5
Rural	318.4	370.7	409.4	477.1	490.2	489.3
TVE employment	30.0	69.8	93.7	92.7	128.6	128.2
Private and individual enterprises	—	—	—	16.0	35.3	40.7
Household workers	288.4	300.9	315.7	368.4	326.3	320.4
Employment	423.6	498.7	553.3	647.5	680.7	720.8
Percentage of total						
Labour force	100.0	100.0	100.0	100.0	100.0	100.0
Urban	25.8	26.0	26.5	26.7	28.9	33.7
Unemployed	1.3	0.5	0.7	0.6	1.2	2.3
Employed	24.5	25.6	25.8	26.2	27.6	31.4
SOEs	18.7	17.9	18.1	15.9	16.3	11.0
UCEs	5.7	6.6	6.3	5.5	4.6	2.0
Other employment	0.2	1.0	1.4	4.8	6.7	18.4
Rural	74.2	74.0	73.5	73.3	71.1	66.3
TVE employment	7.0	13.9	16.8	14.2	18.7	17.4
Private and individual enterprises	—	—	—	2.5	5.1	5.5
Household workers	67.2	60.0	56.7	56.6	47.3	43.4
Employment	98.7	99.5	99.3	99.4	98.8	97.7

Notes: 1. There was a major revision in the figures between 1989 and 1990, based on the 1990 census of population.

    2. In the 1990s the number of urban employees who are attributed to particular ownership categories falls increasingly short of the total; the difference is included in the 'other employment' category.

Source: PRC, SSB (1998: 130), PRC, NBS (2002: 120–1), PRC, MOL (2001: 67, 401).

growing at 3.5 per cent per annum, absorbed 30 per cent of the additional workers. This picture stands in contrast to that for the 1990s, when no less than 86 per cent of the increment to the labour force went into the urban economy. This happened despite the collapse of employment in the state and urban collective sectors. Urban 'other employment' (new enterprises or old enterprises with new forms of ownership) accounted for more than the entire addition to labour supply. The faster

TABLE 2.3 *Change in the labour force, China, 1980–9 and 1990–2000, millions, percentage distribution, and percentage change per annum*

	Millions		Percentage of labour force		Percentage change per annum	
	1980–9	1990–2000	1980–9	1990–2000	1980–9	1990–2000
Labour force	128.1	86.5	100.0	100.0	2.9	1.3
Urban	37.1	74.2	29.0	85.8	3.3	3.6
Unemployed	−1.6	13.1	−1.2	15.1	−3.8	16.1
Employed	38.7	61.1	30.2	70.6	3.5	3.1
State	20.9	−22.5	16.3	−26.0	2.6	−2.4
Urban collectives	10.7	−20.5	8.4	−23.7	4.1	−8.3
Other employment	7.1	104.1	5.5	120.3	30.7	15.7
Rural	91.0	12.2	71.0	14.1	2.8	0.2
TVE employment	63.7	35.5	49.7	41.0	10.2	3.3
Private and individual enterprises	—	24.7	—	28.6	—	9.8
Household workers	27.3	−48.0	21.3	−55.5	1.0	−1.4
Employment	129.7	73.3	101.2	84.7	3.0	1.1

Notes: As for Table 2.2. The interval 1980–9 is used instead of 1980–90 because these years are estimated on a consistent basis.

Source: As for Table 2.2.

growth of the urban than of the rural labour force (3.6 versus 0.2 per cent per annum) reflected rural–urban migration and some reclassification of areas becoming urban. The number of agricultural workers declined by 1.4 per cent per annum: They numbered fewer than 48 million in 2000 than in 1990. This fall in the labour force dependent mainly on the land suggests that China was at least moving in the right direction: If the trend were to continue, the neoclassical stage of the development process would eventually be reached.

Rawski and Mead (1998) reach a more optimistic conclusion. They argue that agricultural employment was exaggerated, and increasingly so, in the official statistics, basically because the number of farm workers was derived as a residual and the number of rural workers entering non-farm activities was increasingly underestimated. It is clearly difficult to determine the main activity of rural workers who combine farm and non-farm activities. Rawski and Mead (1998) measure agricultural employment in a different way, using estimates of labour input per (crop) area and of areas and yields. On this basis, the full-time labour force fell sharply (by 22 per cent) during the period of rural reform (1979–84), when incentives were improving, and thereafter (1984–93) rose very little (by 5 per cent). The implication is that the pressure of population on the land began to ease earlier than we have suggested. However, the authors' evidence that the residual labour force entered unreported non-farm activities rather than underemployment is inconclusive.

There is a general agreement that, prior to the redundancy programme that was introduced in the mid-1990s, there was surplus labour, that is, underemployment of workers, in urban enterprises. It is not easy to estimate the extent of surplus labour. In theory, it might be defined as employment in excess of the profit-maximizing level of employment. In practice, it is generally measured as the excess over the employment 'required' for maximum production, at a given capacity. Various estimates of surplus labour in SOEs were made for the early 1990s (Knight and Song 1995: 101). These included: 25 per cent (by officials in charge of planning and systems reform), 10–12 per cent (a Ministry of Labour survey of 15,000 enterprises), 20–25 per cent (estimates of research institutions), 20 per cent (45 reforming SOEs in Shanghai), 11 per cent (a World Bank survey in two cities), and 23–32 per cent (Jefferson and Xu 1991, for Wuhan). We conclude that the public sector could bear substantial redundancies without loss of output. Since the same pressures for providing jobs were to be found in urban collective enterprises (UCEs), we expect similar urban underemployment to have existed in all but the small private wage sector.

It is fairly clear that urban unemployment was higher in 2000 than at the start of the economic reform, largely because much previously disguised unemployment had become open. Yet registered urban unemployment peaked at 4.9 per cent in 1980 as a result of the young people sent to the countryside during the Cultural Revolution returning to the cities, stayed below 3 per cent for many years, and rose very little—from 2.9 per cent in 1995 to 3.1 per cent in 2000—during the period of widespread retrenchment of urban workers. This series does not reflect the true unemployment situation because of the restrictions on registration. There is an upper age limit (50 for men and 45 for women); it excludes laid-off (*xia gang*) workers, who are treated as nominally still employed by their former work-units; workers who do not qualify for unemployment benefit payments, and those who have been forced into early retirement and receive a pension, cannot register; and migrants (without urban *hukou*) are excluded. There are administrative data also on the number of *xia gang* employees. State employees on permanent contracts who are made redundant remain *xia gang* for a period of three years or until they are formally re-employed. However, the stock of *xia gang* employees may overstate unemployment if some of them become self-employed or take temporary jobs.

The sum of registered unemployment plus *xia gang* employment is the best administratively reported measure of urban unemployment in China, but it leaves out many persons who would qualify to be unemployed on the conventional International Labour Organization (ILO) definition (persons without work, available for work, and seeking work). A more reliable measure of urban unemployment should be available from the population census returns, relating to 1982, 1990, 1995 (a 1 per cent sample), and 2000. Unfortunately, the definitions of unemployment change significantly from one census to another: Only the 2000 census

TABLE 2.4 *Census and administrative estimates of urban unemployment in China, 1982–2000*

	1982	1990	1995	1996	1997	1998	1999	2000
Millions								
Census	3.52	4.90	11.40					24.80
Registered unemployment	3.79	3.83	5.20	5.53	5.70	5.71	5.75	5.95
Xia gang employment	—	—	3.37	4.55	6.34	4.46	4.69	10.92
Total administrative unemployment	3.79	3.83	8.57	10.08	12.04	10.17	10.44	16.87
Percentage of urban labour force								
Census	3.0	2.9	5.6					11.5
Registered unemployment	3.2	2.5	2.9	3.0	3.1	3.1	3.1	3.1
Xia gang employment	—	—	1.4	1.8	2.4	1.4	3.2	4.8
Total administrative unemployment	3.2	2.5	4.3	4.8	5.5	4.5	5.6	7.9

Notes: 1. Many 'youth waiting for higher education' were effectively unemployed. Their inclusion would raise the census unemployment rate in 1982 to 4.2% and in 1990 to 4.2%.

2. In the administrative data the urban labour force is measured as the employed plus the administratively unemployed.

Source: Knight and Xue (2003: tables 1–4, 6).

corresponds to the ILO definition of unemployment. These inconsistencies mean that we cannot be precise about the increase in unemployment.

Knight and Xue (2003) attempted to collate and standardize both the census and the administrative estimates of unemployment (Table 2.4). We see that, largely because of the increasing number of *xia gang* employees, administratively measured urban unemployment rose over the 1990s, from 2.5 per cent of the urban labour force in 1990 to 4.3 per cent in 1995 and to 7.9 per cent in 2000. The equivalent figures for the unemployment rate based on census data were 2.9, 5.6, and 11.5 per cent, respectively.

2.6.2 Rural–urban migration

The leadership of the Communist Party created and sustained an 'invisible Great Wall' between rural and urban China. During the period of central planning, the two societies, each with its own economy, were isolated from each other, institutionally distinct and separately governed. The state intermediated in any trade between them. It prevented the transfer of more labour than was necessary, yet it effected a hidden transfer of capital from the poorer rural to the richer urban sector. As economic reform proceeded, the invisible Great Wall became more permeable in various ways. Nevertheless, its foundations were retained. A set

Introduction

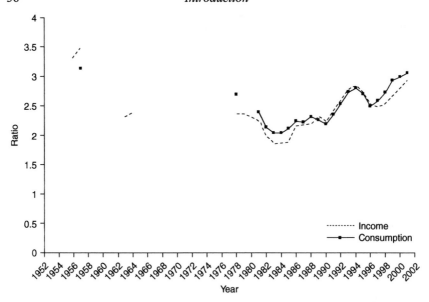

Ratio

Year

FIG. 2.2 *Ratio of average urban/rural income, and consumption, per capita, 1952–2002*

of institutions, policies, and restrictions prevented equilibrating market forces
from eliminating rural–urban disparities. The fascinating story of why and how
rural–urban disparities were created, maintained, and indeed exacerbated is the
subject of our previous book *The Rural–Urban Divide. Economic Disparities and
Interactions in China* (Knight and Song 1999). This divide is a huge obstacle to
the creation of a unified and effective labour market in China.

Figure 2.2 shows the ratio of average urban to rural household income, and
consumption, per capita over both the planning and reform periods. The ratio had
been high throughout the period of central planning, being 2.36 (income) and 2.90
(consumption) in 1978. The ratio fell dramatically as the peasants benefited from
decollectivization and marketization in the period 1978–84. However, by 1984 the
major rural reforms were in place; urban reforms now took centre stage. Thereafter,
and right up to 2000, the disparity between urban and rural China grew larger.
By that year the income ratio had reached 2.79 and the consumption ratio 3.48.
The size of the urban/rural disparity in living standards, and its growth over time,
could be expected to induce an equilibrating movement of labour. Rural–urban
migration did indeed increase, especially after 1990. However, the various controls
on, and deterrents to, the employment of rural migrants in the towns and cities
meant that the factor governing its extent was more one of urban needs than rural
choices.

Rural–urban migration, albeit mainly of a temporary nature, became a growing,
and eventually a major, phenomenon in the Chinese labour market over the period
of economic reform. Unfortunately, it is difficult to make a quantitative estimate of

rural–urban migration. China's censuses of population should be the appropriate source, but the censuses of the past placed people by *hukou* registration, and more recently a certain length of urban residence (more than 12 months in the 1990 census) was required for rural people to be enumerated in urban areas. Rural-based household surveys can accurately record the number of household members absent but lack information on their urban experience. Urban-based household surveys are unlikely to cover the many migrants who stay in hostels, factories, shanties, or the streets.

To arrive at a precise figure, location, duration, and activity have to be specified. A rural migrant might be defined as someone who works 'outside', be it outside the village, or the 'township' (a collection of villages, corresponding to the former 'commune'), or the county. It would be sensible, for instance, to exclude daily commuters. A distinction should be made between rural–urban and other sorts of migrant (rural–rural, urban–urban, urban–rural), and this requires definitions of rural and urban areas. What is the minimum period to count as migration: A week, a month, a year? We need to distinguish between work-related migrants and those who migrate for other reasons, for instance to visit relatives. The difference between stocks and flows of migrants should be recognized. A stock of migrants is the number on any particular date, whereas a flow is the number who migrate during a particular period, say a year. If the average length of time in the city is six months, then the number of migrant-years is half the number who migrate; twice as many people are classified as migrants (the flow) as there are migrants on any day (the stock).

These conceptual and measurement problems help to explain why there is no agreement on the number of Chinese rural–urban migrants. For instance, at a 1996 conference on rural migration in China, a variety of figures were cited, ranging from 30 to 150 million.[3] There is no single 'correct' concept. The choice of concepts, and thus of definitions, should depend on the research questions being asked.

A survey of the 'floating' (i.e. temporary migrant) population of twenty-five large cities in 1988 showed that it came to 23 per cent of the permanent population, having been 9 per cent in 1980 (Li and Hu 1991). Using further information about origins and labour force participation, it was estimated that rural–urban temporary migrants amounted to 12 per cent of the total labour force of these cities in 1988 (Knight and Song 1999: 271–2). From a rural perspective, a national rural household survey conducted in 1993 can be used to estimate the number of rural people working in urban areas. We define rural–urban migrants as those who went outside the township for at least a month to work in an urban area. On this basis, the total annual flow represented 39 million, and the stock of those working in the urban areas at any time in 1993 (given an average work duration of 205 days) was 22 million. These represent 21 and 12 per cent, respectively of the urban labour force (Knight and Song 1999: 273–4). Rozelle et al. (1999) used a survey of households in 200 villages in six provinces in 1995 (with recall to 1988) to estimate the number of out-migrants. These were defined as people who left the village for at least a month in the year for a wage-earning job but retained direct ties to the village. Extrapolated to a national basis, the number of migrants rose from 20 million in 1988 to 54 million in 1995. However, no distinction was made between rural and urban destinations: We expect that most, but not all, of this number were rural–urban migrants.

It is difficult to know whether rural–urban migration rose or fell in the second half of the 1990s. There were two counteracting forces at work. In the face of the radical programme of redundancies in the state sector (with 34 million workers becoming *xia gang* over the period 1996–2000), many city governments restricted the recruitment and re-employment of migrants if they were perceived to be in competition with unemployed urban residents. We see this in the number of 'rural employees in urban registered units'. This peaked at 14.3 million in 1995, when it represented 9.4 per cent of all employees in these units. By 2000, the number had fallen by 5.3 million to 9.0 million, when it represented 7.7 per cent of the total (PRC, MOL 1996: 39; 2001: 8, 14, 29). Over the same period, urban employment in registered units collapsed by 37 million, but outside registered units (in private enterprises and self-employment) it rose by 59 million. City governments had less control over the entry of migrants to the private and self-employment sectors. Johnson (2003) noted the widening gap between the official estimate of total urban employment and the sum of employees recorded in the different forms of ownership. The difference grew from 20 million in 1995 to 62 million in 2000. He suggests that this growth of the residual represents greater use of temporary migrant workers. These pointers indicate that rural–urban migration may have risen despite government intentions and efforts. In line with this, an estimate based on a sample of the 2000 national population census indicates that there were 88 million rural migrants present in the urban areas at that time (Cai 2003: 32).

The late 1990s saw an increase in the number of migrant settlers in the big cities. These were often found in distinct migrant communities from a particular sending area, semi-autonomous and well structured. Such migrants—still registered as rural-dwellers—continued to be at a blatant policy disadvantage with respect not only to jobs but also to such facilities and services as housing and schools. However, they were becoming urbanized de facto, and their reference groups were switching from rural to urban.

2.6.3 *Urban wage behaviour*

In contrast to the stagnation of urban wages over the planning period, wage growth was substantial over the reform period. The average real wage of 'staff and workers' in 1978 was 110 per cent of its 1952 level (implying average annual growth of 0.4 per cent). In 2000, it was 319 per cent of its 1978 level (5.4 per cent). Figure 2.3 illustrates the annual movements of this index over the reform period. These were erratic, with spurts and troughs. The rapid growth in the years 1978–80 (averaging 6.4 per cent per annum) represented a policy change after the long wage

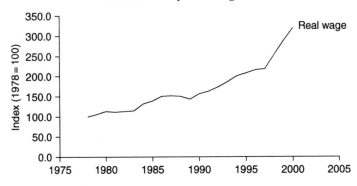

F I G. 2.3 *Average real wage in urban units, 1978–2000*

stagnation, 1981–3 was a period of consolidation (0.5 per cent per annum), the spurt in 1984–6 (9.4 per cent per annum) reflected the initial reform of SOEs, and the halt in 1987–9 (−1.6 per cent per annum) tardy government response to inflation. The resumption of real wage growth over the years 1990–4 (6.9 per cent per annum) indicates a catching-up as inflation decelerated, and a political response to the events of 1989. The pace was moderate (2.9 per cent per annum) during 1995–7, when inflation was serious, but unprecedented (13.6 per cent per annum) from 1998 onwards, reflecting negative inflation, rising profits after radical enterprise reform, and possibly monetization of previous subsidies and payments-in-kind. These wage fluctuations are not amenable to statistical analysis as real wage behaviour was largely a matter of changing government policy, which was more exogenous than endogenous (Knight and Song 1995: 101–2).

The general rise in the urban wage was unlikely to be the result of market forces. First, the rural supply price—insofar as it was relevant—lagged well behind the urban wage. Real income per worker in rural households grew by only 3.4 per cent per annum over the period of urban economic reform, 1985–2000, compared with urban real wage growth of 5.7 per cent per annum. Secondly, there was insuffi-cient labour turnover among urban workers to generate labour market forces. It is difficult to obtain good information on labour turnover but some administratively gathered statistics are available. In 1988, 2.1 per cent of state-sector employees resigned or had their employment terminated. In 1995 this had risen to 5.4 per cent and in 2000 to 6.9 per cent, largely because of the *xia gang* redundancy programme. (PRC, MOL 1990: 268, 320; 1996: 17, 42; 2001: 13, 406). In 1988 urban employ-ment increased by 4.84 million. The number of new assignments was 8.44 million, 4.12 million being of workers already in the urban labour force, that is, who did not enter from education or the rural areas. Assignment of existing urban workers represented 3.2 per cent of urban employment (PRC, MOL 1990: 268, 288–9). In 2000 the corresponding figures were 2.60, 10.09, and 3.31 million, respectively; the last figure representing 1.6 per cent of urban employment (PRC, MOL 2001: 8, 68–9). Thus the rate of labour mobility—that is, transfers from one urban job to

Introduction

T ABLE 2.5 *The composition of wages in state-owned units,*
1978–93 (total = 100), total and basic real wages (1978 = 100)

	1978	1988	1993
Time wage and piece rate standard wage	85.7	56.1	46.6
Bonus and above-quota payments	2.4	19.5	23.3
Subsidies	6.5	21.4	25.1
Other	5.4	3.0	5.1
Total	100.0	100.0	100.0
Total real wages (1978 = 100)	100	153	186
Real 'time wage and piece rate standard wage' (1978 = 100)	100	100	101

Note: The series was discontinued after 1993, reflecting the fact that employers had acquired control over all components of wages.

Sources: PRS, SSB (1991: 107; 1994: 115), PRC, MOL (1996: 47).

another—appeared to be extremely low and not to have increased over the period. It is possible that there were pockets of high labour mobility, for instance among workers with scarce skills, especially if they were demanded in the growing private sector and the most dynamic provinces, but these could not have explained the general rise in real wages.

The share of the 'basic wage' in state-owned work-units declined over the period of economic reform: from 86 per cent in 1978 to 56 per cent in 1988 and to 47 per cent in 1993 (Table 2.5). Both the bonus and the value of subsidies grew correspondingly in importance. The basic wage remained constant in real terms over that period: the near-doubling of the real wage was entirely due to the non-basic components. The extra payments which *danwei* managers were permitted, and chose, to make to their employees were the driving force in pay determination. The distinction between the basic wage and other components became less relevant after 1993 (the last year for which the breakdown was reported) because SOEs acquired control of the wage as a whole. Nevertheless, managerial motivation and action remained the underlying determinant of wage behaviour.

The explanation for the general increase in real wages in this labour-surplus economy is thus likely to be found in the particular characteristics of the Chinese *danwei*. It is arguable that *danwei* leaders identified with their employees and were willing to share profits with them. Management took advantage of the widening scope for them to set wages, initially through the payment of a profit-related bonus or subsidy but later more generally. It is difficult to distinguish empirically between the profit-sharing and the efficiency–wage explanations for wages above the competitively determined market level. The former implies that workers have power in wage bargaining and the latter that workers have control over effort. However, in the Chinese case the two mechanisms may well be intertwined. Workers expect to share in any profits of their *danwei*, and managers expect to encounter diminished effort and weaker compliance unless profits are indeed shared.

2.7 CONCLUSIONS

The task that we set ourselves in this chapter was to provide the skeleton that will be fleshed out in the chapters to come. China has embarked on a journey from plan to market. In some spheres that journey is not far from completion; in the sphere of labour, China has a long way to go.

It was necessary to understand the labour system—involving direction of labour and administration of wages—which was established in the 1950s and continued throughout the period of central planning and beyond. We explained both the Soviet origins of the labour system and its distinctive Chinese characteristics, moulded by tradition and differing circumstances. The labour system avoided open unemployment and serious urbanization problems, it provided employees with security, and it achieved egalitarian objectives. However, it scored badly in terms of the mobility, flexibility, incentives, and efficiency of labour.

It was helpful to compare the process of economic reform in rural and in urban China. Rural China was ready for reform. Once they were given a signal, the peasants, acting in an uncoordinated way, took the initiative. There were few losers, and thus there was little opposition from vested interests. By a process of cumulative causation, reform begat further reform, and so on. The major elements of rural reform were fairly complete within half-a-dozen years. By contrast, urban reform efforts ran up against two main obstacles. One was the vested interests of the SOEs and their privileged urban employees. The other was the need for coordination of various interrelated reforms, giving rise to problems of sequencing. Both obstacles were relevant to the tardy process of moving from a labour system to a labour market.

Central to this issue is the *danwei*, a social institution very different from an employer in the Western sense. It was not going to be possible to create an urban labour market while the *danwei* continued to perform its functions of lifetime employer, mini welfare state, and—after wage-setting became decentralized—profit-sharer. Labour reform has involved de jure, and some de facto, ending of lifetime employment, and such functions as the provision of housing, health-care, pensions, and social security have been transferred elsewhere or are in the process of being transferred. Nevertheless, the continuing influence of the *danwei* is apparent in the extremely low mobility of labour between employers and in the profit-related behaviour of wages in recent years.

Because China has had a surplus labour economy, it was helpful to adopt the theoretical framework of the Lewis model. The model proved to be appropriate for the period of central planning, except in one respect: surplus labour, in the form of overmanning, was found in the urban as well as the rural sector. The model proved to be less appropriate for the period of economic reform.

The growth of rural industry and the growing differentiation among urban workers did not fit the simple distinction between a rural, agricultural sector and an urban, industrial sector. Moreover, the rapid urban real wage growth was inconsistent with the predictions of the model. The evidence for claiming that urban wages rose in response to market forces is weak. Explanations in terms of worker threat, efficiency wages, and *danwei* objectives are nearer the mark. Insofar as a labour market was being formed in China over the 1980s and 1990s, it appeared to be a highly segmented one.

The empirical analysis of this chapter has highlighted the need for good data if we are to understand and assess the workings of the Chinese labour market. Some of the official data are gathered from censuses and surveys, and some are gathered within an administrative framework. There is potential for a large and widening gap between these two sorts of estimate in an economy that is both grow-ing and changing rapidly. This we saw in the case of the residual categories urban 'other employment' and rural 'household workers', and in the different measures of unemployment. The extrapolation of census estimates between and beyond census years involves substantial revisions when new census results become available. The official censuses have not adequately measured the extent and dimensions of the growing phenomenon of rural–urban migration. The official statistics of aver-age wages cover only 'staff and workers' (corresponding roughly to employees of registered work-units)—a diminishing fraction of urban employment. Thus, on several of the key issues, Chinese official statistics are found wanting. They need to be supplemented, or replaced, with sample surveys which are specifically designed to answer the research questions. This is the approach that, for the most part, we adopt in the chapters to come.

NOTES

1. This account of the urban labour system prior to reform draws on various sources, primarily Howe (1973), Korzec and Whyte (1981), Takahara (1992), Shirk (1981), Walder (1987), White (1988, 1993), and Knight and Song (1991).
2. This account of the urban labour reforms draws on various sources, primarily World Bank (1991, 1992), Knight and Song (1991, 1995, 1999), Lim and Sziraczki (1995), Maurer-Fazio (1995), Takahara (1992), Warner (1995), White (1993), Zhu (1995), and OECD (2002).
3. The International Conference on the Flow of Rural Labour in China, organized by the Research Centre for Rural Economy, Ministry of Agriculture, and the Ford Foundation, was held in Beijing in June 1996.

REFERENCES

Bo, Yibo (1991). *Review of Some Important Policies and Events*, Beijing: Shong Gong Zhong Yong Dang Xiao Publication House (in Chinese).

Cai, Fang (2003). 'Reform of labour policy in China: a perspective of political economy', *China and World Economy*, 11, 4: 30–7.

Deng, Xiaoping (1983). *Deng Xiaoping's Collected Works, 1938–1965*, Beijing: People's Publication House (in Chinese).

Du, Runsheng (1989). *China's Rural Economic Reform*, Beijing: Foreign Languages Press.

Jefferson, G.H. and W. Xu (1991). 'The impact of reform on socialist enterprises in transition: structure, conduct and performance in Chinese industry', *Journal of Comparative Economics*, 15: 45–60.

Johnson, D. Gale (2003). 'Provincial migration in China in the 1990s', *China Economic Review*, 14: 22–31.

Howe, Christopher (1973). *Wage Patterns and Wage Policy in Modern China, 1919–1972*, Cambridge: Cambridge University Press.

Knight, John and Song Lina (1991). 'The determinants of urban income inequality in China', *Oxford Bulletin of Economics and Statistics*, 53, 2: 123–54.

—— —— (1995). 'Towards a labour market in China', *Oxford Review of Economic Policy*, 11, 4 (Winter): 97–117.

—— —— (1999). *The Rural–Urban Divide. Economic Disparities and Interactions in China*, Oxford: Oxford University Press.

—— —— (2001). 'Economic growth, economic reform, and rising inequality in China', in Carl Riskin, Zhao Renwei, and Li Shi (eds), *China's Retreat from Equality. Income Distribution and Economic Transition*, Armonk, NY: M.E. Sharpe, 84–124.

—— and Xue Jinjun (2003). 'How high is urban unemployment in China?', typescript.

Korzec, Michael and Martin King Whyte (1981). 'Reading notes: the Chinese wage system', *China Quarterly*, 86 (June): 248–73.

Lee, Jung-Hee (1997). 'Debates over labour reforms in post-Mao China (1978–1995)', *Global Economic Review*, 26, 4 (Winter): 109–35.

Lewis, W. Arthur, (1954). 'Economic development with unlimited supplies of labour', *The Manchester School*, 22 (May): 139–92.

Li, Jinquan (1989). 'The reward system', in *Almanac of Labour and Personnel, 1949–1987*, Beijing: Labour and Personnel Press, 447–61 (in Chinese).

Li, Mengbai and Hu Xing (1991). *The Impact of the Floating Population on the Development of Big Cities in China*, Beijing: Institute of Urban and Rural Construction (in Chinese).

Li, Weiyi (1992). *China's Wage System*, Beijing: China Labour Publishing House (in Chinese).

Lim, Lin Lean and Gyorgy Sziraczki (1995). *Employment Challenges and Policy Responses: Chinese and International Perspectives*, Beijing: International Labour Office.

Mao, Zedong (1969). 'On the People's Democratic Dictatorship', in *Collected Works of Mao Tse-Tung (Mao Zedong)*, Vol. iv, Beijing: Foreign Languages Press.

Maurer-Fazio, Margaret (1995). 'Labour reform in China: crossing the river by feeling the stones', *Comparative Economic Studies*, 37, 4 (Winter): 111–23.

Naughton, Barry (1995). *Growing Out of the Plan*, Cambridge: Cambridge University Press.

Organisation for Economic Co-operation and Development (OECD) (2002). *China in the World Economy. The Domestic Policy Challenges*, Paris: OECD.

People's Republic of China, Ministry of Labour (and Social Security) (PRC, MOL) (various years). *China Labour Statistical Yearbook*, Beijing: China Statistical Press.

People's Republic of China, State Statistical Bureau (PRC, SSB) (various years up to 1998). *China Statistical Yearbook*, Beijing: Statistical Publishing House.

People's Republic of China, National Bureau of Statistics (PRC, NBS) (various years from 1999). *China Statistical Yearbook*, Beijing: Statistical Publishing House.

Rawski, Thomas G. and Robert W. Mead (1998). 'On the trail of China's phantom farmers', *World Development*, 26, 5: 767–81.

Rozelle, Scott, Li Guo, Minggao Shen, Amelia Hughart, and John Giles (1999). 'Leaving China's farms: survey results of new paths and remaining hurdles to rural migration', *China Quarterly*, 158 (June): 367–93.

Shirk, Susan L. (1981). 'Recent Chinese labour policies and the transformation of industrial organisation in China', *China Quarterly*, 88 (December): 575–93.

Takahara, Akio (1992). *The Politics of Wage Policy in Post-Revolutionary China*, London: Macmillan.

Taylor, Jeffrey R. (1988). 'Rural employment trends and the legacy of surplus labour 1928–86', *China Quarterly*, 116 (December): 736–66.

Walder, Andrew G. (1987). 'Wage reform and the web of factory interests', *China Quarterly*, 116 (December): 733–66.

Wang Lina (2001). 'Urban housing welfare and income distribution', in Carl Riskin, Zhao Renwei and Li Shi (eds), *China's Retreat from Equality. Income Distribution and Economic Transition*, Armonk, New York: M.E. Sharpe, 167–83.

Warner, Malcolm (1995). *The Management of Human Resources in Chinese Industry*, London: Macmillan.

White, Gordon (1988). 'Evolving relations between state and worker in the reform of China's urban industrial economy', in Stephan Feuchtwang, Athar Hussain, and Thierry Pairault (eds), *Transforming China's Economy in the Eighties, vol. ii*, Boulder CO.: Westview Press.

——(1993). *Riding the Tiger. The Politics of Economic Reform in Post-Mao China*, London: Macmillan.

World Bank (1991). 'China labour and wage reform: recent progress and issues for the future', China and Mongolia Department, seminar paper, October: 1–15.

—— World Bank (1992). *China. Reforming the Urban Employment and Wage System*, Washington DC: World Bank.

Zhu Ying (1995). 'Major changes under way in China's industrial relations', *International Labour Review*, 134: 37–49.

PART II

THE URBAN LABOUR MARKET

3

Increasing Wage Inequality

In this chapter we shall examine the extent of wage inequality in urban China, and how it changed over time. We argued in Chapter 2 that the reform of the urban labour market was tardy, being held back by ideology, by the latent power of urban workers, and by policy interdependence and sequencing. Nevertheless, from small beginnings in the early 1980s, government permitted relaxation of the extremely egalitarian wage policy that held sway under central planning. Its new objectives were to provide incentives, promote labour efficiency, and foster rapid economic growth. To what extent did labour market reform increase wage inequality? What were the sources of the increase? To answer these questions we shall analyse changes in the urban wage structure between 1988 and 1995.

Policies of egalitarianism in the labour market are likely to curtail economic efficiency. The efficiency–equity trade-off can be illustrated in Figure 3.1. The efficiency frontier Y shows the effect of a higher Gini coefficient (G) on output: It is assumed that greater inequality resulting from the move from an administered labour system towards a labour market permits or encourages higher efficiency, although the effect is subject to diminishing returns. More wage inequality, resulting for instance from greater rewards for productive characteristics, can have allocative and incentive effects which raise average labour productivity. The curve W_1 illustrates the pre-reform egalitarian social welfare function: its curvature implies that the additional output required to compensate for a rise in inequality is an increasing function of inequality. The initial optimum is therefore at a, the point of tangency between the efficiency frontier and the highest attainable social welfare curve. With the economic reform came a change in the social welfare function, say, to W_2. The optimum was now at d, the new point of tangency, involving more efficiency and less equity. The labour market observed in our surveys may well be in transition between points a and d, say point b in 1988 and c in 1995. It is possible, however, that the partial and imperfect reform of the labour market involved a within-frontier trade-off, such as the curve Y', in which case the points b' and c' are observed. It is also possible that the economic reform, by creating new attitudes, institutions, and interest groups, itself carried the social welfare function (as expressed by evolving government objectives) along with it. The grand issues underlying this chapter can be expressed in terms of the figure. Is there evidence that increased wage inequality is associated with increased labour efficiency?

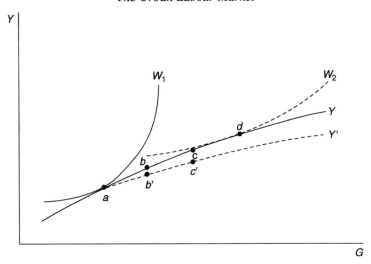

FIG. 3.1 *The efficiency–equality trade-off*

To what extent did the reform improve the operation of the labour market? Has the wage structure become economically more rational? Although our data do not permit us to answer these questions, we shall try to illuminate them by examining changes in the returns to productive and unproductive characteristics.

We shall show that the inequality of wages in urban China has increased sharply in recent years: the Gini coefficient rose from 22.9 to 30.7 per cent between 1988 and 1995. However, wage inequality has widened in many countries: China's experience is part of a broader phenomenon. In the United States 'a large descriptive literature has documented the rise in inequality, while a smaller behavioral literature has sought to delineate the causes of this rise' (Gottschalk 1997: 21). The two main hypotheses put forward to explain the rise are in terms of trade or technology. However, the argument (put forward, for instance, by Wood 1993) that increased trade widens the wage structure in skill-intensive economies would imply a narrowing of the wage structure in China, given its comparative advantage in unskilled labour-intensive production. Moreover, the weight of empirical evidence for developed countries suggests that the rising inequality of wages is demand-driven: Technical progress has favoured skilled labour in production, and the supply of skills has not kept pace with the rising demand (Topel 1997: 72). This is an explanation of movement from one market equilibrium to another. In China the reforms may well have produced a movement from market disequilibrium towards equilibrium. However, rapid economic growth and structural change may also have increased the scarcity of skilled labour and widened the equilibrium wage structure.

Svejnar (1999: 2852–3) concluded from his survey of labour markets in the European transition economies that market pressures forced a greater dispersion of wages, and that the returns to education generally rose but those to experience generally fell. Few studies could identify an effect of ownership on wages but there was evidence that wages started to vary by firm performance (with the implication of rent-sharing). It will be interesting to discover the ways in which the Chinese transition is similar to and the ways in which it is different from the European transition.

We propose to examine these issues by analysing the IE, CASS national household surveys referred to in Chapter 1. These are two cross-section surveys, relating to the years 1988 and 1995, with samples selected and questionnaires designed so as to make them directly comparable. They were subsamples of the sample used for the annual national household income survey of the State Statistical Bureau (SSB), now known as the National Bureau of Statistics (NBS): they covered ten of the thirty-one provinces in 1988 and eleven (the same ten plus Sichuan) in 1995.[1] Separate urban and rural samples were drawn, reflecting the organization of the SSB and the need to administer different questionnaires. The questionnaires were in various ways much more detailed than those used in the official surveys, reflecting our concern not only with description but also with explanation. The results from the 1988 survey were published primarily in Griffin and Zhao (1993), and those of the 1995 survey primarily in Riskin, Zhao, and Li (2001).

We see in Table 3.1 that the mean real wage increased by 52 per cent (6.1 per cent per annum) over the period 1988–95. The table also shows what happened to the inequality of earnings over the seven years. Two types of inequality measures are used: Measures which embody all the data in one statistic (the Gini coefficient,

TABLE 3.1 *Measures of central tendency and dispersion of earnings per worker, 1988 and 1995, at 1995 prices: urban China*

	1988	1995	1995 minus 1988	1995 (1988 = 100)
Mean	4,151	6,294	2,143	152
Median	3,793	5,598	1,805	148
10th percentile	2,343	2,479	136	106
90th percentile	6,045	10,596	4,551	175
Ratio of 90th to 10th percentile	2.58	4.27	1.69	166
Ratio of 90th percentile to median	1.59	1.89	0.30	119
Ratio of median to 10th percentile	1.62	2.26	0.64	140
Gini coefficient (%)	22.9	30.7	7.8	134
Coefficient of variation (%)	57.2	62.2	5.0	109
Log variance	0.179	0.484	0.305	270
Number of observations	17,830	10,626		

Note: The data refer to the urban samples of employed (not retired) individuals aged 16 and above and receiving earned income.

Source: Of this and subsequent tables in this chapter, Knight and Song (2003).

the coefficient of variation, and the variance of log earnings) and measures of the dispersion of earnings structure (the ratios of the 90th to the 10th percentile, of the 90th to the median, and of the median to the 10th). Not only did inequality increase on all three measures but structure widened on all three measures. Whereas the median increase in real earnings was 48 per cent, the pay of the 10th percentile (the worker ranked 10 per cent from the bottom) rose by only 6 per cent, and that of the 90th percentile by 75 per cent. The ratio of the 90th to the 10th percentile earnings rose by 66 per cent; this widening was greater below the median than above it.

It will be helpful to explain our approach to the analysis of the growing inequality. The underlying hypothesis is that it represents a move towards wages which reward efficiency. The household-based data sets enable us to estimate earnings functions but not production functions: We cannot, therefore, provide a direct test of the hypothesis by relating payments for worker characteristics to their marginal products. Our test is necessarily indirect and no more than suggestive. Can the observed changes plausibly be interpreted as the consequence of strengthened labour market forces and of increased rewards for productive characteristics? Our sweep is broad-brush and we have deliberately sacrificed analytical rigour and the full complexities of equation specification in order to draw out the big picture and to conduct decompositions. All the observable determinants of wages are therefore covered. We attempt in one chapter what could only be done thoroughly and with best-practice methods in several chapters. The chapter is best seen as an exploratory data analysis establishing associational patterns and not necessarily causal relationships. Fortunately, however, the initial direction of workers to jobs and their subsequent immobility mean that our data sets are not beset by problems of endogeneity and selection bias to the same extent as in competitive labour markets.[2]

In order to analyse these changes in the structure and inequality of earnings that occurred in urban China between 1988 and 1995, it is important to assess the extent to which a labour market was created over those seven years. Recall the evolution of labour market policy examined in Chapter 2. During the period of central planning there was no labour market. The centralized control of enterprises provided no inducement for the efficient use of labour, and indeed surplus labour was imposed on enterprises. Workers had few material incentives to acquire human capital, to work efficiently, or to improve work methods. The system enabled the state to pursue its egalitarian objectives. The year 1988 was an early year in the process of economic reform, and 1995 a late year. However, the move had been towards decentralization of labour management rather than towards a properly functioning labour market. In 1995, the state sector was still dominant and labour turnover remained low, and many wages appeared to be governed institutionally or by ability to pay rather than by market forces. Nevertheless, the reforms corresponded to a change in the objective function of the Chinese Government away from equality and towards efficiency objectives; and economic agents were freer in 1995 to pursue their interests than they had been in the early stage of the urban reforms.

3.2 THE CHANGE IN WAGE STRUCTURE

We estimate earnings functions of the form $y = f(x)$ where y is the logarithm of individual earnings and x is a vector of characteristics. Table 3.2 presents estimates for both 1988 and 1995, using the urban individual samples. The specifications are identical to facilitate comparisons, and earnings in both years are expressed in 1995 prices. The explanatory variables that might represent discrimination are gender, minority status, and Communist Party membership; those that might reflect segmentation are ownership and province; and the potential human capital variables are educational level, age group, and skill-based occupation.

There are important differences in the coefficients for the two years. Consider the variables that might represent discrimination. The coefficient on female sex, negative in 1988, became larger, while the disadvantage of minority status and the apparent advantage of Communist Party membership increased over the period. All three coefficients were significant in 1995. Although the association of Communist Party membership and earnings may be at least partly due to members having superior personal qualities, it is unlikely that the rise in the coefficient is due to increased superiority in the personal qualities of the slow-changing stock of members over the seven years. It appears that the decentralization of wage setting and recruitment made it possible for employers to discriminate more on non-economic grounds. The relative wage advantage of employees in state-owned enterprises and institutions generally increased: only foreign-owned enterprise pay rose relative to state pay. Again, although state employees may possess unobserved personal qualities which contribute to their wage advantage, it is unlikely that the growth in this advantage is due to a relative improvement in such qualities. This growing segmentation suggests that a large part of the urban economy remained immune to labour market forces. The spatial dispersion of wages increased considerably: in 1995 the standard deviation of the province coefficients was 2.3 times its 1988 level. The growing wage segmentation among provinces was not offset by equilibrating labour mobility.

By contrast, there is also some evidence to suggest that market forces have become more important in certain respects. In particular, the returns to education rose sharply. For instance, the earnings difference between college graduates and primary school-leavers, *ceteris paribus*, was 9 per cent in 1988 and 42 per cent in 1995. Moreover, the coefficients of the occupation terms indicated some increase in the earnings premium on occupation-specific skills. This is best seen by comparing the omitted category, production workers, with cadres and professional and technical workers: The percentage skill premium rose from 5 to 17 per cent in each case. The age–earnings profile changed in an interesting way. The earnings of those under 26 fell drastically relative to the omitted category (age 26–30). In 1995 the profile peaked earlier (at age 41–45 instead of 51–60) and fell dramatically after age 60. This is consistent with a move to a more productivity-based and a less bureaucratically based earnings structure. The age groups that suffered a relative fall were young people, now having to compete for jobs and possibly

TABLE 3.2 *Earnings functions for individual workers in urban China, 1988 and 1995*

Variable	Notation	Mean value		Ln earnings	
		1988	1995	1988	1995
Intercept		1.000	1.000	7.957**	8.230**
Female sex	S_2	0.476	0.472	−0.093**	−0.148**
Minority status	M_2	0.038	0.047	−0.020	−0.065*
Communist party member	CP_1	0.235	0.251	0.041**	0.086**
State-owned	OW_1	0.388	0.271	0.132*	0.239**
Local publicly owned	OW_2	0.387	0.529	0.062*	0.072
Urban collective	OW_3	0.202	0.149	−0.018	−0.076
Sino-foreign joint venture	OW_5	0.003	0.011	0.325**	0.298**
Foreign-owned	OW_6	0.001	0.001	−0.152	0.726**
Other	OW_7	0.005	0.006	−0.147	−0.016
Beijing	P_{11}	0.049	0.082	0.160**	0.119**
Shanxi	P_{14}	0.108	0.107	−0.059**	−0.405**
Liaoning	P_{21}	0.104	0.119	0.012	−0.249**
Anhui	P_{34}	0.099	0.081	−0.095**	−0.321**
Henan	P_{41}	0.118	0.095	−0.150**	−0.409**
Hubei	P_{42}	0.109	0.119	−0.098**	−0.209**
Guangdong	P_{44}	0.119	0.097	0.239**	0.437**
Yunnan	P_{53}	0.102	0.109	0.073**	−0.216**
Gansu	P_{62}	0.066	0.063	−0.005	−0.440**
College or above	E_1	0.061	0.079	0.151**	0.401**
Professional school	E_2	0.067	0.156	0.100**	0.328**
Middle-level professional, technical, vocational school	E_3	0.110	0.165	0.092**	0.309**
Upper-middle school	E_4	0.247	0.247	0.102**	0.251**
Lower-middle school	E_5	0.385	0.300	0.100**	0.181**
Primary school	E_6	0.104	0.048	0.065**	0.021
Owner of private or individual enterprise	OC_1	0.011	0.013	0.168**	0.063
Owner and manager of private enterprise	OC_2	0.002	0.002	0.043	0.057
Professional or technical worker	OC_3	0.157	0.213	0.043**	0.162**
Cadre	OC_4	0.064	0.117	0.057**	0.155**
Office worker	OC_5	0.234	0.204	0.010	0.065**
−20	A_1	0.054	0.022	−0.210**	−0.545**
21–25	A_2	0.109	0.089	−0.081**	−0.217**
31–35	A_4	0.174	0.153	0.117**	0.152**
36–40	A_5	0.178	0.192	0.186**	0.233**
41–45	A_6	0.128	0.199	0.272**	0.290**
46–50	A_7	0.123	0.117	0.314**	0.250**
51–55	A_8	0.077	0.069	0.334**	0.188**
56–60	A_9	0.034	0.040	0.336**	0.110**
61–65	A_{10}	0.005	0.008	0.331**	−0.635**
66–	A_{11}	0.002	0.002	0.136	−0.606**
Adj. R^2				0.313	0.352
F-value				209.253**	148.812**
Dependent mean		8.240	8.563		
Number of observations		17,830	10,627		

Notes: The omitted categories in the dummy variable analysis are S_1 (male sex), E_7 (no education), M_1 (Han), OW_4 (private or individually owned), A_3 (age 26–30), P_{32} (Jiangsu province), CP_2 (not a Communist Party member), and OC_6 (production worker). Statistical significance is based on robust standard errors corrected for heteroscedasticity. ** denotes statistical significance at 1% and * at 5% level.

having effectively to pay for skill acquisition in this more competitive market, and older people, becoming less productive.

3.3 DECOMPOSING THE WAGE INCREASE

Using the earnings functions of Table 3.2, the growth of earnings between 1988 and 1995 can be decomposed as:

$$\bar{y}_1 - \bar{y}_0 = f_1(\bar{x}_1 - \bar{x}_0) + (\bar{f}_1 - \bar{f}_0)\bar{x}_0 \tag{3.1}$$

where the first term reflects the effect of differences in characteristics and the second the effect of differences in coefficients. The alternative decomposition is:

$$\bar{y}_1 - \bar{y}_0 = f_0(\bar{x}_1 - \bar{x}_0) + (\bar{f}_1 - \bar{f}_0)\bar{x}_1 \tag{3.2}$$

Table 3.3 presents a decomposition of the growth in mean real wages over the seven years, using the two alternative decomposition formulae. When the coefficients of 1988 are used to measure the effect of the change in mean characteristics (column (1)), the effect is slight: 92 per cent of the growth in wages is due to the change in the income-generation mechanism. Using the coefficients of 1995 (column (2))—when skill was better rewarded—the improved characteristics of the labour force account for 28 per cent of the wage increase, the human capital variables as a group for 30 per cent, and increased education alone for 12 per cent.

The table shows that some changes in the earnings function raised the mean wage and some lowered it. The contribution of a variable or a set of variables is arbitrary because the choice of omitted category in a dummy variable analysis alters the relative contributions of the intercept and the dummies. The intercept term rose by 31 per cent over the seven years.[3] This relates to the pay of those possessing the characteristics of the omitted categories (uneducated, male, Han, 26–30 year old, production worker, in the private sector, in Jiangsu). This might be thought of as the unskilled, market wage except in one respect: It is better measured as the change in all the provinces rather than in prosperous Jiangsu. At the national level this standardized unskilled, market wage lagged well behind the average wage, rising in real terms by only 15 per cent.[4] On the one hand, the greater discrimination against women, the relative fall in the pay of young and old workers, and the fall in wages elsewhere relative to Jiangsu pulled down the wage. On the other hand, the higher returns to education can explain some 40 per cent of the entire increase in the wage, the greater payment to workers in the state-owned relative to the private sector can explain about 10 per cent, and the higher premia on occupational skills about 15 per cent. The most interesting conclusion to be drawn from this decomposition analysis is that education—both its expansion and the increase in returns—was important in raising the mean real wage of urban workers between 1988 and 1995.

TABLE 3.3 *Decomposition of the increase in mean real wages: urban China, 1988–95*

Percentage due to	(1)	(2)
Mean characteristics		
Total	8.5	27.5
Discrimination variables	0.0	0.1
Segmentation variables	−1.3	−2.9
Ownership	−1.0	−3.8
Province	−0.3	0.9
Human capital variables	9.9	29.7
Education	1.3	12.3
Age	7.0	12.3
Occupation	1.6	5.1
Coefficients		
Total	91.5	72.5
Discrimination variables	−4.2	−5.3
Gender	−7.9	−8.2
Segmentation variables	−43.1	−41.4
Ownership	8.5	11.4
Province	−51.6	−52.8
Human capital variables	47.2	27.2
Education	47.2	36.1
Age	−16.1	−21.5
Occupation	16.1	12.6
Intercept term	92.0	92.0

Notes: The difference in (geometric) mean wages (in 1995 prices) that is to be explained is 1,445 yuan per annum (=100.0%). The decompositions are based on Table 3.2. Column (1) shows the decomposition based on the means of 1995 and the coefficients of 1988, and column (2) the decomposition based on the means of 1988 and the coefficients of 1995.

3.4 DECOMPOSING THE RISE IN INEQUALITY

One approach to understanding the rise in earnings inequality is to examine the contribution of particular characteristics, or sets of characteristics, to the change in a summary measure of inequality. We choose the Gini coefficient, which rose sharply over the seven years—from 22.9 to 30.7 per cent. This increase is decomposed into the contributions of the various characteristics which enter the earnings function.

Consider the income sources of individual i: $y_i = \sum_k y_{ik}$. Shorrocks (1982) has shown, for a large class of inequality measures, that the share of inequality contributed by income source k is given by:

$$\pi_k = \frac{\text{cov}(y_k, y)}{\text{var}(y)} = r_k s_k / s \tag{3.3}$$

where r_k and s_k are respectively the correlation coefficients with total income and the standard deviation of income source k, s is the standard deviation of income, and $\sum_k \pi_k = 1$. The contribution of the income source k thus depends on its degree of correlation with income (r_k) and its relative degree of inequality (s_k/s). In fact, π_k is simply the ordinary least squares (OLS) regression of y_k on y.

Jenkins (1995), Fields (1996), and Ravallion and Chen (1999) adapt this formula to calculate the contribution of income source k to the change in inequality over time:

$$\mu_k = \frac{\pi_{k1} I_1 - \pi_{k0} I_0}{I_1 - I_0} \tag{3.4}$$

where I_j $(j = 1, 0)$ is a measure of inequality and $\sum_k \mu_k = 1$. How can this equation be applied when characteristics determine income through a stochastic process? We have $y_i = \sum_k \beta_k x_{ik}$ where x_k is characteristic k (one of this set being an error term, for which $\beta_k = 1$). The contribution of characteristic k to inequality of income is

$$\pi_k = \frac{\beta_k \text{cov}(x_k, y)}{\text{var}(y)} \tag{3.5}$$

This is equivalent simply to the partial regression coefficient of income on characteristic k, holding all other variables constant (β_k) multiplied by the total regression coefficient of characteristic k on income, holding nothing else constant $(\text{cov}(x_k, y)/\text{var}(y))$.[5]

The decomposition is based on the equations reported in Table 3.2. Table 3.4 shows the percentage contribution of each variable to inequality in 1988 and in 1995, and its contribution to the increase in inequality over the seven years. It also provides corresponding information for the sets of variables representing productive characteristics and market imperfections. Only a third of earnings inequality can be explained by the independent variables available, that is, the sum of π_k for all the explanatory variables is 31.5 per cent in 1988 and 34.9 per cent in 1995: The unexplained residual is important in both cases. The contribution of each independent variable to the change in overall inequality is obtained by estimating μ_k. Only a minority of the increase in inequality is accounted for (this is the net contribution as some components have an equalizing effect). The final column of the table decomposes the part that can be explained.

Given that women were less well-paid than men initially, their enlarged negative coefficient contributed a little to the increase in inequality, as measured by the Gini coefficient. However, the discrimination variables as a group could explain only 3 per cent of the increase in inequality. The segmentation variables accounted for 10 per cent of inequality in 1988 but for as much as 17 per cent in 1995, mainly because of the more dispersed province coefficients. Although ownership form also contributed, province alone accounted for 33 per cent of the growth in inequality.

T A B L E 3.4 *Decomposition of earnings inequality by the determinants of earnings: urban China, 1988, 1995, and 1988–95*

	1988	1995	1988–95	
			Total increase	Explained increase
Human capital	18.0	14.8	5.2	8.6
Education	0.3	3.0	10.7	24.0
Age	16.5	9.1	−12.7	−28.5
Occupation	1.2	2.7	7.2	16.2
Disequalizing components	6.8	11.1	29.4	64.6
Discrimination	3.2	3.2	2.9	6.4
Gender	2.2	1.9	1.0	2.2
Communist Party membership	1.0	1.2	1.7	3.7
Minority status	0.0	0.1	0.2	0.4
Segmentation	10.3	16.9	36.4	79.9
Ownership form	2.2	2.6	3.8	8.3
Province	8.1	14.3	32.6	71.6
Residual	68.5	65.1	55.5	

Notes: The decomposition of the change in inequality is based on the Gini coefficient. The disequalizing components of human capital are education beyond secondary school, the professional, technical, and administrative occupations, and age below 26 and above 60.

The human capital variables are the second-most important identifiable disequalizing force. Education contributed 11 per cent and skill-based occupation 7 per cent. By contrast, age had an equalizing effect overall. The relative fall in the earnings of well-paid prime-age workers (aged 45–60) reduced inequality considerably, whereas the relative fall in the earnings of workers under 25 and over 60 raised it. This last effect plus the relative rise in the earnings of those with more than secondary education and those in professional, technical, and administrative occupations together accounted for 29 per cent of the increase in inequality. These particular changes are likely to represent the stirring of labour market forces and a move towards efficiency-based pay determination. This decomposition analysis suggests that there is indeed an efficiency–equity trade-off to be made.

3.5 THE RISE IN WAGE INEQUALITY: QUANTILE REGRESSION ANALYSIS

In Section 3.4 as much as two-thirds of earnings inequality, and just over half of the increase in inequality, could not be explained by the independent variables at our disposal. The unobserved determinants of earnings are clearly important, and deserve investigation. Quantile regression analysis might be able to provide the means: It can be used to compare the earnings function at different points in the conditional wage distribution (Buchinsky 1994; Mwabu and Schultz 1996; Koenker and Hallock 2001). Quantiles are defined in terms of the conditional wage distribution. Where $0 < q < 1$ is the quantile (percentage from the bottom) of interest, the regression is obtained by minimizing the sum of the absolute deviations of the equation residuals, weighted according to q. This effectively requires that the proportion q of the error terms are negative and $(1 - q)$ are positive.[6] The error term represents measurement error, or chance, or unobserved individual characteristics attracting payments ('ability' for short), or unobserved characteristics of the employer or of the locality that affect the wage. Quantile differences in the coefficients on an explanatory variable may therefore reveal a relationship between it and the unobserved influences. Quantile regressions are estimated for values of $q = 0.125, 0.375, 0.625,$ and 0.875 (corresponding to the midpoints of the quarters) in both years. A full set of explanatory variables (corresponding to those in Table 3.2) is included, but only those coefficients which reveal interesting patterns are shown in Table 3.5.

Consider education: With only trivial exceptions, in both years and at each quantile, the coefficients on the education terms (no education being the omitted dummy variable) are ranked according to educational level. In relation to no education, the coefficient on each educational level tends to decline as we move up the quantiles. With only one exception, the coefficient is greater at the 0.125 than at the 0.875 quantile. For instance, from the first row of Table 3.5 we see that in 1988 the coefficient on college education was 0.17 at the former quantile and 0.08 at the latter. One interpretation of these results is that unobserved personal characteristics are a substitute for education (for instance, education is less valuable for those with ability). However, the normal expectation is that education and ability are complements, that is, the coefficient on education should be greater at the higher quantiles.[7]

An alternative interpretation is that unobserved employer characteristics (such as ability to pay) can raise conditional pay but lower the returns to education. In China the more profitable enterprises raise wages by paying bonuses and subsidies over and above basic wages (Chapter 7). Such payments tend to be more equally distributed within the enterprise than are basic wages, at least in 1988.[8] This reduces the returns to education in the log wage equation for profitable enterprises, which are likely to be near the top of the conditional distribution. It is relevant that Meng (2002), analysing an enterprise-based survey in 1999, found that the pay of urban workers was positively related to the profitability of their enterprises, and also that the returns to education were lower for profit-making enterprises (PMEs) than for loss-making enterprises (LMEs). This is consistent with our hypothesis.[9] Another indirect test was to distinguish the basic wage and the bonus. In 1988—when the distinction was clear—in the case of the bonus, education was not rewarded at the median: The returns accrued only at the bottom

TABLE 3.5 *The coefficients on selected variables in quantile regressions, 1988 and 1995*

		Quantile											
		0.125			0.375			0.625			0.875		
		1988	1995	1995 minus 1988	1988	1995	1995 minus 1988	1988	1995	1995 minus 1988	1988	1995	1995 minus 1988
College or above	E_1	0.1714**	0.6583**	0.4869	0.1420**	0.4882**	0.3462	0.1471**	0.4882**	0.3411	0.0754**	0.3829**	0.3075
Professional school	E_2	0.1365**	0.5958**	0.4593	0.0930**	0.3951**	0.3021	0.0858**	0.4408**	0.3550	0.0276	0.3320**	0.3044
Middle level professional, technical, vocational school	E_3	0.1440**	0.5461**	0.2021	0.0898**	0.3847**	0.2949	0.0658**	0.4237*	0.3579	0.0012	0.3210**	0.3198
Upper middle school	E_4	0.1160**	0.4778**	0.3618	0.0880**	0.3285**	0.2405	0.0805**	0.3785**	0.2980	0.0320	0.3142**	0.2822
Lower middle school	E_5	0.1190	0.4056**	0.2866	0.0925	0.2598**	0.1673	0.831	0.3295**	0.2464	0.0278	0.2615**	0.2337
Primary school	E_6	0.0730	0.0517**	-0.0213	0.0467	0.0520	0.0053	0.0601	0.1913*	0.1312	0.0324	0.1470	0.1146
State-owned	OW_1	0.4828**	0.1691**	-0.3137	0.1707**	0.2043**	0.0336	0.0022	0.1949**	0.1927	-0.3462**	0.1619**	0.5081
Local public owned	OW_2	0.4305**	0.0271	-0.4034	0.1220**	0.0605	-0.0615	-0.0633**	0.0323	0.0956	-0.4459**	0.0080	0.4539
Urban collective	OW_3	0.3429**	-0.1751	-0.5180	-0.0577**	-0.1083**	-0.1660	-0.1160**	-0.1340**	-0.0180	-0.4407**	-0.1399**	0.3108
Sino-foreign joint venture	OW_5	0.4314**	0.2490**	-0.1824	0.3177**	0.2512**	0.0665	0.3636**	0.2699**	-0.0937	-0.0564	-0.2218**	0.2782
Foreign-owned	OW_6	0.1683	0.6525**	0.4842	-0.0928	0.4992**	0.5920	-0.2274**	0.6095**	0.8369	-0.4534**	0.9998**	1.4532
Other	OW_7	-0.0348**	-0.0903	-0.0555	-0.2506**	-0.0154	0.2352	-0.2953**	-0.0182*	0.2771	-0.4078	-0.1363**	-0.2715
-20	A_1	-0.3125**	-0.8023**	-0.4898	-0.2445**	-0.5247**	-0.2802	-0.1847**	-0.3941**	-0.2094	-0.1446**	-0.2929**	-0.1483
21-25	A_2	-0.1283**	-0.3027**	-0.1744	-0.1028**	-0.2204**	-0.1176	-0.0879**	-0.1961**	-0.1082	0.0399**	-0.1392**	-0.0993
31-35	A_4	0.1266**	0.2521**	0.1255	0.0986**	0.1428**	0.0442	0.0933**	0.1058**	0.0125	0.0988**	0.0991**	0.0003
36-40	A_5	0.2225**	0.3578**	0.1353	0.1811**	0.2447**	0.0636	0.1656**	0.1859**	0.0203	0.1557**	0.1464**	-0.0093
41-45	A_6	0.3009**	0.4232**	0.1223	0.2685**	0.3217**	0.0532	0.2463	0.2379**	-0.0084	0.2351**	0.1698**	-0.0653
46-50	A_7	0.3388**	0.3684**	0.0296	0.3240**	0.2942**	-0.0298	0.3023**	0.2513**	-0.0510	0.2792**	0.2067**	-0.0725
51-55	A_8	0.3909**	0.2630**	-0.1279	0.3486**	0.2725**	-0.0761	0.3276**	0.2695**	-0.0581	0.3014**	0.2143**	-0.0871
56-60	A_9	0.3712**	0.0184**	-0.3528	0.3676**	0.2574**	-0.1102	0.3493**	0.2915**	-0.0578	0.3025**	0.2684**	-0.0341
61-65	A_{10}	0.3445**	-0.9554**	-1.2999	0.3471**	-0.6132**	-0.2661	0.3839**	-0.3646**	-0.7485	0.3476**	-0.1210	-0.4686
66-	A_{11}	-0.0351	-0.5847**	-0.6198	0.0949	-0.6050**	-0.6999	0.2572**	-0.4839**	-0.7411	0.1077	-0.2481	-0.3558
Guangdong	P_{44}	0.0854**	0.3427**	0.2573	0.1712	0.3642**	-0.1930	0.2645**	0.4514**	-0.1869	0.3833**	0.5628**	0.1795

Note: ** Denotes statistical significance at 1% and * at 5% level.

end of the conditional distribution. The fall in the education coefficients from the lowest to the highest quantile was much sharper for the bonus than for the basic wage. Our hypothesis appears to be part of the 1988 story, although not the whole of it. However, by 1995 the distribution between the bonuses (representing discretionary pay by the enterprise) and the basic wage (non-discretionary pay) had been lost. For instance, a state directive to raise the basic wage in 1994 led many employers to incorporate some of the bonuses into the basic wage (Knight, Li, and Zhao 2001). Again, the bonus attracted no returns to education (beyond primary school) but the pattern observed in Table 3.5 for the wage as a whole applied also to the (now discretionary) basic wage.

There is a substantial increase in all the education coefficients between 1988 and 1995 but the increase is greatest at the lowest quantile. Illustrating again from the first row of the table, between 1988 and 1995 the coefficient on college education rose by 0.49 at the lowest quantile and by 0.31 at the highest. This divergence between the extreme quantiles implies that the effect became more powerful over the seven years.

In both 1988 and 1995, the lowest quantile conditional wage is the most sensitive to age—showing the most pronounced inverted U-shape—and the highest quantile is the least sensitive. Between the years the hump becomes more pronounced in general but at the lower quantiles in particular. Taking the bowing of the age–earnings profile to be a response to market forces, we might infer that market forces operate more freely on workers with less valuable unobserved characteristics. Insofar as the labour market is divided into a (preferred) protected sector and a (residual) market sector, low-ability workers may be concentrated in the market sector. Alternatively, employers that pay above the market wage may be less sensitive to age (for instance, rents may be shared among employees in an egalitarian way) whereas enterprises subject to market forces pay both at a lower level and more according to productivity. Again, the latter explanation seems more plausible than the former: The very low mobility of workers across employers affords little scope for the sorting of workers by ability. The evidence suggests, therefore, that enterprises less able to share rents with employees, that is, more subject to market discipline, are also more prone to reward human capital, represented both by education and by age.

The coefficients on province differ very little across quantiles except in the case of Guangdong, the province in which economic reform started earliest and went furthest. In both years the coefficient on residence in Guangdong rises as we move up the quantiles. It seems that the reward for unobserved worker ability is more varied in Guangdong, or that enterprises in Guangdong are more varied in their ability or willingness to pay. The effect is maintained over time.

In 1988, for all categories but the small, residual, ownership category, the coefficient relative to private ownership is large and positive at the lowest quantile, and in all cases it falls as we move up the quantiles, being negative at the highest quantile. This suggests that the private sector was initially more sensitive to the unobserved influences on wages (varying pay more over the range of worker ability or firm performance) than were other forms of ownership. In 1995, by contrast, for all but the foreign-owned sector, the coefficient on ownership category is stable across quantiles. The coefficient on foreign ownership, already large (+0.48) at the lowest quantile, is extremely large (+1.00) at the highest. Pay in the state and collective sectors is similar to that in the private sector throughout the range of abilities. It is now the foreign-owned sector which stands out as being willing to pay relatively more for more able workers or as being wage-sensitive to firm performance.

3.6 CONCLUSIONS

This is a pioneering analysis of changes in the Chinese urban wage structure overall, being based on precisely comparable surveys conducted as many as seven years apart.[10] Even its descriptive results are therefore of interest. The consequences of labour market reform were observable in our surveys. The Gini coefficient of earnings rose by 8 percentage points over the seven years. Whereas the mean wage increased by 52 per cent, the pay of the 10th percentile rose by only 6 per cent, and that of the 90th percentile rose by 75 per cent. Moreover, the returns to education rose sharply, as did the returns to occupation-specific skills. The initially slight inverse-U shape of the age–earnings profile became more pronounced—a change consistent with human capital theory. Thus the productive characteristics of workers were increasingly rewarded in the labour market. However, there were also signs of greater wage discrimination—against women and minorities and in favour of Communist Party members. Moreover, the market forces operating in the growing private sector and the relative immunity of the state sector from those forces generated greater wage segmentation among types of ownership, and provincial differences in the pace of reform and in economic growth created spatial segmentation in wages that could not be removed by the equilibrating movement of labour.

Decomposition analyses were conducted in order to illuminate the processes of wage differentiation in China. Our decomposition of the rapid increase in mean earnings showed that, whereas the unskilled market wage rose very little in real terms, the impetus came especially from the rising returns to education and the growing gap between the low-paying local private sector and other ownership sectors. Another decomposition was to examine the contribution of particular characteristics to the rise in the Gini coefficient. Only a third of earnings inequality could be explained, and 55 per cent of its increase: The unobserved determinants are clearly important to the increase in earnings dispersion. The discrimination variables accounted for only a small part of the increase. The segmentation variables made the most important contribution, and that was mainly due to growing wage dispersion among provinces. This result is supported by other evidence of powerful divergence in mean earnings among provinces (Knight, Li, and Zhao 2001). This spatial dimension of wages is examined in Chapter 4.

Some but not all components of human capital were disequalizing. The disequaliz-ing components—education beyond secondary school, the professional, technical, and administrative occupations, and age below 26 or above 60—together account for 65 per cent of the explained increase in the Gini. These particular changes are likely to represent the stirring of labour market forces.

By definition, we cannot know the unobserved determinants of earnings. Nevertheless, quantile regressions were estimated in order to shed light on the relationships between the observable and unobservable determinants. Clear patterns emerged, ruling out chance and measurement error as the explanation. For each of the four characteristics considered, it was possible to provide an explanation in terms of either varying payments to employees for their unob-served abilities or varying willingness of employers to pay wages above market rates. In the case of education and age, however, the explanation in terms of employers was more plausible than that in terms of employees. Those employers that, by virtue of their low conditional pay, appeared more subject to market discip-line, were also more prone to reward these human capital variables. The locally- or foreign-owned private sector, and the most reformed province, were the most sensitive to the unobservables, suggesting that marketization increases the import-ance of the unobserved influences on wages, whether they be employee or employer characteristics. It cannot be assumed that the unobserved determinants of wages in the transitional Chinese labour market necessarily represent unobserved 'skills'.

Did the rise in wage inequality involve a trade-off between efficiency and equity objectives, as implied by Figure 3.1? This underlying question adds piquancy and policy relevance to our descriptive analysis of the growing inequality and its constituent elements. Our data and methodology do not permit a reliable answer but they provide pointers. Some of the new inequalities appear justifiable in the terms of the greater incentives or efficiency to which they give rise. In particular, it is likely that initially the returns to education and occupational skills were too low, and that the pattern of returns to age did not adequately reflect the age–productivity relationship. Other emerging disparities are more difficult to justify in terms of output objectives. For instance, the apparent greater discrimination by gender and the sharper segmentation by ownership type and by province suggest new sources of economic inefficiency. The move of some but not all types of firm towards the payment of competitive market wages is liable to generate inefficiency of the sort associated with 'the theory of the second best'. Insofar as the widening province coefficients represent diverging marginal products, they provide efficient market signals. These signals are, however, not acted upon because labour is insufficiently mobile.

Finally, our surveys of urban-*hukou* households conceal the importance of labour market discrimination between urban residents and the growing number of rural–urban migrants, which corresponds well to the distinction, made in other contexts, between labour market insiders and outsiders (Knight and Song 1999; Knight, Song, and Jia 1999). This issue will be addressed in Chapters 5 and 7.

NOTES

1. A panel element was planned but, as 20% of the SSB sample is replaced each year, none of the households sampled in 1988 remained available in 1995.
2. In 1988, workers were highly immobile and had hardly any freedom of choice, for example, freedom to move to a better-paying job. Even in 1995, the labour market lacked the mobility across employers, occupations, and space that is taken for granted elsewhere. A smaller but comparable urban survey (IE, CASS 1999) showed that even in 1999 no less than 78% of urban workers had never changed employer (Knight and Yueh 2004). The most likely source of selection bias, if any, is that young people who had recently entered the labour market could have been selected into ownership categories or occupations on the basis of unobserved characteristics.
3. $Exp(0.273) - 1 = 0.314$.
4. In each year the intercept is adjusted by the weighted average of the province coefficients.
5. All this is derived from Ravallion and Chen (1999).
6. The technicalities are explained in Deaton (1997: 80–4) and Stata (1995: 100–9). The Stata *qreg* program is used.
7. As found in Buchinsky (1994: 454) and Arias et al. (2001: 36) for the United States.
8. See, for instance, Walder (1987). We have been unable to locate relevant evidence from enterprise-based surveys for the 1990s.
9. However, Knight and Li (2004), using the 1995 data set, were unable to find a significant difference in the returns to education as between (employee-reported) PMEs and LMEs.
10. Other studies of the effects of labour market reform in China have had to rely on comparisons of more and less reformed parts of the labour market at a single point in time (e.g. Knight and Song 1993, based on the 1988 survey) or on shorter-term changes between distinctly different surveys (e.g. Maurer-Fazio 1999). Gustafsson and Li (2001*a*) used the 1988 and 1995 data sets to analyse changes in the wage structure but confined their analysis to the gender gap, and Gustafsson and Li (2001*b*), again using these data sets, measured the rise in wage inequality and conducted a 'mean logarithmic deviation' decomposition of the rise, showing that earnings inequality increased within every category of labour.

REFERENCES

Arias, Omar, Kevin Hallock, and Walter Sosa-Escudero (2001). 'Individual heterogeneity in the returns to schooling: instrumental quantile regression using twins data', *Empirical Economics*, 26, 1: 7–40.

Buchinsky, Moshe (1994). 'Changes in the U.S. wage structure 1963–1987: application of quantile regression', *Econometrica*, 62, 2: 405–58.

Deaton, Angus (1997). *The Analysis of Household Surveys. A Microeconometric Approach to Development Policy*, Baltimore: The World Bank and Johns Hopkins University Press.

Fields, Gary S. (1996). 'Accounting for differences in income inequality', Cornell University, processed.

Gottschalk, Peter (1997). 'Inequality, income growth and mobility: the basic facts', *Journal of Economic Perspectives*, 11, 2 (Spring): 21–40.

Griffin, Keith and Zhao Renwei (eds) (1993). *The Distribution of Income in China*, London: Macmillan.

Gustafsson, Björn and Li Shi (2001*a*). 'Economic transformation and the gender earnings gap in urban China', in Carl Riskin, Li Shi, and Zhao Renwei (eds) *China's Retreat from Equality. Income Distribution and Economic Transition*, Armonk, New York: M.E. Sharpe, 184–209.

—————— (2001*b*). 'The anatomy of rising earnings inequality in urban China', *Journal of Comparative Economics*, 29: 118–35.

Jenkins, Stephen P. (1995). 'Accounting for inequality trends: decomposition analysis for the UK, 1971–86', *Economica*, 62: 29–64.

Knight, John and Li Shi (2004). 'How does firm profitability affect wages in urban China?' Department of Economics, University of Oxford, September, mimeo.

Knight, John and Lina Song (1993). 'Why urban wages differ in China', in Keith Griffin and Zhao Renwei (eds) *The Distribution of Income in China*, London: Macmillan, 216–84.

—————— (1995). 'Towards a labour market in China', *Oxford Review of Economic Policy*, 11, 4: 97–117.

—————— (1999). 'Employment constraints and sub-optimality in Chinese enterprises', *Oxford Economic Papers*, 51, 2: 284–99.

—————— (2003). 'Increasing urban wage inequality in China: extent, elements, and evaluation', *The Economics of Transition,* 11, 4: 597–619.

—————— and Linda Yueh (2004). 'Job mobility of residents and migrants in urban China', *Journal of Comparative Economics*, 32: 637–60.

——— Li Shi and Zhao Renwei (2001). 'A spatial analysis of wages and incomes in urban China: divergent means, convergent inequality', in Carl Riskin, Li Shi, and Zhao Renwei (eds) *China's Retreat from Equality. Income Distribution and Economic Transition*, Armonk, NY: M.E. Sharpe, 133–66.

Knight, John, Lina Song, and Jia Huaibin (1999). 'Chinese rural migrants in urban enterprises: three perspectives', *Journal of Development Studies*, 35, 3: 73–104.

Koenker, R. and K. Hallock (2001). 'Quantile regression', *Journal of Economic Perspectives*, 15, 4: 143–56.

Maurer-Fazio, Margaret (1999). 'Earnings and education in China's transition to a market economy. Survey evidence from 1989 and 1992', *China Economic Review*, 10, 1 (Spring): 17–40.

Meng, Xin (2002). 'Profit-sharing and the earnings gap between urban workers and rural–urban migrants in Chinese enterprises', Australian National University, mimeo.

Mwabu, Germano and T. Paul Schultz (1996). 'Education returns across quantiles of the wage function: alternative explanations for the returns to education in South Africa', *American Economic Review*, 86: 335–9.

Ravallion, Martin and Shaohua Chen (1999). 'When economic reform is faster than statistical reform: measuring and explaining income inequality in rural China', *Oxford Bulletin of Economics and Statistics*, 61, 1: 33–56.

Riskin, Carl, Zhao Renwei, and Li Shi (2001). *China's Retreat from Equality. Income Distribution and Economic Transition*, Armonk, NY: M.E. Sharpe.

Shirk, Susan L. (1981). 'Recent Chinese labour policies and the transformation of industrial organisation in China', *China Quarterly*, 88: 575–93.

Shorrocks, Anthony F. (1982). 'Inequality decomposition by factor components', *Econometrica*, 50: 193–211.

Stata (1995). *Reference Manual, Release 4*, Vol. 3, College Station, TX: Stata Corporation.

Svejnar, Jan (1999). 'Labor markets in the transitional central and east European economies', in Orley Ashenfelter and David Card (eds) *Handbook of Labor Economics*, Vol. 3B, Amsterdam: Elsevier, ch. 44, 2809–57.

Topel, Robert H. (1997). 'Factor proportions and relative wages: the supply side determinants of wage inequality', *Journal of Economic Perspectives*, 11, 2 (Spring): 55–74.

Walder, Andrew G. (1987). 'Wage reform and the web of factory interests', *China Quarterly*, 109: 22–41.

4

The Spatial Behaviour of Wages

4.1 INTRODUCTION

The urban economic reforms, commencing in the early 1980s and gaining pace in the mid-1990s, occurred at different times and at different rates across the provinces and cities of China. The decentralization of decision-making and the introduction of market forces were sure to affect the behaviour of wages. A spatial analysis of urban wages and of incomes per capita may therefore reveal interesting patterns and help to explain how the emerging labour market operated.

Although we have conducted the analysis for income per capita as well as for wage per worker, with remarkably similar results (Knight, Li, and Zhao 2001), we concentrate here on wages. We refer only to the basic results for incomes. However, most of the research on convergence or divergence has been concerned with incomes. The first of our questions (what happens to the spatial inequality of inequality?) has been posed rarely if at all, but the second (what happens to the spatial inequality of means?) is now common. There is a lively and growing literature on economic convergence across countries (Barro and Sala-i-Martin 1995: ch. 12). The same authors (1995: ch. 11) also reported a number of regional studies of convergence. They used measures of β-convergence (the relation between changes in the logarithm of income per capita and its initial value) and of σ-convergence (changes in the standard deviation of the logarithm of income per capita). They found evidence of β-convergence among US states, Japanese prefectures, and European regions, both absolute and also conditional convergence (standardizing for other variables). They also generally found σ-convergence.

A likely explanation for these results, along with technological diffusion, is that equilibrating flows of labour and capital tend to equalize incomes. Convergence should accordingly be weaker when the equation is standardized for net migration. However, the authors found, if anything, the opposite result, which they attributed to the endogeneity of migration. As with cross-country convergence, cross-region convergence of mean incomes is a common phenomenon that is not yet well understood.

Research on spatial income inequality in China has generally been conducted at the province level. For instance, Jian, Sachs, and Warner (1996) examined inequality among provinces over the period 1978–93, using data on provincial mean income per capita, based on the official national household survey. Their equations implied convergence during the period up to 1985, but the evidence for the period after 1985 was weak. In neither case was there evidence of conditional convergence or divergence, that is, the effect of initial income on its growth became insignificant when other explanatory variables were introduced into the equation.

A good deal of spatial economic research is now being done on China, but the results so far do not add up to a clear pattern—varying as they do according to time period, unit of analysis, data set, and dependent variable. One of the obvious complications is that some areas which had a distinct locational and policy advantage—like Guangdong and Fujian—and therefore have grown very rapidly, started off poor but in recent years have been rich.

With few exceptions (including Knight and Song 1993) the literature does not distinguish between urban and rural areas, yet the administrative and economic divide between urban and rural China makes it important to analyse the two sectors separately. Such an analysis would be possible at the province level using data from the urban or the rural samples of the official national household survey. However, as official data at the household level are not available to researchers, only the IE, CASS 1988 and the IE, CASS 1995 surveys permit an analysis of the change in inequality within as well as among provinces.

Recall that the two surveys were designed by a team comprising of researchers at the Institute of Economics, Chinese Academy of Social Sciences, and foreign scholars. They were conducted by the National Bureau of Statistics (NBS), drawing subsamples from the samples used in the annual official national household surveys. The urban and rural samples were drawn separately, reflecting their administrative and economic differences. Not all provinces could be surveyed: There were ten common provinces in the urban and nineteen in the rural surveys. Our analysis is based on the common provinces in the urban sample and the common cities within them. We draw on Knight, Li and Zhao (2001).

4.2 CONVERGENCE IN INEQUALITY: EVIDENCE

This section contains two exercises. First, we test for divergence or convergence in intra-province inequality across provinces over the period 1988–95. We use as our measure of inequality the Gini coefficient, a well-known standard measure which varies in value from zero (implying complete equality) to unity, which we express as 100 per cent (implying complete inequality).

Table 4.1 shows the Gini coefficient of earnings per worker and household income per capita in 1988 and 1995, and the change in the Gini coefficient, both the percentage change and the change in percentage points. In all provinces except Gansu there was a rise in inequality over the seven years. The increase in the Gini coefficient for the group of ten provinces common to the urban samples was by 7.8 percentage points in the case of earnings and 5.1 percentage points in the case of income. In each case the increase was greater for the four coastal provinces than

TABLE 4.1 *The level and change in the Gini coefficient of earnings per worker and of income per capita in urban China, 1988–95, by province*

Province	Earnings		Change		Income		Change	
	1988	1995	Per cent	Percentage points	1988	1995	Per cent	Percentage points
Beijing	20.4	26.1	27.9	5.7	17.0	21.5	26.5	4.5
Shanxi	24.9	29.7	19.3	4.8	23.0	26.6	15.7	3.6
Liaoning	17.4	28.8	65.5	11.4	15.7	23.4	49.1	7.7
Jiangsu	18.3	28.8	57.4	10.5	17.4	23.2	33.3	5.8
Anhui	24.3	27.8	14.4	3.5	21.5	22.1	2.8	0.6
Henan	22.4	30.1	34.4	7.7	21.6	28.4	31.5	6.8
Hubei	18.5	27.7	49.7	9.2	18.1	22.5	24.3	4.4
Guangdong	27.7	33.1	19.5	5.4	24.9	28.6	14.9	3.7
Yunnan	19.7	23.1	17.3	3.4	19.8	21.5	8.6	1.7
Gansu	27.6	27.1	−1.8	−0.5	26.8	22.5	−16.0	−4.3
Coastal	23.8	32.9	38.2	9.1	21.3	27.7	30.1	6.4
Interior	23.3	28.1	20.6	4.8	22.0	24.3	10.5	2.3
Total	24.1	31.9	32.4	7.8	23.2	28.3	22.0	5.1
Standard deviation	3.84	2.64	−31.3	−1.20	3.63	2.77	−23.7	−0.86

Note: The coastal region comprises Beijing, Liaoning, Jiangsu, and Guangdong; the interior region comprises Shanxi, Anhui, Henan, Hubei, Yunnan, and Gansu.

Source: Of this and subsequent tables in this chapter, Knight, Li, and Zhao (2001).

for the six inland provinces (9.1 versus 4.8 percentage points for earnings, and 6.4 versus 2.3 percentage points for income). There was a good deal of variation among the provinces.

In order to discern patterns we estimated the following relationship:

$$G_1 - G_0 = a + bG_0 \qquad (4.1)$$

where G is the Gini coefficient and the subscripts 0, 1 are the years 1988 and 1995, respectively. The coefficient b is a test of convergence ($b < 0$) or divergence ($b > 0$). The coefficient indicates whether the initial level of inequality hinders or assists its growth.

Table 4.2 tests across provinces for convergence or divergence in the intra-province Gini coefficient (columns (1) and (3)). We see that the coefficient on initial inequality is significantly negative. For both earnings per worker and income per capita, a reduction in the initial Gini coefficient by 10 percentage points raises its subsequent growth over seven years by 7 percentage points. When the proportionate growth in earnings or income is added as an explanatory variable, its coefficient is positive but small and not statistically significant (columns (2) and (4)). When

TABLE 4.2 *The inter-province relationship between initial Gini coefficient of earnings, and income, and its growth: urban China, 1988–95*

| | Increase in Gini coefficient (percentage points) | | | |
| | Earnings | | Income | |
Equation	1	2	3	4
Intercept	21.993***	19.190***	17.147	13.426*
Initial Gini coefficient	−0.715**	−0.669**	−0.666**	−0.582*
Proportionate growth in earnings/income		0.041		0.040
Adj. R^2	0.512	0.542	0.422	0.410
F-value	10.449**	6.332**	7.556**	4.123*
Mean value of dependent variable	6.110	6.110	3.450	3.450
Number of observations	10	10	10	10

Note: *** Denotes statistical significance at the 1%, ** at the 5%, and * at 10% level.

TABLE 4.3 *The growth of the Gini coefficient of income per capita and earnings per worker, 1988–95, as a function of their initial values, by city, urban China*

| | Change in the Gini coefficient | |
	Income	Earnings
Intercept	0.197***	0.202***
Initial value (G_0)	−0.922***	−0.793***
Adj. R^2	0.589	0.489
F-value	84.158***	56.443***
Mean of dependent variable ($G_1 - G_0$)	0.015	0.031
Number of observations	60	60

Note: *** Indicates statistical significance at the 1% level.

initial mean earnings or income is included, the coefficient is positive but not at all significant (equations not shown).

Because there are only ten provinces in the urban sample, our results might be due to the particular or idiosyncratic behaviour of one or two provinces. The same analysis cannot be conducted on all thirty provinces because official intra-province inequality measures are not available. However, we can estimate equation (4.1) for the sixty cities common to our two surveys. Our second exercise, therefore, is to test for divergence or convergence in intra-city inequality among cities.

Table 4.3 shows powerful and statistically significant evidence of convergence in inequality among cities. The coefficient b on G_0 is no less than -0.92 in the case of income and -0.79 in the case of earnings, that is, a 10 per cent lower initial value of the Gini coefficient raises its increment by 8 percentage points or more. A pattern is therefore established: The convergence of inequality is a general phenomenon, applying not only among provinces but also, even more powerfully, among cities.

4.3 CONVERGENCE IN INEQUALITY: EXPLANATION

In all but one province urban inequality rose between 1988 and 1995, but it rose more rapidly in those provinces which started with low inequality in 1988. The provinces were becoming more similar in their degree of urban inequality. How is this trend to be explained? How is it related to the process of economic reform, and what does it imply for inequality in the future?

One possibility is that the observed convergence is merely a statistical illusion: The regression of the change in a variable on its initial value is subject to errors-in-variables bias. Assume that measurement errors in the initial year and the final year are uncorrelated. If the initial value is under-reported, the change is equivalently over-reported. This reduces the estimated coefficient on the initial value, biasing it towards -1 and thus towards convergence. The extent of the bias increases with the proportion of the variance in the initial value that is attributable to measurement error. A common method of attempting to correct for such bias—instrumenting the initial value by means of the value of a contiguous year—is not open to us. Nor do we possess good proxies for the initial value (such as a coastal dummy) that are not correlated with the error term of the dependent variable. However, there are two pieces of evidence against the bias explanation.

First, we conducted a simple experiment to answer the question: What proportion of the variation in the initial value would have to be the result of measurement error for convergence to disappear? Accordingly, we set each initial province value first 20 per cent, and then 50 per cent, closer to the initial mean value. The coefficient on the initial Gini remained significantly negative in the former case, and had a negative value exceeding -0.3, albeit not significant, in the latter. Secondly, β-convergence is a necessary but not a sufficient condition for σ-convergence (Barro and Sala-i-Martin 1995: 385). The former tends to generate the latter, although this process can be offset by new disturbances that increase dispersion. We find that between 1988 and 1995 σ-convergence occurred in every case. Whether we consider earnings or income, the standard deviation of the Gini coefficient fell sharply among provinces (Table 4.1) and also among cities; and the coefficient of variation even more. This is a further indication that the β-convergence observed is not an illusion.

Our second approach is to conduct a decomposition analysis of the Gini coefficient in each province in 1988 and 1995 by component of earnings, and then to decompose the rise in the Gini coefficient between 1988 and 1995 into the contributions made by the different components. We make use of the following property:

$$G = \sum \pi_i = \sum u_i C_i \tag{4.2}$$

where G is the Gini coefficient of wage inequality, u_i is the ratio of the ith component of wages to total wages, that is, its share of the total, C_i is the concentration ratio of the ith component of wages, and π_i is the contribution of the ith component to the Gini coefficient.

The concentration curve $C_i(x)$ represents the share of component i received by the lowest x proportion of recipients of *total* wages. The concentration ratio C_i is then derived from the concentration curve in exactly the same way as the Gini coefficient is derived from the Lorenz curve. The contribution made by each component of wages to the Gini coefficient is given by $\pi_i = u_i C_i$.

Table 4.4 shows the percentage shares (u_i) of the different components of earnings. We see that the main component was basic wages (E_1), representing 54 per cent in 1988 and 59 per cent in 1995. Contrary to expectations, the share of bonuses (E_2) fell, from 19 per cent in 1988 to 15 per cent in 1995. The main distinction between the coastal and the interior provinces was the greater importance of bonuses and the lesser importance of basic wages in the former. Despite their relative decline, bonuses may well have been the driving force behind earnings in the period up to 1993 as the wage reform of 1994 consolidated part of the bonus into basic pay.

We decompose the rise in the Gini coefficient of earnings in each province between 1988 and 1995 (Table 4.5). The contribution of each component is given by $\pi_{i1} - \pi_{i0}$, and the proportion due to each component by $(\pi_{i1} - \pi_{i0})/(G_1 - G_0)$. For the sample as a whole, the major contribution is made by the basic wage (70 per cent), followed by the cash subsidy (33 per cent). However, the contribution of the basic wage is greater for the interior than for the coastal region (113 versus 49 per cent) and that of the bonus correspondingly smaller.

We are now in a position to examine the proximate causes of the inter-province convergence of intra-province inequality. We estimate variants of equation (4.1):

$$\pi_{i1} - \pi_{i0} = a + bG_0 \tag{4.3}$$

$$\pi_{i1} - \pi_{i0} = c + d\pi_{i0} \tag{4.4}$$

Equation (4.3) indicates whether, and to what extent, a particular component of earnings contributed to convergence in the Gini coefficient. Equation (4.4) indicates whether, and to what extent, the contribution of a particular component was itself subject to convergence. Table 4.6 shows that the coefficients of all components were negative in equation (4.3) but none was significantly so. The basic wage

TABLE 4.4 *Percentage shares of earnings components in total earnings: urban China, 1988 and 1995*

Province	E_1	E_2	E_3	E_4	E_5	Total
1988						
Beijing	52.2	17.2	17.8	0.3	12.5	100
Shanxi	59.7	17.2	15.4	0.7	7.1	100
Liaoning	55.0	18.2	17.3	0.2	9.4	100
Jiangsu	52.5	18.7	15.2	1.2	12.6	100
Anhui	54.0	20.2	14.7	1.2	9.9	100
Henan	63.8	14.2	12.5	0.5	9.0	100
Hubei	57.1	17.1	16.2	0.5	9.2	100
Guangdong	41.8	30.8	14.9	1.9	10.6	100
Yunnan	53.0	18.6	16.1	1.0	11.3	100
Gansu	59.1	9.6	17.9	1.5	11.8	100
Coastal	48.9	23.0	15.8	1.1	11.1	100
Interior	57.5	16.5	15.4	0.9	9.7	100
Total	53.7	19.4	15.5	1.0	10.3	100
1995						
Beijing	52.7	18.3	16.3	0.1	12.6	100
Shanxi	68.3	12.5	14.1	0.4	4.7	100
Liaoning	65.1	10.3	17.3	0.6	6.9	100
Jiangsu	60.5	16.0	16.7	0.3	6.6	100
Anhui	71.5	9.6	10.4	0.2	8.4	100
Henan	63.5	9.9	17.1	2.4	7.1	100
Hubei	63.2	12.2	16.1	0.7	7.9	100
Guangdong	43.6	28.5	16.5	1.7	9.8	100
Yunnan	59.8	10.1	24.2	1.1	5.0	100
Gansu	73.7	6.7	18.6	0.2	6.1	100
Coastal	52.1	19.4	16.6	0.8	9.0	100
Interior	65.0	10.6	17.1	0.9	6.5	100
Total	59.3	15.3	16.8	0.8	7.8	100

Notes: E_1 = Basic wage of workers; E_2 = bonus of workers; E_3 = cash subsidy of workers; E_4 = earnings of private owners and self-employed; E_5 = other income. Coastal region includes Beijing, Liaoning, Jiangsu, and Guangdong; interior region includes Shanxi, Anhui, Henan, Hubei, Yunnan, and Gansu.

made the greatest contribution to the convergence in the Gini coefficient. However, we see in equation (4.4) that the minor components of earnings (the cash subsidy, earnings from self-employment, and 'other earnings') were themselves subject to powerful convergence, whereas the basic wage was weakly convergent and the bonus weakly divergent. Convergence was thus common to all earnings components with the exception of bonuses. Even this last result is not secure: Bonuses may have played a larger role than our estimates suggest, but this role could have

TABLE 4.5 *Contribution of earnings components to change in earnings inequality: urban China, 1988–95*

Province	E_1	E_2	E_3	E_4	E_5	Change in Gini coefficient of earnings
Beijing	88.6	−2.7	7.8	−3.2	9.6	100
Shanxi	135.5	−53.4	33.9	−8.9	−7.1	100
Liaoning	86.8	−11.4	24.5	0.1	0.1	100
Jiangsu	39.7	23.3	37.5	−8.3	7.8	100
Anhui	176.9	−86.5	26.1	−8.6	−7.9	100
Henan	70.2	−5.5	41.2	3.5	−9.3	100
Hubei	83.8	−11.4	28.9	−0.9	−0.4	100
Guangdong	9.4	13.0	66.3	−11.2	22.5	100
Yunnan	78.9	−38.5	90.6	11.6	−42.6	100
Gansu	−741.2	199.4	−109.6	178.3	573.2	100
Coastal	48.9	9.7	33.9	−5.3	12.8	100
Interior	112.8	−32.1	48.3	−4.1	−24.9	100
Total	69.9	2.0	32.8	−4.4	−0.3	100

Notes: E_1 = Basic wage of workers; E_2 = bonus of workers; E_3 = cash subsidy of workers; E_4 = earnings of private owners and self-employed; E_5 = other income. Coastal region includes Beijing, Liaoning, Jiangsu, and Guangdong; interior region includes Shanxi, Anhui, Henan, Hubei, Yunnan, and Gansu.

TABLE 4.6 *The inter-province relation between the contribution of a component to the change in earnings inequality and the initial contribution of the component or the initial Gini coefficient*

	The coefficient on the initial value of	
	G_0	π_{i0}
Basic wage	−0.302	−0.008
Bonus	−0.101	0.101
Cash subsidy	−0.105	−1.233**
Income from self-employment	−0.074	−1.020**
Other earnings	−0.147	−1.028***

Note: *** Denotes statistical significance at the 1%, ** at the 5%, and * at the 10% level.

been disguised insofar as the wage reform of 1994 produced a consolidation of part of the bonus into the basic wage.

An analysis of household income per capita, corresponding to that of earnings per worker presented in Tables 4.4–4.6, produced the following main results.

TABLE 4.7 *The inter-province and inter-city relation between the Gini coefficient of earnings and the proxy for the extent of reform: urban China, 1988*

	Provinces	Cities
Intercept	26.704	27.663***
Basic wage as a percentage of earnings	−0.084	−0.115*
Adj. R^2	−0.106	0.029
F-value	0.135	2.701*
Mean of dependent variable	22.120	21.431
Number of observations	10	60

Note: *** Denotes statistical significance at the 1%, ** at the 5%, and * at the 10% level.

Wages were the dominant source of income, contributing 80 per cent of the total in 1988 and 77 per cent in 1995. Wage income made the largest contribution to income inequality in both years. Moreover, it accounted for 76 per cent of the rise in income inequality, but this was concentrated in the coastal provinces. Wages also made much of the largest contribution to the inter-province convergence in the Gini coefficient.

Our attempt to understand the proximate reasons for the inter-province convergence of inequality has thrown only a little light on the processes at work. It was the basic wage which made the greatest contribution to the convergence of earnings inequality. We can be confident only that bonuses were not part of the explanation. How then can we explain convergence, if it depended mainly on wage income and, within wage income, on the basic wage? It is possible that convergence was due to the uneven timing of reforms. Those provinces and cities which reformed early—during the period up to 1988—had higher inequality by 1988. In these cases inequality did not rise much more between 1988 and 1995. Those provinces and cities which commenced reforms later had lower inequality in 1988 but higher increases in the ensuing seven years.

To test this hypothesis, we need to measure the progress in reform that had been achieved by 1988. To a considerable extent, the proportion of earnings other than basic wages represents the degree of decentralized freedom to determine earnings that employers then possessed. We use this as our proxy for the extent of labour market reform in a province in 1988. Accordingly, Table 4.7 shows inter-province and inter-city estimates of the equation:

$$G_0 = a + bW_0 \qquad (4.5)$$

where W is basic wages as a percentage of earnings. The hypothesis is that $b < 0$. Indeed, we find that b is negative in three of the four cases but significantly so only

TABLE 4.8 *The coefficient on the initial value of the Gini coefficient of earnings in the inter-province equations predicting the change in the Gini coefficient: urban China, 1988–95*

	Coefficient on the initial Gini coefficient
Production worker	−0.573***
Non-production worker	−0.713**
State sector	−0.576**
Non-state sector	−0.853***

Note: *** Denotes statistical significance at the 1% and ** at the 5% level.

in the equations for cities. Our evidence that the reforming provinces had higher initial inequality is weak but it remains our favoured explanation for convergence.

A further approach was to examine the pattern of variation in convergence among various subgroups. A distinction was made between non-production and production workers ('staff' and 'workers'), and between the state and non-state sectors. We see from Table 4.8 that convergence is stronger for staff than for workers, and for the non-state sectors than the state sectors. Provinces have come more rapidly into line in their extent of earnings inequality in the case of staff and of non-state employees, both of which are more likely to be subject to market forces.

4.4 DIVERGENCE IN MEANS: EVIDENCE

We approach the analysis of the growth in intra-province mean earnings in the same way as for intra-province inequality. First, we test for convergence or divergence in the means across provinces. Secondly, we extend the analysis to the sample of cities. We then go on to explore the underlying reasons for the powerful divergence evident in our equations.

Table 4.9 provides the basic data on mean real earnings from employment and mean household real income per capita for each of the ten provinces common to our urban samples of 1988 and 1995, and the corresponding percentage increases. It is notable that provinces diverged sharply over the seven years. For instance, earnings per worker rose by 84 per cent in Beijing and 79 per cent in Guangdong but only by 3 per cent in Gansu and 27 per cent in Yunnan. The percentage growth in earnings in the coastal provinces is double that of the interior provinces. Very similar results are obtained for income per capita. These results square with the widening province dummy coefficients in the earnings functions over the same period, reported in Chapter 3.

TABLE 4.9 *The mean values of earnings per worker and income per capita, 1988 and 1995, at constant (1988) prices, urban China, by province, and their percentage rates of growth*

Province	Earnings			Income		
	1988	1995	Percentage change	1988	1995	Percentage change
Beijing	2,022	3,722	84.1	1,612	2,933	81.9
Shanxi	1,632	2,088	27.9	1,093	1,538	40.7
Liaoning	1,835	2,449	33.5	1,402	1,872	33.5
Jiangsu	1,895	2,950	55.7	1,459	2,403	64.7
Anhui	1,725	2,160	25.2	1,249	1,764	41.2
Henan	1,531	2,044	33.5	1,144	1,604	40.2
Hubei	1,749	2,590	48.1	1,307	1,994	52.6
Guangdong	2,723	4,876	79.1	2,053	3,673	78.9
Yunnan	1,988	2,514	26.5	1,321	1,926	45.8
Gansu	1,898	1,972	3.9	1,327	1,467	10.6
Coastal	2,144	3,300	53.9	1,584	2,502	58.0
Interior	1,739	2,205	26.8	1,177	1,632	38.7
Total	1,900	2,646	39.3	1,336	1,995	49.3

Notes: The coastal region comprises of Beijing, Liaoning, Jiangsu, and Guangdong; the interior region comprises Shanxi, Anhui, Henan, Hubei, Yunnan, and Gansu. The income concept used throughout excludes the housing subsidy and the imputed rent of privately owned housing. Because these are based on market rents, which tend to be high in prosperous provinces irrespective of the quality of housing, their inclusion would raise income misleadingly in those provinces.

Again, we test for convergence or divergence using the equation:

$$y_1 - y_0 = a + by_0 \tag{4.6}$$

where y is the natural logarithm of mean earnings or income. Table 4.10 (columns (1) and (5)) shows equations for the growth of earnings and income, respectively over the seven-year period. In both cases the coefficient on the base year value is significantly positive. In the case of earnings it implies that a 10 per cent higher initial earnings involves growth that is faster by 6 percentage points; and in the case of income the growth is 5 per cent faster. This constitutes strong evidence of inter-province divergence in earnings and income levels. Note the corresponding result in Table 4.9: Comparing the coastal and interior groups of provinces, we see that the coastal region had both higher initial mean values and faster growth in earnings per worker and income per capita than the interior region.

Table 4.10 also shows the equivalent equations using official data for all twenty-nine provinces (columns (2) and (6)). Evidence of divergence is again found, although it is not quite so powerful, nor is it statistically significant in the case of

TABLE 4.10 *The inter-province relationship between initial mean earnings, and income per capita, and their growth: urban China*

	Proportionate growth in earnings per worker				Proportionate growth in income per capita		
	CASS	SSB			CASS	SSB	
Equation	1988–95	1988–95	1988–95	1978–88	1988–95	1988–95	1978–88
	1	2	3	4	5	6	7
Intercept	−4.184	−1.715	0.501	3.768***	−3.302*	−2.144***	2.843**
Initial income	0.600*	0.269	−0.059	−0.479**	0.511**	0.366***	−0.351*
Percentage bonus			0.011**				
Percentage private employment			0.012*				
Adj. R^2	0.201	0.040	0.685	0.178	0.314	0.357	0.062
F-value	3.265*	2.175	18.803**	7.050**	5.125**	16.534***	2.858*
Mean of dependent variable	0.335	0.292	0.292	0.382	0.389	0.446	0.553
Number of observations	10	29	29	29	10	29	29

Notes: 1. *** Denotes statistical significance at the 1% level, ** at the 5%, and * at the 10% level.

2. The 1995 data on earnings and incomes are deflated to 1988 figures using the urban consumer price index (which rose by 128 per cent).

3. Inflation was very similar across the ten provinces, the mean annual rate being 13.0 and the standard deviation 1.0 per cent. Use of the province price indices had a negligible effect on the divergence coefficient, raising it from 0.600* to 0.610* in equation 1 and lowering it from 0.511** to 0.475* in equation 5.

Sources: IE, CASS 1988 and 1995 household surveys, urban samples; State Statistical Bureau (SSB): official data on household incomes and earnings from employment.

earnings. We are observing a general phenomenon, which is not just the result of outliers in our ten-province sample.

The same equation estimated for the previous decade (1978–88), using official data for the twenty-nine provinces, is reported in columns (4) and (7) of Table 4.10. The results are quite different for this period: they indicate strong and statistically significant convergence of both earnings per worker and income per capita. Something happened to set different forces in motion during the later period. The most likely explanation is the urban economic reforms—involving the decentralization of control and the dismantling of planning—which gained pace in the mid-1980s.

A further pointer to this explanation is provided by the addition of two proxies for labour market reform in the twenty-nine-province equation for 1988–95 (column (3)): The bonus as a percentage of total earnings, and employment other than by the state or urban collectives as a percentage of total employment. Both reflect the extent of managerial autonomy; both coefficients are positive and significant. Moreover, the initial earnings coefficient becomes slightly negative and not at all significant. It appears that the differential growth of bonus payments and of the private sector was responsible for the divergence of earnings among provinces.

The equation was re-estimated using the sample of sixty cities. In contrast to Table 4.10, Table 4.11 shows no sign of divergence in mean earnings or mean income among cities. The coefficient is slightly negative but not significantly different from zero. How is the difference in the results for cities and for provinces to be explained? One possibility is that labour is more mobile among the cities of a province than among cities of different provinces. Such mobility would tend to equalize incomes, so producing convergence among the cities of a province.

We test this hypothesis by estimating intra-province equations for the seven provinces which contain at least six cities (Table 4.12). Given such small

TABLE 4.11 *The growth of income per capita and earnings per worker, 1988–95, as a function of their initial values, by city: urban China*

	Proportionate growth in	
	Income	Earnings
Intercept	0.845	1.167
Initial value (y_0)	−0.068	−0.112
Adj. R^2	−0.014	−0.010
F-value	0.198	0.446
Mean of dependent variable ($y_1 - y_0$)	0.362	0.324
Number of observations	60	60

Note: None of the coefficients is significantly different from zero even at the 10% level.

TABLE 4.12 *The growth of income per capita and earnings per worker, 1988–95, as a function of their initial values, by cities within provinces: urban China*

	Shanxi	Jiangsu	Anhui	Henan	Hubei	Guangdong	Yunnan
Growth of income per capita							
Intercept	1.252	15.181**	4.165	1.999	4.040	7.984*	1.594
Initial income	−0.146	−2.037**	−0.543	−0.248	−0.511	−0.992*	−0.173
Adj. R^2	−0.239	0.480	0.235	−0.140	0.105	0.278	−0.076
F-value	0.034	8.387**	2.540	0.140	1.702	3.698	0.508
Mean of dependent variable	0.250	0.443	0.326	0.286	0.421	0.520	0.359
Number of observations	6	9	6	8	7	8	8
Growth of earnings per worker							
Intercept	0.665	17.251**	4.735	4.245	1.615	11.596	0.906
Initial earnings	−0.063	−2.236**	−0.605	−0.543	−0.167	−1.404**	0.152
Adj. R^2	−0.248	0.554	0.186	−0.075	0.182	0.613	0.006
F-value	0.006	10.954**	2.143	0.512	0.077	12.107**	1.041
Mean of dependent variable	0.206	0.421	0.230	0.290	0.369	0.539	0.424
Number of observations	6	9	6	6	7	8	8

Note: ** Denotes statistical significance at the 5% and * at the 10% level.

samples, it is hardly surprising that only two of the earnings coefficients are significantly different from zero. These are in the two provinces—Jiangsu and Guangdong—which have grown fastest and moved furthest towards a market economy. However, six of the seven coefficients are negative and four of them exceed −0.5. In these cases, a 10 per cent lower initial income raises the growth rate by over 5 percentage points. Very similar results are obtained for the income equations. Again, convergence is most powerful within Jiangsu and Guangdong.

4.5 DIVERGENCE IN MEANS: EXPLANATION

We investigate the reasons for the divergence in province mean earnings in three main ways. First, we decompose the mean increases into their component parts, in order to discover which components of earnings contribute to the divergence. Secondly, we examine different subsamples, in order to explore variation in the divergence. Third, we decompose the mean differences between four samples (coast, interior; 1988, 1995) in order to throw light on the reasons for these differences.

TABLE 4.13 *Percentage growth of real earnings components, urban China, by province, 1988–95*

	E_1	E_2	E_3	E_4	E_5	Increase in real earnings
Beijing	85.5	95.9	68.6	−38.6	85.6	84.1
Shanxi	46.4	−7.0	71.1	−26.9	−15.3	28.0
Liaoning	58.0	−24.5	33.5	300.4	−2.0	33.5
Jiangsu	79.4	33.2	71.0	−61.1	−18.5	55.7
Anhui	65.8	−40.5	−11.4	79.1	6.3	25.2
Henan	32.9	−6.9	82.6	540.8	5.3	33.5
Hubei	63.9	5.7	47.2	107.3	27.2	48.1
Guangdong	86.8	65.7	98.3	60.2	65.6	79.1
Yunnan	42.7	−31.3	90.1	39.1	−44.1	26.5
Gansu	24.3	27.5	−5.4	−86.2	−46.3	3.9
Coastal	64.0	29.8	61.7	11.9	24.8	53.9
Interior	43.3	−18.5	40.8	26.8	−15.0	26.8
Total	53.8	9.8	50.9	11.4	5.5	39.3

Notes: E_1 = basic wage of workers; E_2 = bonus of workers; E_3 = cash subsidy of workers; E_4 = earnings of private owners and self-employed; E_5 = other income. Coastal region includes Beijing, Liaoning, Jiangsu, and Guangdong; interior region includes Shanxi, Anhui, Henan, Hubei, Yunnan, and Gansu.

Table 4.13 shows the percentage growth in the components of earnings in each province between 1988 and 1995. The growth in basic wages (E_1) generally exceeded that in total earnings, as did the growth in the cash value of subsidies (E_3), whereas bonuses (E_2) grew less rapidly, and they actually fell in the interior region. When the absolute increase in earnings is analysed, we find that Beijing and Guangdong had the largest increase not only in basic wages but also in bonuses and cash subsidies. The decline in the share of wages paid in the form of bonuses may be misleading. Bonuses were unimportant prior to the urban economic reforms that commenced in 1984. The proportion rose from 13 per cent in 1983 to 19 per cent in 1988; this trend was not confined to the state sector. The proportion rose further, to 22 per cent, in 1993. However, in 1994 a dramatic increase in the basic wage occurred in the government sector, and this was generally followed in the enterprise sector. Employers responded to the wage reform by paying the basic increase partly from bonus funds. In 1994, the average wage rose by 8 per cent in real terms, but this comprised a rise in 'non-bonus income' (mainly the basic wage) by 18 per cent and a fall in the bonus by 13 per cent. The consolidation was not reversed in 1995: the share of the bonus was down to 16 per cent. It is plausible, therefore, that the bonus, being the payment most subject to managerial and least subject to government control, was the dynamic element primarily responsible for the growth of earnings, and its spatial divergence, over much of our seven-year period.

TABLE 4.14 *The contribution of earnings components to the divergence of real earnings across provinces: urban China, 1988–95*

Explanatory variable	Coefficient on the explanatory variable	
	Initial earnings (y_0)	Initial component earnings (y_{i0})
Basic wage	0.481*	0.018
Bonus	1.296	0.466
Cash value of subsidy	0.747	0.218
Earnings from self-employment	−0.715	−0.788
Other earnings	0.825	0.215

Notes: * Denotes statistical significance at the 10% level. The dependent variable is the proportionate growth of the earnings component ($y_{i1} - y_{i0}$).

We estimate the inter-province equations:

$$y_{i1} - y_{i0} = a + by_0 \tag{4.7}$$

$$y_{i1} - y_{i0} = c + dy_{i0} \tag{4.8}$$

where y_{ij} is the log of earnings component i per worker in year j, y_j is the log of total earnings per worker in year j.

Equation (4.7) indicates whether each component contributes to the divergence of earnings ($b > 0$), and equation (4.8) whether each component itself diverges over the period ($d > 0$).

Table 4.14 shows the contribution made by each component of earnings to the divergence in the growth of earnings across provinces. Only self-employment earnings have the wrong sign and the contributions of bonuses and subsidies are important. For instance, a 10 per cent higher initial level of earnings raises the growth of bonuses by 13 per cent, and that of subsidies by 7 per cent. However, the importance of the basic wage in total earnings means that it contributes more in absolute terms to the divergence. We see from the second column that bonuses and subsidies, rather than basic wages, are themselves subject to the strongest divergence.

A decomposition of household mean income per capita by source showed that wage income grew in percentage terms almost as rapidly as total income, and that it accounted for 72 per cent of the absolute real increase. Moreover, the divergence of income per capita across provinces was overwhelmingly due to the behaviour of mean wages; indeed, the other sources of income actually converged across provinces. Our analysis of wage divergence therefore has direct implications for household welfare.

Our second approach is to examine the divergence of earnings in different sub-sectors. Production and non-production workers are distinguished, as are the three ownership categories: non-state enterprises, state enterprises, and government (almost all non-enterprise activities being in state hands). There is no difference at all in the degree of divergence as between staff and workers, and very little as between the three ownership categories. It appears that divergence among provinces occurred irrespective of occupation and of whether employers were subject to government control and of whether they were in a position to make profits and engage in rent-sharing with their employees.

We decided to pursue the distinction between the coastal and the interior provinces. In 1988, the ratio of coastal to interior mean earnings was 123 per cent, and in 1995 it was 150 per cent. The ratio of 1995 to 1988 mean earnings was 154 per cent in the coastal provinces, and 127 per cent in the interior provinces. To what extent was the growing divergence between the two regions due to growing regional differences in the mean income-earning characteristics of workers and to what extent was it due to growing regional differences in the income-generation process itself?

We attempt to answer this question by conducting standard decomposition analyses of the difference in mean earnings both between the two regions and between the two years:

$$\bar{y}_i - \bar{y}_j = f_i(\bar{x}_i) - f_j(\bar{x}_j)$$
$$= f_i(\bar{x}_i) - f_j(\bar{x}_j) + f_i(\bar{x}_j) - f_j(\bar{x}_j)$$
$$= f_i(\bar{x}_i - \bar{x}_j) + f_i(\bar{x}_j) - f_j(\bar{x}_j) \qquad (4.9)$$

where i, j are 1995, 1988 or coast, interior, a bar over a variable indicates its mean value, and x is a vector of explanatory variables. The first term measures the component attributable to the difference in mean characteristics and the second term the component attributable to differences in earnings functions. The alternative decomposition is:

$$\bar{y}_i - \bar{y}_j = f_j(\bar{x}_i - \bar{x}_j) + f_i(\bar{x}_i) - f_j(\bar{x}_i) \qquad (4.10)$$

The competitive market prediction is that the income-generation mechanism should be the same everywhere. However, endowments of workers' characteristics could differ spatially, and it is this that would produce spatial differences in means (and in inequality) in a fully competitive economy. China does not have such an economy: We see in Table 4.15 that the earnings difference between the coast and the interior in both years was due entirely to differences in coefficients and not at all (the effect was negative) to differences in characteristics. Similarly, we see that changes in coefficients were overwhelmingly important to the increase in mean real earnings between 1988 and 1995 in both regions.

It is worth exploring further which explanatory variables contributed most to that part of the mean earnings gap which was attributable to the difference in coefficients (Table 4.16). In comparing the coastal and interior regions, we see that the intercept term was crucial in 1988, accounting for some 95 per cent of the total. This represented the characteristics omitted from the earnings function

TABLE 4.15 *Decomposition analysis of the difference in mean earnings in urban China: coast–interior, 1988–95*

	Percentage of the difference in mean earnings that is due to	
	Coefficients	Mean values
1988–95		
Coastal provinces		
Equation (4.9)	68.8	31.2
Equation (4.10)	90.0	10.0
Interior provinces		
Equation (4.9)	67.1	32.9
Equation (4.10)	81.1	17.9
Coast–interior		
1988		
Equation (4.9)	110.4	−10.4
Equation (4.10)	109.6	−9.6
1995		
Equation (4.9)	101.0	−1.0
Equation (4.10)	106.4	−6.4

TABLE 4.16 *The percentage contribution of each worker characteristic to the regional difference in mean earnings attributable to coefficients: urban China, 1988 and 1995*

Equation used	1988		1995	
	(4.9)	(4.10)	(4.9)	(4.10)
Intercept	94.1	94.9	57.7	54.7
Sex	−0.9	−1.0	−1.2	−1.1
Age	13.8	13.1	−12.8	−13.3
Education	−13.9	−14.5	53.0	49.0
Party membership	−4.5	−4.0	4.3	3.8
Minority status	−1.9	−1.1	−3.0	−1.6
Ownership category	−19.9	−22.9	17.1	20.5
Occupation	5.1	4.6	−2.9	−2.9
Employment status	11.4	12.0	−17.2	−15.0
Sector	16.7	18.9	5.0	5.9
Total	100.0	100.0	100.0	100.0

analysis (male, aged 25–29, 0–3 years of education, Han, not a party member, production worker, in state-sector manufacturing, self-employed), that is, what might be regarded as basic urban unskilled labour.

The mean real earnings difference between the regions attributable to coefficients rose from 450 to 1,140 yuan per annum over the seven years. In 1995, education accounted for no less than half of this difference, having had a slight negative effect in 1988. The intercept term accounted for the other half. In addition, ownership had a positive effect and age a negative effect. Age was less well rewarded at the coast than in the interior.

Of crucial importance were the differential returns to education. The premium on higher education relative to 0–3 years of primary school was 92 per cent at the coast, and 49 per cent in the interior. This helped to raise the relative mean earnings of coastal workers. It appears that pressure of demand for educated workers in the coastal provinces raised their pay and contributed to the divergence of earnings among provinces.

4.6 CONCLUSIONS

Using the urban samples of the IE, CASS national household surveys of 1988 and 1995, we established two interesting results which deserve attention and explanation. First, there was a tendency for intra-province inequality in both earnings per worker and household income per capita not only to rise in each province but also to converge across provinces. Secondly, there was a tendency for both province mean earnings per worker and household mean income per capita not only to rise in each province but also to diverge across provinces. The same tendencies were to be found at the regional (coastal–interior) and city levels. This chapter was concerned to establish these patterns and then to explain them. We did better in achieving our first objective than in achieving our second. We explored various avenues but could not produce conclusive explanations.

Our analysis to decompose inequality by source of income indicated that the basic wage was the most important reason for the general increase in earnings inequality. Moreover, the basic wage made the greatest contribution to the convergence of earnings inequality across provinces although other sources were themselves more powerfully convergent. The one exception was bonuses, which were divergent. With regard to inequality of income, wage income was the main reason for the increased inequality in the coastal region but it made no contribution in the interior region, where pensions were crucial. Wages made the greatest contribution to the convergence of income inequality across provinces.

The fact that convergence of earnings inequality appeared to be stronger for 'staff' than for 'workers' and for non-state than for state employees suggests that market forces played a role in producing convergence. It is likely that the uneven timing of reforms also played a role: Those provinces and cities that reformed early had greater inequality in 1988 but a smaller increase in inequality thereafter.

Our proxy measure of the extent of labour market reform in 1988 did indeed have a positive effect on inequality in that year.

Our analysis of the inequality of inequality appears to break new ground. Given competitive markets all round, the spatial convergence of income or earnings inequality would require that economies become more alike in their distribution of productive characteristics among households or workers. However, markets in China have by no means been competitive throughout. They became more competitive between 1988 and 1995, although the process was both limited and spatially uneven. We explained convergence in terms of the process and timing of market reforms.

The decomposition of the growth in mean earnings showed basic wages to be the main, and the most dynamic, component. Basic wages also made the largest contribution to divergence, although bonuses and subsidies were themselves subject to stronger divergence. The most dynamic component of income growth was income from capital but wage income made the greatest contribution and pensions were also important in the interior. The divergence of income per capita across provinces is due to the behaviour of wage income, as all other components actually converged.

Divergence in earnings occurred irrespective of occupation or of type of employer. A decomposition analysis of the difference in mean earnings in coastal and interior provinces showed that it was due entirely to the difference in their income-generation processes. The widening of the difference over the seven years was partly due to the relative improvement in the pay of unskilled labour and partly to the sharper rise in the premium on education in the coastal provinces. This last finding suggests that market pressures for scarce labour were a driving force. Another indication that market forces were at work is the finding that mean earnings converged among the cities of a province but diverged among provinces, that is, mobility of labour limits divergence and assists convergence.

Bonuses were the component of wages over which enterprises probably had greatest autonomy. Their part in our story therefore deserves scrutiny. Being dependent on the profitability and negotiating power (over soft budgets) of enterprises, bonuses tend to segment the labour market by enterprise. Walder (1987) argued that bonuses were fairly equally distributed within the enterprise, reflecting worker pressures and preferences. However, there may be as many work units as households in our urban sample. We found bonuses to be the most disequalizing component of earnings. Bonuses were more unequally distributed among workers, and also among provinces, in 1995 than in 1988, probably because of greater segmentation among enterprises. Bonuses do not help to explain the interprovince convergence of earnings inequality that we observed; indeed, their effect is divergent. Bonuses are also an important source of the inter-province divergence of mean earnings. The share of bonuses in earnings fell over the seven years. They may nevertheless have been the driving force behind the growth of earnings, a role which could have been concealed by the consolidating wage reform of 1994.

The policy of permitting state-owned enterprises to pay bonuses was intended to improve incentives for efficiency, at least at the level of enterprise. However the continuing weakness of both product market and labour market forces made possible large differences in enterprise profitability and thus in enterprise pay—a relationship which we explore in Chapter 7. Bonuses weakened the convergence in the inequality of wages and incomes and strengthened the divergence of mean wages and incomes.

Convergence of mean incomes among economies is consistent with models of technological diffusion and with neoclassical growth models of closed economies. It is also consistent with increased factor mobility across economies. There is much evidence of conditional economic convergence around the world. However, we found economic divergence among the regions of urban China. The most plausible explanation is the relative lack of factor mobility and the weakness of market forces. The former permitted very different income-generation functions to exist, and the latter permitted wages in general, and bonuses in particular, to be influenced by rent-sharing behaviour as well as by local supply and demand conditions.

If our interpretations of the results are correct, two policy conclusions follow. First, economic reform may have a once-for-all and finite effect on inequality. At the least, there is a once-for-all component. The growth of inequality is limited by the processes that produced cross-province convergence in inequality. Secondly, although divergence in mean earnings and incomes may continue across provinces, further reform of the labour market—assisting labour mobility, and giving more rein to market forces in the slower reforming provinces—can slow it down and may eventually reverse it. Nevertheless, forces of cumulative causation appear to be at work in the Chinese economy, which may keep divergence going for some years yet.

REFERENCES

Barro, Robert J. and Xavier Sala-i-Martin (1995). *Economic Growth*, New York: McGraw-Hill.

Jian, Tianlun, Jeffrey Sachs, and Andrew Warner (1996). 'Trends in regional inequality in China', *China Economic Review*, 7, 1 (Spring): 1–22.

Knight, John and Lina, Song (1993). 'The spatial contributions to income inequality in rural China', *Cambridge Journal of Economics*, 17: 195–213.

——, Shi Li, and Zhao Renwei (2001). 'A spatial analysis of wages and incomes in urban China: divergent means, convergent inequality', in Carl Riskin, Zhao Renwei, and Li Shi (eds), *China's Retreat from Equality: Income Distribution and Economic Transition*, Armonk, NY: M.E. Sharpe, 133–66.

Walder, Andrew (1987). 'Wage reform and the web of factory interests', *China Quarterly*, 109 (March): 22–41.

5

Rural Migrants in Urban Enterprises

5.1 INTRODUCTION

During the period of the communes and central planning, the movement of labour in China was tightly controlled and restricted. This was achieved through a combination of, inter alia, a household registration (*hukou*) system, commune controls, and food rationing. The restrictions were intended to ensure that agriculture would fund rapid but orderly urban industrialization and to maintain political control over society (Knight and Song 1999). During the period of economic reform and transition to a market economy, the communes were disbanded and food rationing was phased out, and rural–urban migration became an important phenomenon. This reflected a growing urban need for migrant labour but also the weakened power to control movement. According to a representative rural household survey, there were in 1993 perhaps 39 million rural workers in the urban areas at any time (RDI, CASS 1994: 111).

Despite their greater freedom, it remained difficult for rural workers to acquire urban registration and permanent urban residence. Government attempted to maintain continuing control over the 'floating' population of temporary rural–urban migrant workers. Generally, rural workers are permitted only in the 'residual' urban jobs not wanted by urban residents. These tend to be the lowest-wage, lowest-skill, least pleasant jobs. Although rural households have a strong economic incentive to send out members to the cities and towns as temporary workers (Knight and Song 2003), the migrants are at a considerable disadvantage in the urban labour market by comparison with urban residents—with regard to job opportunities, skill acquisition, wages, and employer-provided benefits such as housing, healthcare, and pensions.

Are the productive characteristics of migrants rewarded in the urban labour market? How do migrants compare with non-migrants in their productive characteristics, occupational attainment, and pay? Do migrants have an incentive to remain with the enterprise and in the city, and what factors influence these attitudes? What determines the extent of migrant employment? Do enterprises have an incentive to employ more migrants, and how do they value migrants relative to non-migrants? How does policy influence migrant flows: Does government impede or encourage the growth of 'floating' workers? These are the questions that we pose.

We utilize a survey of rural–urban migrants employed in city enterprises (MOL 1995). This is described in Section 5.2. We analyse the determinants of their pay (Section 5.3) and compare their pay with that of urban residents employed in the same enterprises (Section 5.4). We proceed to view migrant employment from three distinct perspectives: That of the migrants themselves (Section 5.5), that of the urban enterprises which employ them (Section 5.6), and that of the Chinese Government (Section 5.7). Section 5.8 concludes.

5.2 THE SURVEY

The survey that we analyse was planned, and the questionnaires designed, by researchers in the Ministry of Labour (now the Ministry of Labour and Social Security), guided by the authors, in order to investigate rural migrants employed in urban enterprises, about whom little had hitherto been known. The survey was conducted in January 1996 and much of it relates to the year 1995. It covers 2,900 migrants employed in 118 enterprises located in four cities. The cities were chosen to be reasonably representative of large- and medium-sized cities in China. They include a huge city (Beijing), a rapidly growing coastal city (Shenzhen), a traditional interior city (Wuhan), and a smaller city (Suzhou). It was hoped that comparisons among the cities would assist the interpretation of results and the projection of trends.

Within each city, enterprises were chosen by a random procedure from a sample frame stratified by ownership and by sector. Each sampled enterprise was required to complete an enterprise questionnaire. The number of migrants sampled depended on the number of migrants employed; there is some bias in favour of enterprises employing migrants.[1] We suspect that there is also bias towards larger enterprises. In 1994, the average number of 'staff and workers' (non-migrants) in urban industrial firms was 222 and in urban construction firms 620 (427 and 1,128 in state-owned enterprises (SOEs) respectively) (PRC, SSB 1996: 375–6, 429–31), whereas the sample estimates were 1,489 in industry and 1,189 in construction. The bias could be due either to the choice of cities or to sampling within the cities. The survey tells us about only a part of the urban labour market for migrants but one which, we shall argue, is substantial and likely in the long run to grow in importance.

Table 5.1 presents basic data from the migrant questionnaire. Most of the migrants are male and single. The average age is 26; only a minority are household heads. Women are on average five years younger than men; there are very few married women. Nearly two-thirds of the migrants have junior middle school education (nine years). Most farmed previously; few consider themselves to come from the poor households of their village. Turning to their experience of migration, we find that many have visited a large- or middle-sized city before, and half have previously migrated for work. Their average length of current migration employment is twenty-nine months. This implies that, provided the flow of migrant employment is

The Urban Labour Market

TABLE 5.1 *Basic data on the migrants*

	Percentage of respondents*
Migrant characteristics	
Male	62.9
Single	62.4
Male	50.7
Married	37.6
Male	83.3
Household head	28.6
Average age (years)	
All	25.6
Male	27.5
Female	21.9
Professional education or above	4.1
Senior middle school	25.9
Junior middle school	63.6
Primary school or below	6.4
Household income level within village	
Rich	23.0
Average	62.6
Poor	14.5
Previous occupation	
None	3.2
Farming	61.1
Rural industry	15.0
Migration experience	
Visited a big city before	63.6
Previous migration experience	52.0
Months of migration experience	
Total	40.9
Current	29.3
If married	
Spouse with migrant	36.1
Spouse not with migrant	63.9
Employment in 1995	
Hours per day	8.4
Days per month	25.3
Months per year	10.6
Average income (yuan per month)	551.4
Employer pays medical insurance	24.4
Employer pays injury insurance	31.8
Employer provides accommodation	78.5
Accommodation per migrant (sq. m)**	3.8

Notes: * Unless otherwise specified. ** Excluding the 170 cases who must have lived in the factory itself.

Source: Of this and subsequent tables in this chapter, Knight, Song, and Jia (1999).

TABLE 5.2 *Basic data on the enterprises*

	Percentage of enterprises
Manufacturing	38.8
Construction	13.8
Services	29.4
Other sectors	18.1
State-owned	54.7
Collective	20.5
Other ownership categories	24.8
Enterprise established	
–1979	47.0
1980–89	34.2
1990–	18.8
Average number of employees	
All*	1,319
Migrants	327
Non-migrants	992
Migrants as percentage of employees	
All	24.8
Aged 16–25	54.3
Aged 26–35	25.4
Aged 36–	7.1

Note: * This differs from the number reported for the sample as a whole because it covers the 108 enterprises recording both their migrant and non-migrant numbers.

regular, the average length of completed migrant employment is twice that length, that is, almost five years. Nearly two-thirds of the married migrants have not brought their spouse. They worked intensively throughout 1995, for an average wage of 550 yuan per month. Few employers provide insurance but most provide accommodation, albeit extremely rudimentary and meagre (averaging less than 4 sq. m per migrant).

Table 5.2 presents basic data taken from the enterprise questionnaire. We see that manufacturing is the most important sector, and that SOEs account for more than half the total. However, the collective sector and the new private sector each account for more than a fifth of the sample. Many of the enterprises are long established. The average enterprise employs 327 migrants and 992 non-migrants, yielding a total of 1,319 employees. The breakdown by age group reveals an interesting pattern: Migrants account for a quarter of the sample overall but for more than half of the 16–25 year-olds.

Information on the four cities is provided in Table 5.3. We see, for instance, the much greater size of the Beijing labour market, the importance of the state

TABLE 5.3 *Basic data on the four cities*

	Beijing	Shenzhen	Wuhan	Suzhou
Official statistics				
Population, 1994 (million)				
Total*	10.62	0.94	7.00	3.27
Non-agricultural*	6.84	0.70	3.95	1.07
City and town employment, 1994 (million)*	5.09	0.26	2.69	0.42
Employment as percentage of total				
State-owned enterprises	76.07	45.19	68.76	59.33
Collective enterprises	15.31	12.17	28.08	27.28
Other enterprises	8.62	42.64	3.16	13.49
Construction sector	12.25	9.22	11.72	3.49
Manufacturing sector	29.45	48.17	67.00	55.09
Other sectors	58.30	42.61	21.26	41.42
Migrant statistics				
Average age (years)	23.8	26.4	26.3	26.5
Average income (yuan per month)	529.2	822.2	412.1	430.7
Average living expenses (yuan per month)	274.5	454.8	239.9	241.8
Length of current employment (months)	24.2	29.2	33.6	32.7
Length of employment contract (months)	24.0	12.6	16.6	26.4
Percentage of total migrants				
Male	68.5	64.3	63.2	52.7
Single	68.6	59.7	59.4	59.0
Senior middle school or above	35.7	48.9	20.3	10.2
With skill	70.7	61.6	65.7	57.0
Received training for more than a month	48.0	40.0	33.0	24.6
Production or supporting worker	73.7	66.1	80.6	89.7
Skilled worker	11.0	12.9	7.3	5.3
Managerial or sales staff	15.3	21.0	12.1	5.0
From this province	1.3	45.7	77.7	83.0
From neighbouring provinces	32.9	13.6	17.5	6.9
From other provinces	65.8	40.7	4.6	10.1
Recruited by				
Relatives or friends	44.4	81.4	80.8	47.8
Rural labour department	24.2	3.0	7.7	32.7
Directly by employer	23.0	3.8	3.3	10.2
Enterprise statistics				
Average number of employees				
Total	2,825	557	996	1,230
Migrant	561	193	193	213
Non-migrant	2,264	363	803	1,016

TABLE 5.3 (*continued*)

	Beijing	Shenzhen	Wuhan	Suzhou
Migrants as a percentage of total city employment				
All	19.9	34.6	19.3	17.3
Production or supporting worker	22.7	44.7	26.9	26.4
Skilled worker	25.5	30.3	15.2	6.7
Managerial and technician staff	2.0	1.3	0.7	0.6

Notes: * The area extends beyond the city proper to include surrounding rural areas under the administration of the city. Farming and rural households are generally excluded from the 'non-agricultural' and 'city and town' statistics, respectively.

Sources: PRC, SSB (1993: Vol. 1, 82, 218, 238, 256, 264; 1996: 312–3), PRC, MOL (1996: 82, 85, 92, 94).

sector in Beijing and of the private sector in Shenzhen, and the predominance of manufacturing in Wuhan and Suzhou, and of services in Beijing. From the sample, it is notable that wages are highest in Shenzhen. This is explained partly by the higher cost of living: Living expenses are also reported to be highest in this new city neighbouring Hong Kong. The Beijing migrants tend to be younger, to have arrived more recently, to come from distant provinces, to have been formally recruited, and to have longer contracts. Beijing contains the highest proportion of male, single, skilled, and trained migrants. On the other hand, Shenzhen has the most educated migrants and the highest proportion in skilled manual and non-manual occupations. This reflects the fact that Shenzhen has much the highest proportion of migrants in total employment: There are better jobs available for migrants to fill. By contrast, in the more traditional and more representative cities, Wuhan and Suzhou, the migrants are largely from within the province, and they are almost entirely production or supporting workers—less well educated, less often trained, and less well paid.

5.3 THE REWARDS FOR MIGRANT LABOUR

In this section we seek to understand the determinants of migrant pay. Is the human capital of migrants valued by the employers? Do migrants have the opportunity to work in the sorts of jobs which reward skills? Table 5.4 presents mean values and the coefficients of an earnings function for the sample as a whole. As the dependent variable is the logarithm of the wage per month ($y = \ln Y$), the coefficients can be interpreted as proportionate effects. Table 5.5 presents equivalent earnings functions for the four cities separately. The differences among them may help to explain the general results.

TABLE 5.4 *Earnings function for migrants: mean values and coefficients*

	Mean value	Coefficients
Intercept		5.497**
Junior middle school	0.636	−0.061**
Primary school and lower	0.065	−0.086*
No skill	0.329	−0.037*
Has not received training	0.293	−0.059**
Age (years)	25.554	0.034**
Age squared		−0.0005**
No previous city experience	0.357	−0.050**
Time with the enterprise (months)	29.591	0.002**
Production worker	0.539	−0.089**
Supporting worker	0.208	−0.093**
Female	0.368	−0.107**
Married	0.376	0.023
Disabled	0.027	−0.034
Minority group	0.035	0.101*
Length of job search (months)	12.023	0.001**
Recruitment through:		
Official channels	0.171	0.052*
Labour market	0.090	0.068*
Enterprise	0.110	−0.075**
Working hours per month	211.455	−0.0000
Shenzhen	0.235	0.456**
Wuhan	0.210	−0.157**
Suzhou	0.220	0.029
Construction	0.140	0.298**
Communication and transport	0.078	0.088**
Commerce and food trade	0.114	0.208**
Services	0.148	0.101**
Other sectors	0.107	−0.159**
Collective ownership	0.199	0.123**
Private ownership	0.076	0.161**
Foreign ownership	0.125	0.152**
Other ownership	0.024	0.035
Number of employees in the enterprise (00)	19.121	0.004**
Number squared		−0.0000
Mean value of ln wage	6.183	
Adjusted R^2	0.409	
F-value	59.109	
Number of observations	2,775	

Notes: ** Denotes statistical significance at the 1% level and * at the 5% level. The omitted categories in the dummy variable analysis are senior middle school and above, skilled, has received training, previous city experience, skilled manual or non-manual worker, male, single, healthy, Han, recruitment through family or friends, Beijing, manufacturing, state ownership. The dependent variable is the logarithm of the average wage of migrant workers.

TABLE 5.5 *Earnings functions for migrants, by city: mean values and coefficients*

	Mean values				Coefficients			
	Beijing	Shenzhen	Wuhan	Suzhou	Beijing	Shenzhen	Wuhan	Suzhou
Intercept					5.751**	6.690**	5.172**	5.845**
Junior middle school	0.621	0.482	0.705	0.758	−0.098**	−0.060	0.048	−0.028
Primary school and lower	0.025	0.032	0.086	0.142	−0.257**	−0.022	−0.099	−0.008
No skill	0.276	0.337	0.310	0.421	−0.008	−0.009	−0.014	−0.022
Has not received training	0.167	0.299	0.346	0.429	−0.056*	−0.088	−0.040	−0.025
Age (years)	23.832	26.530	26.330	26.383	0.022*	0.005	0.008	0.016
Age squared					−0.0003*	−0.0001	−0.0001	−0.0003*
No previous city experience	0.337	0.210	0.449	0.457	−0.044*	−0.045	−0.056	−0.010
Time with the enterprise (months)	24.152	29.917	34.217	33.074	0.002**	0.002**	0.000	−0.002
Production worker	0.513	0.464	0.539	0.658	−0.072**	−0.050	−0.073	−0.089**
Supporting worker	0.208	0.150	0.235	0.242	−0.064*	−0.147*	−0.008	−0.052
Female	0.314	0.341	0.363	0.484	−0.033	−0.159**	−0.110	−0.178**
Married	0.317	0.412	0.411	0.393	0.011	0.010	0.031	0.008
Disabled	0.020	0.014	0.051	0.029	−0.036	0.052	−0.002	−0.107
Minority group	0.080	0.011	0.022	0.003	0.078*	−0.029	−0.138	0.034
Length of job search (months)	10.364	17.025	12.611	8.635	0.001**	0.001	0.000	−0.000
Recruitment through:								
Labour department	0.079	0.029	0.067	0.324	0.021	−0.056	0.059	0.010
Labour market	0.222	0.115	0.080	0.092	0.007	0.069	0.004	−0.048
Enterprise	0.167	0.037	0.029	0.093	−0.038	−0.259*	0.096	0.044
Working hours per month	214.531	210.120	212.705	207.020	−0.0002	0.0003	0.0012**	0.0007**
Mean of dependent variable	6.150	6.608	5.934	6.015				
Adjusted R^2	0.718	0.337	0.408	0.543				
F-value	45.522	8.207	9.211	18.688				
Number of observations	926	653	584	611				

Notes: As for Table 5.4.

Consider the potential human capital variables in Table 5.4. Education is little rewarded. By comparison with senior secondary school graduates, junior secondary school graduates (having three fewer years of schooling) receive only 6 per cent less pay, and primary school or lower graduates (six or more years less schooling) only 8 per cent less. The education coefficients are greatest in the skilled manual and non-manual occupations and in the private sector (equations not shown). On that basis we would expect Shenzhen (with relatively most of both) to show the highest returns to education, but these are to be obtained in Beijing. Self-assessed skills and training are little rewarded (making differences of 4 and 6 per cent, respectively). Finally, both production workers and supporting workers receive 9 per cent less than the more skilled workers. Various measures of experience are significantly rewarded although their effects are relatively small. One measure is age: The age–earnings profile has the familiar inverted U-shaped relationship. A migrant aged 25 has 13 per cent more pay than one aged 18, and earnings continue to rise throughout the relevant age range. Age is rewarded most in Beijing and least in Shenzhen. Pay also increases with the length of service, being 5 per cent higher at the average length of current tenure than at the start.

The relatively low returns to human capital no doubt reflect the lowly and tenuous nature of migrant employment. No less than 54 per cent of the sample are production workers and 21 per cent supporting workers, that is, only 25 per cent of the migrants are skilled manual or non-manual workers. The limited length of stay in the enterprise (on average 30 months of incomplete service, suggesting 60 months of complete service) reduces the incentive for firms to train workers. Nevertheless, the great majority of migrants (71 per cent) had received some training, mainly after migration, mainly in the enterprise (Table 5.6). However, it was generally brief: Only 22 per cent had received training for more than three months. Training in its various dimensions was strongly positively correlated with education and, to a lesser extent, with occupation. The great majority of migrants (80 per cent) wanted more training, and many (68 per cent) would be prepared to pay for it. Why is training so popular when it is so little rewarded? Asked what had been the effect of their training, 84 per cent of the respondents said it had improved their skills whereas 16 per cent said it had raised their wages. Migrants may well regard training as an investment with long-run benefits, not necessarily reaped in their current employment.

Women are paid 10 per cent less than men, *ceteris paribus*, and non-Han people 10 per cent more than Han. Discrimination against women is the least, and discrimination in favour of minorities the greatest, in Beijing. This probably reflects the importance of state ownership (73 per cent of migrants) in the Beijing sample. The process of job search also affects pay. Length of search raises the subsequent wage slightly but significantly, as is to be expected if job search is an investment. Direct rural recruitment by the enterprise reduces pay whereas recruitment in the city labour market raises it—results which may reflect the degree of competition for migrant services.

TABLE 5.6 *The training of migrants*

	Percentage of respondents			
	Total	Upper middle school or above	Lower middle school	Primary school or below
Has received training	71	80	68	39
Non-manual or skilled manual worker	79			
Production worker	71			
Supporting worker	62			
Has received training for ≥3 months	22	31	20	5
Non-manual or skilled manual worker	27			
Production worker	23			
Supporting worker	13			
Has received training				
Before migration	19			
After migration	81			
Was trained by*				
Enterprise	67			
Government	30			
Other	19			
Number of times received training	1.2	1.5	1.1	0.6
Average days per time	21	29	19	5
Total cost paid by self (yuan)	121	225	81	35
Wants to receive (further) training	80	85	80	51
Would be prepared to pay for further training	68	74	68	41
Can training raise work efficiency? Yes	61	69	58	40
Consequence of your training*				
Improved skill	84			
Raised wage	16			
Other	17			

Note: * Denotes that figures can add up to more than 100% because more than one answer was permitted.

The characteristics of the enterprise are important influences on the pay of migrants. Consider the equation for the sample as a whole (Table 5.4). Wages in construction are 35 per cent higher than in manufacturing, probably on account of the arduous nature of construction work. Private and foreign firms pay 17 and 16 per cent more, respectively, than state-owned firms: They may be more responsive to 'efficiency wage' considerations or to charges of exploitation. Wages also tend to rise with the number of employees in the enterprise: This frequently observed firm-size effect thus extends to migrants in China. Wages in fast-growing

Shenzhen exceed those in Beijing by 58 per cent, *ceteris paribus*. To some extent this reflects a higher cost of living: The reported difference in mean living expenses accounts for 61 per cent of the difference in mean wages. It may also reflect a tighter market for migrants and a consequent bidding up of wages in Shenzhen. Migrants represent 35 per cent of total employment in the Shenzhen sample but only 20 per cent in Beijing and even less in the other two cities (Table 5.3). Finally, it is notable that the earnings function for Beijing has more explanatory power (higher R^2, more coefficients significant) than the others, especially Shenzhen (Table 5.5). It is possible that the greater absolute number of migrants in Beijing has generated more competition in the labour market and hence greater economic rationality in the structure of wages.

5.4 MIGRANT AND NON-MIGRANT EARNINGS COMPARED

In order to understand the residual role of migrants in the urban labour market, it is necessary to compare them with urban-*hukou* residents. The employer question-naire permits such a comparison: It sought summary information on the average earnings and employment of both rural and urban workers in the enterprise. It did so by occupation, and also occupation interacted with age, education, and gender, one at a time, in the case of employment; and on occupation alone in the case of average earnings. Thus a comparative earnings function analysis for migrants and non-migrants and a consequent decomposition analysis can be conducted only rather crudely at the enterprise level and not at all at the individual level.

Table 5.7 shows the average earnings and employment of migrants and non-migrants for the four occupational categories. The managerial and technical category is roughly equivalent to non-manual, and the other three categories are manual occupations. We see that the ratio of rural to urban workers' average earnings ranges from 74 per cent (in the managerial and technical occupation) to 89 per cent (for supporting workers), the weighted average being 79 per cent. This percentage would be considerably lower if the various payments-in-kind (such as subsidized housing, medical, and pension benefits) could be included. Urban and migrant workers are likely to receive the same money wage for doing identical jobs in an enterprise but often their jobs are not identical. For instance, the urban worker may be a cook and the migrant worker an assistant cook receiving lower pay. The difference in pay may or may not correspond to a difference in personal skill. In any case, it is likely that migrants fresh from the countryside lack the social and communication skills that are acquired by growing up and living in a city.

The occupational composition of migrants and non-migrants is rather different: Only 1 per cent of the former but 19 per cent of the latter are managerial and technical staff, whereas 68 per cent of the former and 48 per cent of the latter are production workers. We isolate the effect of occupational composition on the difference in average earnings by standardizing for occupation in the following

TABLE 5.7 *Average earnings and employment by occupation: urban, rural, and total workers*

	Urban workers	Rural workers	Total workers	Rural workers (urban = 100)	Rural workers (rural plus urban = 100)
Average earnings (yuan per annum)					
Managerial and technical staff	10,918	8,120	10,653	74.4	
Skilled workers	9,569	7,952	8,489	83.1	
Production workers	7,682	6,589	6,805	85.8	
Supporting workers	6,988	6,192	6,367	88.6	
Total	8,679	6,877	7,752	79.2	
Employment (percentage)					
Managerial and technical staff	19.1	1.0	15.5		0.1
Skilled workers	23.5	22.5	23.2		19.9
Production workers	48.1	68.0	52.2		27.0
Supporting workers	9.3	8.5	9.1		19.3
Total	100.0	100.0	100.0		20.7

TABLE 5.8 *Decomposition of the differences in average earnings between rural and urban workers*

	Yuan per annum	Percentage
Difference in average earnings	1,802	100.0
of which, due to:		
Occupational composition	350	19.4
Within-occupation earnings differences	1,452	80.6

Note: Where $G = \bar{w}_u - \bar{w}_r$, G is decomposed into $\sum i\bar{w}_{ui}\rho_i - \sum i\bar{w}_{ri}\rho_i$, within-occupation earnings differences, and the residual, due to occupational composition (w_u, w_r is average earnings of urban and rural workers, and ρ_i is the proportion of total workers in occupation i).

way. We calculate the weighted average earnings of rural and urban workers using as weights the occupational composition of the sample as a whole. Table 5.8 shows the result of this exercise: 19.4 per cent of the gross difference in average earnings is due to occupational composition and 80.6 per cent to intra-occupation earnings differences. No doubt a finer occupational classification would show a greater role for occupational composition. Occupational differences can often be subtle, as in the distinction made above between a cook and assistant cook.

TABLE 5.9 *Earnings functions for urban and rural workers using enterprise-level data*

	Urban	Rural
Intercept	−14682.000	9753.000**
Education (years)	578.719	264.407
Age (years)	906.907	−129.920
Age squared	−12.183	2.283
Managerial and technical staff	4440.127	3080.764
Skilled workers	1995.277	−153.559
Production workers	−449.535	523.137
Beijing	−5271.906**	−4539.844**
Wuhan	−6692.684**	−6435.688**
Suzhou	−4727.641**	−4194.246**
Collective ownership	1204.905	454.853
Private ownership	165.973	951.711
Foreign-owned, joint venture	1549.886	−234.663
Other ownership	−3793.184	−1362.480
Mining	−2004.415	−1311.996
Manufacturing	1670.964	−663.561
Communication and transport	4704.053*	−266.375
Commerce and food	3269.122	−755.049
Service trade	2780.750	−2314.976
Other sectors	2528.579	−1503.603
Adj. R^2	0.428	0.506
F-value	4.106**	4.452**
Mean of average wage (yuan)	8209.458	6205.998
Number of observations	80	65

Notes: The dependent variable is the average wage in the enterprise, w_u and w_r. The absolute form of the dependent variable was superior to the logarithmic form by various criteria. The omitted categories in the dummy variable analysis are Shenzhen, state ownership, and construction. The occupational variables show the proportion (between 0 and 1) of urban (or rural) workers employed in the occupation; supporting workers are the omitted category. ** Denotes statistical significance at the 1% level and * at the 5% level.

It is possible to isolate the effect of education, age, and occupation on the earnings of migrants and of non-migrants by means of an earnings function based on enterprise-level data (Table 5.9). Although only the city coefficients are significant, the coefficients suggest that: The education of urban workers is valued more than that of migrants; the contrasts among the city labour markets differentiate wages; and the age of urban workers is powerfully rewarded whereas that of migrants is actually penalized. Age, our best proxy for employment experience, should reward non-migrants better because their employment experience is more likely to be relevant to their current work than is that of migrants. The negative age coefficient of the latter may represent a decline in productivity with age in arduous manual work; for example, many older migrants can get only low-status sedentary jobs.

We pose the counterfactual question: What would the average earnings of migrants be if they had the same average characteristics as non-migrants? In this way we can decompose the difference in group mean wages ($w_u - w_r = 2,003$ yuan). What proportions of this difference are due to group differences in productive characteristics and in other factors, including their income-generation mechanisms? Urban workers average 2.0 years more in schooling and 7.8 years more in age than migrants. Differences in these human capital variables account for 22 per cent of the difference in mean earnings, and differences in occupational composition for 34 per cent. Of course, part of the difference in occupational distribution is due to the greater human capital of urban workers: Occupation is positively correlated with education and age. The education of the workers is rewarded partly because it improves their access to higher-paying occupations. Thus, for instance, the omission of the occupation terms from the migrant earnings function raises the contribution of the human capital variables to the group mean wage difference to 33 per cent. However, the higher human capital of urban workers cannot explain much of their occupational advantage. The collinearity with occupation is considerably weaker for migrant workers. Thus, for instance, raising the educational level of migrants to that of urban workers increases the proportion of migrants in non-manual occupations from 23 to only 33 per cent—well short of the 43 per cent in the urban sample.[2]

A substantial residual remains to be accounted for after we have standardized as best we can for the quality differences which help to make urban workers a different factor of production. A large part of the residual appears to be due to 'job discrimination', that is, equally productive people have differential access to the better jobs. The institutional arrangements suggest that there is also 'wage discrimination', that is, equally productive people are paid differently in similar jobs. This can result from differences in supply prices. Urban workers are protected by institutional wage determination and, in 1995, by the government commitment to provide them with employment. The wages of migrants are more market-determined and their reservation wages are weakened by lack of village opportunities, of information, and of security. The urban labour market is segmented between migrants and non-migrants, and there is little competition between them.

5.5 *THE PERSPECTIVE OF THE MIGRANTS*

The future of rural–urban labour migration in China depends on the wishes and needs of three economic actors: The prospective migrants, the urban enterprises, and the government at different levels. Migrant employment will grow in quantity and quality if all three parties are in favour: Any one could hinder such a development. We examine what light the migrant and enterprise questionnaires throw on these three perspectives, beginning in this section with that of the migrants. We pose the following main questions. Why did the migrants come to the city? How did they rate their migration experience? Did they want to remain in their jobs? How close were their rural ties? Did they want to remain in the city? What were the factors influencing their future plans?

Migrants were asked to give the reasons for their migration. These can be loosely classified into four categories. 'Surplus labour' denotes economic push, 'more income' economic pull, 'more experience of life' suggests social motivation, and 'more skill' an economic investment. We see from Table 5.10 that the four reasons are of roughly equal importance. Beijing stands out as attracting the curious and the investors. Women are less concerned than men about income and more concerned to experience life. Age has a powerful and predictable effect, almost monotonic, on motivation: The importance of the income motive increases with age and the social and investment motives decrease. Marriage has the same effects on motivation; as does length of migration. Curiously, neither education nor occupation is related to the reasons for migration.

TABLE 5.10 *Reasons for migrating: percentage of respondents reporting each reason*

| | Reason for migration | | | |
	Surplus labour	More income	More experience of life	More skill
Total	31	46	38	44
Beijing	30	41	47	57
Male	33	57	29	40
Female	26	28	54	51
Age				
−20	30	29	63	60
20–24	31	38	50	52
25–29	29	54	26	39
30–34	33	64	13	30
35–	34	70	7	15
Spouse present	28	58	23	30
Spouse absent	33	61	19	32
No spouse	31	34	54	55
Migration for (years)				
<2	31	43	42	48
2–4	32	43	44	45
>4	33	56	22	36

Note: Row percentages may add up to more than 100 because more than one reason was permitted.

There is considerable evidence from the survey that many migrants were fairly pleased with their migration experience. For instance, asked to rate their degree of satisfaction, 50 per cent were satisfied or very satisfied, whereas only 9 per cent were dissatisfied or very dissatisfied. Asked the reasons for their satisfaction, the former group stressed the possibility of working for a long period (51 per cent), followed by the possibility of learning skills (36 per cent), rather than high income in itself (19 per cent). Many of the migrants were also satisfied with their current jobs. A high proportion (42 per cent) wanted to work as long as possible in the current job, and only 21 per cent for less than two years, 27 per cent wanted to change their current job but 73 per cent did not or had not considered the question. Asked what they would prefer, the former group stressed jobs offering higher wages (51 per cent) or more suitable to their skills (54 per cent).

We estimated a multinomial logit model of tenure choice. Migrants were asked: How long do you want to work in this enterprise? Three answers were possible: Leave after a certain period (several were specified), stay as long as possible, and have no plans. Table 5.11 reports the coefficients on 'stay as long as possible', 'leave' being the omitted category. Three basic explanatory variables are included: The migrant wage, rural household income per capita, and the length of current tenure. Although the equation predicts poorly, all three determinants have the expected sign and are statistically significant. The higher the migrant's wage and the poorer his rural household, the keener he is to stay as long as possible. Although the relationship is likely to reflect two-way causation, the longer a migrant stays, the greater the probability that he wants to stay

TABLE 5.11 *Multinomial logit analysis of tenure choice: the determinants of indefinite stay*

	Mean value	Coefficient		Marginal effect on percentage probability	
Intercept		−0.058	−0.225*		
Migrant wage (00 yuan per month)	5.374	0.048**	0.038*	1.356	1.103
Rural household income per capita (00 yuan per month)	7.815	−0.008*	−0.007*	−0.136	−0.103
Months in current employment	29.312		0.007**		0.187
Pseudo-R^2		0.004	0.012		
Percentage of correct predictions		42.6	42.8		
Number of observations		2,859	2,859		

Notes: The coefficients show the determinants of the wish to stay as long as possible in the enterprise, the omitted category being the wish to leave after some specified period; the coefficients for 'no plan' are not reported. The marginal effects show the impact of a unit increase in the explanatory variable on the probability of wishing to stay as long as possible in the enterprise. ** Denotes statistical significance at the 1% and * at the 5% level.

indefinitely. The marginal effects suggest that tenure choice is somewhat responsive to its determinants over a plausible range. Not only do many migrants want to stay indefinitely but this attitude appears to be amenable to economic incentives, for example, the wage offered by the enterprise and its use of seniority payments.

Did the migrants want to settle in the city? Responses to questions are difficult to interpret here because it is unclear what implicit assumptions were being made, for example, as to whether they could get an urban *hukou*, or bring their families. Ties with the rural household were clearly being maintained: 74 per cent of migrants had returned home for the previous Spring Festival and 71 per cent intended to return for the coming one. A high proportion of migrants' income was remitted to their rural households. In 1995 the average migrant remittance was 1,230 yuan. This represented 21 per cent of the urban income for the year, or 50 per cent of urban income minus estimated living expenses. Asked their plans for the future, 57 per cent of the migrants planned to return home, although only a few (8 per cent) intended to return to farming. Only 14 per cent planned to remain in the city or to move to another, and 33 per cent had made no plans.

How is this evidence to be reconciled with the high proportion of migrants who wanted to stay in their current job for as long as possible? The current job offered security whereas life in the city without it appeared hazardous and insecure. City governments tend to be concerned about the welfare of workers only if they possess a city *hukou*. Asked what difference it would make if they obtained an urban *hukou*, only 20 per cent envisaged no change, 36 per cent expected to work for a longer period, and 39 per cent expected to get a higher wage.

Less than a third of migrants remitted none of their urban income in 1995. The non-remitters tended to be young, single, female, well-educated, and in non-manual jobs, that is, probably keener to become urbanized. It is possible to analyse the determinants of remittances by means of a tobit regression equation (Table 5.12). The marginal propensity to remit income, *ceteris paribus*, is 0.28 for those who already remit and 0.20 for the sample as a whole. Household responsibilities appear to play an important role: Household heads, married people, and males (often expected to fund housebuilding and marriages) remit substantially more, even when other things, including income, are held constant. Remittances may be higher, the fewer the number of workers in the rural household. Less is remitted to non-farming households (the richest rural group) but more to mixed activity households (which may have greater need for finance) than to farming households (the poorest group). Recruitment through official channels raises subsequent remittances, possibly because of the facilities provided for transferring money. Links with the village appear to be stronger for less well-educated migrants, probably because they are more likely to return. Remittances decline significantly with the duration of current migrant employment but the effect is minor (92 yuan over one standard deviation for those who remit). We conclude, therefore, that the migrants generally remain part of their rural households: Only a small proportion seem to have severed their ties.

TABLE 5.12 *The determinants of migrant remittances: tobit regression equation*

	Coefficient
Intercept	−1,541.693**
Migrant income	0.279**
Male	318.402**
Married	314.465**
Household head	343.058**
Lower middle school	291.055**
Primary school or below	981.927**
Household workers	−14.569
Non-farming household	−107.438
Mixed-activity household	444.151**
Recruitment through:	
Labour department	230.062*
Labour market	−5.158
Employer	−70.226
Months in current employment	−2.743*
Mean of dependent variable	1,226.252
Number of observations	2,873
Number of zero observations	844

Notes: ** Denotes statistical significance at the 1% and * at the 5% level. Both migrant income and migrant remittances relate to the year 1995. The multiplicative factor for the derivative—to answer the question: What is the effect on the remittances of the sample as a whole?—is 0.706.

5.6 THE PERSPECTIVE OF THE ENTERPRISES

How important are rural migrants to urban enterprises, and how do they value their rural employees by comparison with their urban employees? We explore these questions in three ways: By analysing managerial attitudes towards the employment of migrants and by estimating two types of equations, both based on the enterprise. We estimate employment functions, in which the numbers of migrant and non-migrant employees are the dependent variables; and production functions, which contain both migrant and non-migrant employees among the explanatory variables.

Table 5.13 reveals managerial attitudes towards the employment of rural migrants. The most frequently cited reason for recruiting migrants was their greater suitability: They can bear hardship and are easily manageable. In many cases migrants were employed because no urban workers could be found. The lower cost of migrants was less frequently perceived to be the reason. Two-thirds of managers claimed that it would not be possible to replace migrants with redundant

TABLE 5.13 *Managerial attitudes towards migrants*

	Percentage of respondents
Why do you recruit rural workers?*	
Lower cost	29.6
They can bear hardship	60.9
They are more manageable	33.0
Urban workers are not available	40.0
Can rural workers be replaced with redundant urban workers?	
Yes	25.5
No	66.0
If not, why not?*	
Urban workers are inadequate for the job	14.9
The work is too hard for urban workers	50.7
Urban workers do not want to do the job	49.3
Why do you recruit trans-provincial migrants?*	
Lower cost	15.9
More skilled and more capable	18.7
Not enough local migrants	42.0
Are you satisfied with the quality of migrant workers?	
Yes	60.2
No	38.9
Training of migrant workers	
Must be trained strictly before starting	47.0
Short-term training is enough	40.0
No training is needed	13.0
Length of employment	
Skills require long-term employment	57.7
Short-term employment is an advantage	6.3
Enterprise is indifferent	36.0

Note: * Denotes that figures may add up to more than 100% because more than one answer was permitted.

urban workers. There were two main reasons: Urban workers could not do the hard, demanding jobs for which migrants were engaged,[3] nor would they want to. When enterprises were asked why they recruited migrants from other provinces, the main explanation was that there were not enough local migrants, rather than lower cost or higher quality. This suggests that local and distant migrants are paid the same wages, and that the additional wage costs of attracting more locals would exceed the additional recruitment costs of looking further afield.

The majority of enterprises (60 per cent) were satisfied with the quality of their migrant employees, although in Beijing only a minority (48 per cent) expressed satisfaction. Very few enterprises claimed that it was unnecessary to train migrants: No fewer than 47 per cent (70 per cent in Beijing) required strict training before commencement of employment. These responses tied in with managerial attitudes towards the duration of migrant employment. Only a small number preferred short-term employment, and 36 per cent were indifferent as to duration. The majority (58 per cent) of enterprises reported that the skills of migrants required them to remain long in employment. This figure was as high as 65 per cent for those that favoured strict training but only 14 per cent for the non-trainers. The employers' responses on training may give a misleading impression: Recall from Tables 5.4 and 5.6 that migrants generally reported only a brief training and were little rewarded for their training. Enterprises may wish some migrants to stay long, but they do not have to make the same commitment to the migrants as perforce they do to urban employees. We conclude from this analysis of attitudes that urban and rural workers are not close substitutes in the production function of urban enterprises, that migrant employment on the then current scale had become fairly indispensable, and that most enterprises have an interest in training and retaining many of their rural workers.

Table 5.14 presents estimates of the determinants of the number of urban residents and the number of rural migrants employed by the enterprise, in both absolute and logarithmic forms. Few of the coefficients of either equation are significantly different from zero (owing to the small size of the enterprise sample and to multicollinearity) but many are large in relation to mean employment (1,029 urban and 330 rural employees). The results on which we comment were robust to changes in specification. Rural workers represented 21 per cent of the total employment in the sample as a whole. The percentage was highest in the foreign-owned and joint venture sector, *ceteris paribus*, and in the construction sector. Both these results have plausible explanations: Profit-motivated foreign firms have more incentive to employ migrants rather than non-migrants, and the arduous, footloose and intermittent nature of construction work encourages the employment of temporary migrants.

The coefficients on the instrumented value of employment (of migrants in the non-migrant equation and of non-migrants in the migrant equation) are large, positive, and (in levels) statistically significant. We would expect the causal relationships between the two labour inputs normally to be negative, for example, the employment of one or more migrants may make one non-migrant redundant. Yet despite standardizing (for both inputs and outputs) and instrumenting as best we can, the coefficients stay positive. Either we are unable to identify the substitution relationship between the two labour inputs (for instance, owing to unobserved influences on joint demand) or the relationship is positive, and in this sense one of complementarity. Only if migrant employment is expressed as a percentage of total employment (the final column) does the coefficient on non-migrant employment become (very slightly and significantly) negative. It is plausible that administrative interventions prevent substitution, for example, the employment of more migrants is not permitted if this puts non-migrant jobs at risk, and the employment of more non-migrants requires the employment of more migrants in the complementary

TABLE 5.14 Estimates of urban and rural employees per enterprise

Dependent variable	Non-migrants		Migrants		
	Levels	Logs	Levels	Logs	As a percentage of the total
Intercept	1430.841**	4.323**	−190.793	4.091**	14.993
Collective ownership	−757.023*	−0.990**	218.959	−0.149	11.836
Private ownership	−222.834	−0.808	−81.633	−0.131	20.472*
Foreign-owned, joint venture	−1094.900	0.132	98.361	0.382	−2.494
Other ownership	193.111	0.747	14.125	−0.996	−30.688**
Mining	446.359	−2.656	78.872	−0.875	48.102
Construction	684.310	0.435	653.098**	2.265**	30.251**
Communication and transport	−84.093	0.362	30.796	−0.721	−4.485
Commerce and food	114.865	−0.694	15.248	−0.840	3.813
Service trade	−984.842	−0.495	306.924	0.426	29.297*
Other sectors	−406.231	−0.171	214.774	0.661	14.595
No surplus labour	−848.897**	−1.013**	−154.285	−0.834**	7.206
Migrants not restricted			213.538	0.505	6.845
Fixed assets (million yuan)	0.042	0.004	0.010	0.004	−0.002
Output (million yuan)	0.114**	0.0278**	0.048**	0.129*	0.0002
Migrant employees (instrumented)	1.341*	0.208			
Non-migrant employees (instrumented)			0.309**	0.038	−0.0004
Adj. R^2	0.359	0.523	0.292	0.328	0.309
F-value	4.440**	7.739**	3.367**	3.796**	3.559**
Mean of dependent variable	1028.977	5.753	329.874	4.690	32.826
Number of observations	87	87	87	87	87

Notes: ** Denotes statistical significance at the 1% and * at the 5% level. The omitted categories in the dummy variable analysis are state ownership, manufacturing, Shenzhen, reported surplus labour, and migrant restricted. Migrant employees in the non-migrant equation and non-migrant employees in the migrant equation are both instrumented using exogenous variables including city. In the equations with logarithmic dependent variables, the continuous variables (fixed assets and employees) are also logged. In the case of 'no surplus labour' the enterprise reported that it had not identified surplus employees, and in the case of 'migrants not restricted' that it was not officially restricted in its recruitment. To maintain sample size gross, rather than net, output data are used.

jobs thereby created. In such circumstances, the two types of labour are likely to become highly imperfect substitutes or even complements.

Up to the time of the migrant survey, the state was concerned to minimize open unemployment in the cities. Through its urban labour allocation policy and its controls over rural–urban migration, the government tried to ensure that all residents of working age are in employment. It preferred unemployment to take a disguised form in the work unit than a visible form on the street. There is an accumulation of evidence that, prior to the redundancy programme of the late 1990s, many urban enterprises contained considerable surplus labour. No less than 37 per cent of the enterprises in our sample claimed to have identified surplus labour. City governments are concerned about the welfare of their own residents but not of outsiders. We therefore expect to find the underemployment to be concentrated among urban residents: The employment of migrants is a business decision. The reported possession of surplus labour in the enterprise does indeed increase the number of urban employees greatly and significantly. However, enterprises with surplus labour also tend to employ more migrants, *ceteris paribus*, possibly because they use non-migrants less effectively.

Our final exercise was to estimate enterprise production functions in which the dependent variable is value added (v) and the arguments are non-migrant labour (n), migrant labour (m), and capital (k), all expressed in logarithmic form:

$$v = a + bn + cm + dk \qquad (5.1)$$

We use the production function to test the hypotheses that urban enterprises in China are constrained in their employment decisions, and that as a result their employment of labour is economically suboptimal. In particular we suggest that the enterprises employ too few rural migrants and too many residents. Where Y is output, M migrant labour, N non-migrant labour, K capital, w_i ($i = m, n$) the wage rate of i, Y_i the marginal product of i, and $*$ indicates the optimal value, we hypothesize,

$$w_m < w_n \qquad (5.2)$$

$$Y_m > w_m \qquad (5.3)$$

$$M^* > M \qquad (5.4)$$

$$Y_n < w_n \qquad (5.5)$$

$$N^* < N \qquad (5.6)$$

In words, the wage of migrants is below their marginal product, and the wage of non-migrants exceeds their marginal product. The production function is used to estimate the marginal products.

The argument can be illustrated by means of Figure 5.1, a conventional isoquant diagram. We hypothesize that the enterprise is constrained to choose point b rather than the optimal point a. However, if there were a competitive urban labour market

The Urban Labour Market

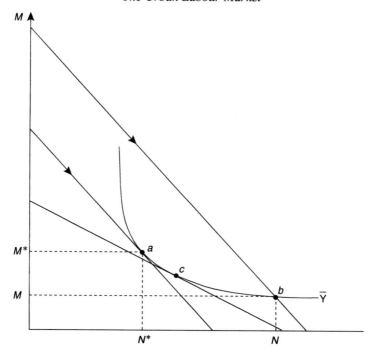

FIG. 5.1 *Employment of migrants and non-migrants*

without wage discrimination against migrants, the optimal outcome would be somewhere between *a* and *b*, say point *c*.

It is possible that the employment of migrants is endogenous. The Hausman specification test indicates endogenity: The error term from the equation predicting employment of migrants (but not of non-migrants) has a significant coefficient in the production function. Accordingly, migrant employment is instrumented in the production function equation (Table 5.15).

Physical capital, migrant employment, and non-migrant employment all have significantly positive coefficients. The coefficient of migrant employment (1.112) implies that, at the mean values, the marginal product of migrant labour is 20,706 yuan per annum, that is, above the (geometric) mean wage of migrant labour (5,368 yuan per annum). By contrast, the coefficient on non-migrant employment is 0.555, implying a marginal product of 5,597. This stands in juxtaposition to the mean wage of non-migrants, which is no less than 6,956 yuan per annum. It appears that the enterprises are indeed widely characterized by surplus urban workers, but that they nevertheless find it profitable to hire migrant workers as well. Indeed, they appear to be constrained from employing as many migrants as they would choose.

These conclusions proved to be robust to various experiments. When m^2 and n^2 were included in the production function, their coefficients were positive and

TABLE 5.15 *Estimates of the enterprise production function*

Dependent variable	Ln value added (v)	
Intercept	3.997*	3.390
Ln physical capital (k)	0.106*	0.099
Ln floating capital	0.028	0.034
Ln migrant labour ($\hat{m}$)	1.112**	1.076**
Ln non-migrant labour (n)	0.555*	0.637*
Adj. R^2	0.342	0.336
F-value	9.824**	7.871**
Mean of dependent variable ($\bar{v}$)	15.425	15.425
Number of observations	69	69

Notes: ** Indicates statistical significance at the 1% and * at the 5% level. Migrant employment is instrumented using an equation very similar to that in Table 5.14.

negative, respectively—consistent with our story—but not significant. Table 5.15 suggests that the introduction of the dummy variable denoting the absence of surplus labour raises the productivity of the enterprise. Moreover, this standardization for surplus labour has the expected effect of raising the marginal product of urban workers (to 6,425 yuan, close to their mean wage).

5.7 THE PERSPECTIVE OF GOVERNMENT

The policy after 1949 was to permit no more urbanization of peasants than was necessary for the strategy of industrialization. After the late 1950s, this meant that there was hardly any permanent urban settlement of rural people. The policy was enforced through the household registration *(hukou)* system, commune controls, food rationing, and the allocation of urban housing. The few exceptions included college graduates and retired soldiers.

Some of the levers of control were lost during the reform period. Moreover, temporary rural–urban migration grew as urban enterprises demanded relatively unskilled workers for the jobs that urban residents did not want. Nevertheless, the permanent urban settlement of rural workers and their families remained very difficult. It was crucially important to obtain an urban *hukou*. This was either impossible or expensive, although somewhat easier in towns and rapidly expanding new cities than in the large established cities.

Responsibility for policy on rural–urban migration is spread among various organs of government. For instance, the *hukou* system, preventing permanent urban settlement, is the responsibility of the urban authorities. However, the Ministry of Labour also plays a central role, overseeing the system of 'floating' migration. The ministry is represented at national, provincial, city, and county *(xian)* levels, and the different levels are sensitive to different problems. The policy framework emanates from the centre. In its implementation, however, offices of the ministry in poor, labour-surplus provinces and counties are keen to promote labour migration from their areas whereas offices in city governments are concerned to protect urban residents against competition from migrants.

City governments have pursued active policies of regulating the inflow of migrants in order to protect their residents. For instance, one of the four city labour bureaux was found to classify jobs into three types: urban-*hukou* jobs, rural migrant jobs, and jobs open to all but with urban workers receiving preference. It also imposes quotas on the number of migrants that each enterprise can employ; these are enforced by inspection teams. The restrictions are sensitive to the state of the city labour market, being tightened if unemployment rises. City governments make price as well as quantity interventions. Enterprises must pay for their quotas, and they must pay an extra charge in order to exceed their quotas. Similarly, enterprises receive subsidies, in the form of tax relief, if they recruit redundant urban workers (*xia gang* employees, who no longer need to attend work but continue to be paid low wages by the relinquishing enterprise).

The general policies laid down at the top include the severe restriction of permanent urban settlement and preferential access to urban jobs for urban residents. These policies have been effectively implemented. Other policies include: Organizing the 'orderly' movement of temporary migrant labour so as to avoid both too much and too little supply in relation to urban demand for migrants, the assistance of potential migrants from poor areas, and maintenance of satisfactory conditions for migrant workers in the urban areas. The degree of official control and influence in these matters is more limited, reflecting the migrants' own preferences as well as the ministry's limited information, resources, leverage, and powers of enforcement. The decentralized nature of government, both among ministries and within the Ministry of Labour, weakens policy interventions. An initiative need not have wide influence unless it is 'red-headed', that is, it is issued by the Central Committee of the Communist Party. Decentralization also gives rise to principal–agent problems: Bureaucratic units may pursue their own agendas, such as the levying of fees for revenue purposes. There is a lack of coherence and cohesion in government policy on migration.

Various pieces of evidence can be adduced to illuminate government policies and their effects. Did these government interventions reduce the number of migrants employed? Eighty-one per cent of the enterprises reported that they were officially restricted in recruiting migrant workers. In Section 5.6, we estimated a regression equation predicting the number of migrants employed by the enterprise (Table 5.14). The introduction of a dummy variable denoting that the government did not exercise restrictive control over the hiring of migrants increased their number substantially but not significantly. It is plausible that many firms are indeed prevented by government from employing as many migrants as they would choose.

No less than 77 per cent of enterprises had to pay fees to employ migrants. Among those that did pay, the average recruitment fee per migrant employee was

213 yuan, representing 44 per cent of the average monthly migrant wage. When the average fee was introduced into the equation predicting migrant employment, its coefficient was negative, as expected, but not significant.

The responses to the migrant questionnaire reveal that a labyrinthine and costly system of permissions has been erected by various organs of government. Ninety per cent of respondents had obtained an identity card before migrating, the average cost of which (for those who obtained a card) was 24 yuan. Eighty-eight per cent of migrants had obtained a temporary residence card in the city. This lasted for 1.2 years and cost 131 yuan on average (but 264 yuan in Shenzhen). Sixty-one per cent of migrants had received an employment registration card, costing 47 yuan. Seventy-five per cent had obtained a migrant identity card, lasting for 1.3 years and costing 49 yuan. A migrant who needed all four permits would have to pay 251 yuan on average, equal to 52 per cent of the average monthly wage.

The underlying purpose of these permissions is to control labour flows out of the rural areas and into the cities. It is possible, however, that the accompanying charges do not simply cover administrative costs. They may serve a deterrent or a revenue function. It is a common practice now for departments of government at the various levels to attempt to raise revenue, from which the department or its members can benefit.

The Ministry of Labour and Social Security has set up rural recruitment agencies for migrants (local employment bureaux) in various parts of China, especially in the poorer areas with much surplus labour. The rationale is to provide would-be migrants with information, contacts, and arrangements—so reducing the high risks and transaction costs that they face. However, only 18 per cent of the sample had been recruited through rural departments of the ministry, the most common form of recruitment being through friends and relatives (62 per cent). One reason for the limited role of government was the limited coverage of employment bureaux, but another was the relatively high charges. Whereas it had cost migrants recruited by friends and relatives on average 50 yuan to get their jobs, those recruited in the city labour market 156 yuan and those recruited directly by the employer 194 yuan, migrants who relied on local employment bureaux spent on average 324 yuan. Given the likely importance of economies of scale in recruitment, it seems that the local employment bureaux were more than covering their costs. They may have been effectively charging for the relatively high pay (5 per cent higher than for those recruited by friends or relatives) of migrants using their services (Table 5.4). The underlying policy is in danger of being subverted by opportunistic behaviour in which revenue motives are important.

5.8 CONCLUSIONS

It is extremely difficult to obtain a representative sample of rural migrants in the urban areas of China. The diversity of their accommodation arrangements—staying in migrant hostels, living in the place of work, lodging with urban households, dwelling in shanties, sleeping rough—means that a residence-based survey is problematic. An employer-based survey, of the sort that we have analysed, is liable to under-represent or omit the more marginal migrants—the unemployed, the self-employed, and those working in small sweatshops. A representative sample of rural–urban migrants is more likely to be obtained from a rural survey. The companion study to our enterprise study was based on a 1994 rural labour force survey of 4,000 households in eight provinces, designed to analyse migrants from a rural perspective (Chapter 8). It revealed the following pattern of migration: 51 per cent of migrants worked in villages or in towns at county level or below, and 49 per cent worked in cities. Of the migrants to cities, 16 per cent were self-employed, 19 per cent were wage-employed in the informal sector, and (depending on what proportion of private enterprises can be classified as formal) between 40 and 64 per cent were wage-employees in the formal sector. Thus our sample of migrants employed in city enterprises represented between two-fifths and two-thirds of rural migrants to cities, and between one-fifth and one-third of all rural migrants.

The average spell of migrant work observed in our survey was considerably longer than that found in another national survey of rural households and their migrants. This study (covering over 14,000 households in 26 provinces) reported that each migrant was away from home for 208 days (6.8 months) during 1993 (RDI, CASS 1994: 110). Rural workers employed by medium- and large-scale enterprises in cities are probably among the more successful migrants: They are likely to be better paid and, judging by their length of tenure, they are more willing to hold onto their jobs and are less rapidly drawn back by the claims of their rural households. Our conclusions are not necessarily applicable to all rural–urban migrants, but they are applicable to a substantial group. Moreover, our projections in Chapter 10 suggest that, as long as China can maintain the rate of economic growth achieved over the reform period, it is a group which is likely to grow in importance.

The human capital of migrants is not well rewarded. This reflects the low-potential jobs in which they are mostly employed, and the disincentive of employers to give more than rudimentary training to temporary workers. Nevertheless, it is interesting that the majority of migrants valued training and wanted more of it, even if they would reap the benefits only later. Migrants are less well-paid than urban residents: On average the migrant wage is 80 per cent of the non-migrant wage (and provision for housing, healthcare, and retirement further favours the urban workers). The large disparity that remains after standardization for differences in characteristics is likely to reflect labour market segmentation and lack of competition between migrants and non-migrants. The former are more subject to market forces. Moreover, their frequent lack of information, contacts, and alternatives serves to depress their supply prices. The latter are protected by preferential access to urban employment, institutional determination of wages and benefits-in-kind, and iron rice bowls.

Many migrants are fairly pleased with their migration experience and with their current jobs. A high proportion want to stay with the enterprise as long as possible, and this attitude is amenable to economic incentives. The apparent inconsistency that few migrants want to settle in the city probably reflects the hazardous nature of city life without an urban *hukou* and a secure job. The extent of remittances and contacts indicates that most migrants remain part of their rural households.

Migrant and non-migrant workers are highly imperfect substitutes or even complements: Migrants do the jobs that non-migrants shun. The majority of enterprises nevertheless reported that the training of migrants requires them to remain long in employment. We found that the average duration of completed tenure with the enterprise is almost five years. Our enterprise production functions imply that the marginal product of migrants is double their wage whereas that of the non-migrants is below their wage. Urban enterprises are therefore generally constrained in the number of migrants and non-migrants they are permitted to employ: Too few migrants and too many non-migrants. Although many enterprises have surplus urban workers, they find it beneficial to hire migrant workers as well, and may be prevented from employing as many migrants as they would choose.

Government has successfully implemented its general policies of severely restricting permanent urban settlement of rural people and ensuring preferential access to urban jobs for urban residents. Our evidence indicates that government at various levels also restricts the formal sector employment of 'floating' migrants by imposing fees and controls on enterprises, and by erecting a labyrinthine system of permissions and fees through which rural migrants must pass. There is a danger that the policy of assisting and controlling labour flows will be subverted by opportunistic behaviour.

We have analysed the employment of rural–urban migrants in urban enterprises in the year 1995. This picture is incomplete for two reasons. First, it excludes the many migrants engaged in urban informal sector activities, whether wage- or self-employed. Secondly, the urban labour market for migrants is changing rapidly. On the one hand, migrant employment in the formal sector suffered from the state's labour retrenchment policies of the late 1990s and, on the other hand, urban informal sector employment grew rapidly in response to growing demand. In Chapter 7, we examine the position of urban-household-based migrants in 1999, comparing them with urban-*hukou* workers, and in Chapter 10 we consider the future of rural–urban migration.

NOTES

1. An enterprise was discarded if it employed fewer than ten migrants. All migrants were sampled if 10–30 were employed, and no more than 50 migrants were sampled in any enterprise.
2. Applying the urban educational attainment distribution to the migrant education–occupation matrix.
3. This reported inability may reflect employers' perceptions of urban workers' status and their refusal to tolerate hardship, rather than physical inability.

REFERENCES

Knight, John and Lina Song (1999). *The Rural–Urban Divide. Economic Disparities and Interactions in China*, Oxford: Oxford University Press.

——— (2003). 'Chinese peasant choices: migration, rural industry or farming', *Oxford Development Studies*, 31, 2: 123–47.

——— and Jia Huaibin (1999). 'Chinese rural migrants in urban enterprises: three perspectives', *Journal of Development Studies*, 35, 3: 73–104.

Peoples' Republic of China, Ministry of Labour (PRC, MOL) (1996). *China Labour Statistical Yearbook 1995*, Beijing: China Statistical Publishing House.

Peoples' Republic of China, State Statistical Bureau (PRC, SSB) (1993). *Tabulation on the 1990 Population Census of the Peoples' Republic of China,* Vols 1–4, Beijing: China Statistical Publishing House (in Chinese).

——— (1996). *China Statistical Yearbook 1995*, Beijing: China Statistical Publishing House.

Rural Development Institute (RDI, CASS) (1994). *Green Report: Annual Report on Economic Development of Rural China in 1993 and Development Trends in 1994*, Beijing: China Social Sciences Publishing House.

6

Redundancies, Unemployment, and Migration

6.1 INTRODUCTION

The previous chapter described the results of a survey of migrants employed in urban enterprises in 1994. This was before the government was forced into pursuing a more drastic policy of reforming state-owned enterprises (SOEs) and requiring large-scale redundancies of their underemployed labour. The policy was launched in the mid-1990s and was in full spate by 1997. Although that was never the intention, it can be viewed as a fascinating policy experiment to find out whether it is possible to create an instant labour market! How did the millions of *danwei* employees who lost their jobs subsequently fare in the labour market? Did they remain unemployed for long? At what wages were they employed? Which workers were particularly prone to retrenchment and which of these were more likely to be re-employed? How did the redundancies affect the employment of migrants? To what extent did retrenched urban workers and rural–urban migrant workers compete for jobs? How did the government handle the social problems created by the redundancy programme? These are the questions that we address in this chapter.

We make use of the IE, CASS 1999 survey, which we and others designed in order to examine the effects of the redundancy policy on the urban labour market and on urban poverty. We also analyse official statistics in order to measure the impact on migrant employment.

Section 6.2 explains employment policies prior to enterprise reform, and their implications. Section 6.3 describes the redundancy programme that became a centrepiece of enterprise reform. Section 6.4 analyses the consequences of that programme, including the determinants of displacement, of re-employment, and of continuing unemployment. The effects of both the incidence and the duration of unemployment on the subsequent wage are the subject of Section 6.5. Section 6.6 explores the nature of the relationship between urban residents and migrant employment. Section 6.7 concludes.

6.2 EMPLOYMENT IN CHINESE ENTERPRISES

Byrd and Tidrick (1987) examined a sample of twenty SOEs in detail in 1982. At that time—before the industrial reforms had begun in earnest—the familiar problems of enterprises under central planning were to be observed. The enterprises were characterized by surplus labour, which they were not trying to remedy. It was the policy that all urban workers should have employment. Employment was often hereditary: Both workers and local governments were keen to secure jobs within the work unit for the workers' children—a widespread practice in China known as *ding ti*. Urban workers were centrally allocated to jobs in urban enterprises; there was little urban employment of rural migrants. It was extremely difficult to dismiss employees, particularly as they depended on the enterprise for housing, pensions, medical, and even educational benefits. For the same reasons, voluntary labour mobility was also very restricted. Workers felt that they had 'property rights' over their jobs. In the pre-reform period the wage rate, employment, and output in SOEs were all determined by the government rather than by the management. We would therefore not expect employment to respond to the wage rate nor would we expect a clear economic relationship between employment and output.

Since the early 1980s there has been a series of enterprise reforms, very limited at first but gaining pace over time, which increased the autonomy and improved the incentives of managers. Administrative allocation of workers to jobs was gradually diminished, and management acquired more control over recruitment and employment. From 1984, lifetime employment—the 'iron rice bowl' (*tie fan wan*)—was phased out for new workers. By 1995, 'contract' workers on fixed-term renewable contracts, represented 41 per cent of urban employees (PRC, SSB 1997: 113). The introduction of limited bonuses and the weakening of job security were intended to motivate workers and provide greater flexibility.

The effect of the reforms was apparent even in the 1980s. Groves et al. (1994) analysed a sample of 769 SOEs over the years 1980–9. They estimated enterprise production functions, introducing among the arguments two variables representing incentives: Bonuses as a percentage of the wage bill, and contract employees as a percentage of the total. Both had significantly positive coefficients, that is, the reforms had met with some success. However, enterprises remained severely constrained. Hay et al. (1994: 126–34, table 4.4), using the same data set, specified an employment equation. They recognized that the wage bill quotas imposed on enterprises by their local labour bureaux would limit managerial control over employment. This was reflected in the fairly complete adjustment of employment to the wage bill (the elasticity being 0.8) and the limited adjustment (elasticity 0.2) of employment to output. Hussain and Zhuang (1994) examined 514 SOEs later in the reform process: Their panel covered the years 1986–91. They estimated an employment function to examine the response of enterprise employment to output and wages. Their estimated output-elasticity of employment was about 0.4, which they interpreted as evidence of existing but diminishing surplus labour. Their wage-elasticity of employment was about −0.35, that is, significantly negative but low by comparison with market economies (their table 7).

How widespread was urban underemployment? The ideal approach is to ask: How much labour would be employed by profit-maximizing enterprises in competitive markets? Surplus labour is then any employment in excess of the profit maximization benchmark. A World Bank report (1993: 8) cites various cross-section estimates of surplus labour from Chinese government sources: 25 per cent of SOE employees (by officials in charge of planning and systems reform); 10–12 per cent of urban SOE employees (Ministry of Labour, based on a survey of 15,000 enterprises in eleven provinces); 20–25 per cent of urban SOE employees (estimates of other research institutes); and 20 per cent of employees (in a survey of 45 reforming SOEs in Shanghai). The World Bank mission itself produced estimates ranging from 3 to 30 per cent but averaging 11 per cent over 19 SOEs. Jefferson and Xu (1991), in a survey of twenty industrial enterprises, estimated that the number of hours worked each day averaged 5.4, whereas the normal day was 7–8 hours, that is, surplus labour was 23–32 per cent. It is difficult not to conclude that, up to the mid-1990s, there remained substantial surplus labour in the public sector in China. Since the same pressures for providing jobs are to be found in the urban collectives, we expect similar problems of urban underemployment to have existed in all but the small private wage sector.

None of the estimates cited above distinguished between urban residents and rural migrants. By 1996, the migration of rural people to work in urban enterprises had gathered momentum and was now substantial. However, it remained impossible or very difficult for rural migrants to settle or take permanent jobs in the cities. The political need to protect urban residents and avoid serious urban unemployment remained compelling. The continuation of 'soft budgets'—fending off bankruptcies—and the pressures on management, emanating from their employees and local governments, made the reduction of employment a slow and difficult process. The controls on migration still insulated the urban labour market from the rural labour market, and segmented the urban labour market between regular employees (with urban *hukous*) and temporary or casual employees (mostly with rural *hukous*). In 1995, registered unemployment was only 2.9 per cent of the urban-*hukou* labour force, and *xia gang* employees (redundant workers who no longer need to attend work but continue to be paid low wages by the relinquishing enterprise) represented a further 3.1 per cent, that is, the combined urban unemployment rate was 6.0 per cent. In the same year rural migrants employed in urban work-units (*danwei*) totalled 8.0 per cent of the *danwei* labour force with urban *hukous* (PRC, MOL 1996: 39, 91, 409).

6.3 THE REDUNDANCY POLICIES

As we explained in Chapter 2, increased product market competition brought tumbling profits and escalating losses to the SOEs, so creating a serious fiscal problem for the state. By the mid-1990s, the Chinese Government was forced to tackle this issue. The redundancy programme, first on trial in 1994 and fully launched in 1997, was intended to resolve the problem of inefficiency in the state sector by laying off a quarter or more of its workers within the four years 1997–2000. By the end of 2000, the gross figure for the accumulated laid-off workers exceeded 60 million, representing some 40 per cent of the 'staff and workers' who had been at risk and 30 per cent of the urban labour force in 1994 (Knight and Xue 2003: table 6).

Redundant urban workers fell into three distinct categories. Those who had been employed before 1984, and thus enjoyed lifetime employment rights, would become *xia gang*, that is, they would remain in the employ of the relinquishing firm and receive a small wage from it but would not be required to attend work. They could remain *xia gang* for three years or until they secured another formal job, whichever was the sooner. Those whose employers had paid unemployment insurance contributions on their behalf could register as officially unemployed. Other contract and casual workers who had lost their jobs were left to their own devices, and they were not recorded in the administratively collected statistics of unemployment.

The administratively recorded urban unemployment rate at the end of 2000 was 7.9 per cent of the urban labour force (3.1 per cent were registered as unemployed and 4.8 per cent were registered as *xia gang*) (PRC, MOL 2001: 67, 401). However, this figure excluded the unemployed who had not qualified, or had ceased to qualify, to be registered as unemployed or as *xia gang*. Broader estimates of the effects of the retrenchment programme can be obtained from the urban household survey of IE, CASS 1999 and the 2000 census of population. In 1999, 11.6 per cent of the urban-*hukou* labour force were unemployed, made up of the officially registered unemployed (1.3 per cent), *xia gang* employees (5.6 per cent), unemployed labour market entrants (2.6 per cent), and persons who had been forced into early retirement (2.0 per cent). The estimate of unemployment among urban-dwellers in 2000 (based on the International Labour Organization definition of being without work, wanting work, and seeking work) was 11.5 per cent (Knight and Xue 2003: tables 7, 9).

Workers who had entered the labour market up to 1984 were entitled to redundancy benefits under the *xia gang* arrangements. These were supposed to be paid in equal parts by the state via local government, the work unit, and semi-private insurance companies (usually run by the local government insurance agents). However, in reality, enterprises and insurance companies may not have had sufficient funds to contribute their share of the benefits, while even the government's share may sometimes not have been paid. Workers who had entered the labour market after 1984 were not entitled to these benefits. They could be paid by an unemployment benefit scheme, run by semi-private insurance companies, provided that they had joined such a scheme before their job contracts were terminated. The system of *xia gang* support ended in 2001. Thereafter, newly redundant workers were not entitled to the *xia gang* redundancy payments, and instead enterprises were required to insure their employees against the possibility of unemployment.

6.4 REDUNDANCY, UNEMPLOYMENT, AND RE-EMPLOYMENT

These developments ended the 'win–win' phase of economic reform and brought about a phase in which there were clear losers, at least in the short term. Who were the losers? Appleton et al. (2002) use the IE, CASS 1999 household survey to pose three main questions about the retrenchment programme. First, what kind of urban workers were most likely to be displaced? Secondly, what is the duration of unemployment of retrenched workers? Thirdly, what kind of unemployed workers were most likely to be re-employed?

6.4.1 The possibility of retrenchment

A number of factors are likely to be relevant to retrenchment decisions. Some concern the enterprise in which the worker is employed. In the worst case, an entire enterprise may be closed and all its employees retrenched regardless of their personal characteristics. More commonly, however, retrenchment is selective—with some workers in an enterprise being laid-off while others are retained. When selecting workers for retrenchment, employers concerned with minimizing costs are likely to take into account their productivity relative to their wages.

The survey deliberately over-sampled households with retrenched workers in order to study the phenomenon. However, within the subsample of 6,102 urban workers from the nationally representative group of 4,000 households, the retrenchment rate among households was 18.7 per cent and among workers 11.4 per cent. Clearly, there has been widespread implementation of the policy of retrenchment by SOEs. Appleton et al. (2002) estimated a binary probit model of whether a worker had been retrenched since 1992. As it was not possible to estimate worker productivity from the household data set, they adopted a reduced form approach, including in the vector of explanatory variables some characteristics that are likely to affect productivity. Given that wages were largely set by the state sector, the hypothesis was that wages were unlikely fully to reflect productivity, so that the least productive workers were at most risk of being retrenched.

The results of the probit estimation are shown in Table 6.1. The model identifies a number of determinants: Most hypothesized explanatory variables are statistically significant. The goodness of fit—measured by the likelihood ratio (0.18) or the percentage of correct predictions (84 per cent)—is respectable. The quantitative importance of each variable is shown by reporting the predicted probabilities of the model at the means of the other explanatory variables. The base probability of retrenchment at the mean of all the explanatory variables is 22.9 per cent. This is higher than the actual 11.4 per cent retrenchment rate among the nationally representative sample.[1] The predicted probabilities should be used to assess the relative effect of explanatory variables rather than to provide measures of the absolute risk of retrenchment faced by individuals with particular characteristics.

The Urban Labour Market

TABLE 6.1 *Probit model for the probability of retrenchment: coefficients and marginal effects, 1999 urban resident sample*

	Coefficient	T-ratio	Marginal
Constant	−1.043	−5.06***	22.9
Male	−0.306	−7.24***	20.4
Female (default)			25.9
Education in years	−0.043	−3.93***	
Experience	0.036	3.81***	
Experience squared	−0.001	−3.35***	
Minority ethnicity	0.81	0.78	24.2
Han Chinese (default)			22.8
Party member	−0.348	−5.48***	18.6
Non-party member (default)			24.5
Bad health	0.252	2.95***	27.4
Good health (default)			22.7
Central SOE	−0.608	−10.90***	16.3
Local SOE (default ownership sector)			26.4
Urban collective	0.357	6.56***	33.8
Urban private	−0.056	−0.30	25.3
Urban individual	−0.431	−3.39	18.9
Foreign invested	−0.615	−2.96	16.2
State listed	−0.125	−0.99	24.0
Other listed	−0.528	−2.84***	17.4
Rural enterprise	0.355	0.54	33.8
Other ownership	−0.118	0.65	24.1
Administrative	0.047	0.49	19.7
Professional/technical (default occupation)			
Clerical	−0.027	−0.34	18.5
Low-skilled industrial	0.584	7.45***	29.5
High-skilled industrial	0.386	5.09***	25.6
Unskilled industrial	0.525	6.81***	28.3
Commercial worker	0.503	535***	27.8
Service worker	0.411	4.19***	26.0
Other occupation	0.342	2.05**	24.7
Beijing (default city)			20.9
Shenyang, Liaoning	−0.122	−1.41	18.9
Jinzhou, Liaoning	0.392	4.19***	28.1
Nanjing, Jiangsu	−0.110	−1.24	19.2
Xuzhou, Jiangsu	0.243	2.44***	25.2
Zhengzhou, Henan	−0.086	−0.82	29.5
Kaifeng, Henan	0.285	2.76***	26.0
Pingdingshan, Henan	−0.140	−1.25	18.7
Chengdu, Sichuan	0.237	2.76***	25.1
Zigong, Sichuan	0.247	2.44***	25.3

T A B L E 6.1 (*continued*)

	Coefficient	*T*-ratio	Marginal
Nanchong, Sichuan	0.266	2.60***	25.7
Lanzhou, Gansu	0.244	2.89***	25.3
Pingliang, Gansu	0.540	5.33***	31.2
Dummy for SOE workers married to retrenched SOE workers	−0.090	−0.98	22.9
Spouse not retrenched (default)			21.4
Log-likelihood	−2500.22		
Restricted log-likelihood	−3128.64		
Likelihood ratio index	0.18		
Number of observations	6,929		

		Predicted	
		0	1
Actual	0	5,658	112
	1	1,018	141

Notes: The marginals show the predicted probabilities of retrenchment at the mean of other explanatory variables. *** and ** denote significance at the 1% and 5% levels, respectively.

Source: Appleton et al. (2002: table 2).

Workers employed in urban collectives bore the greatest risk of retrenchment, followed by local SOEs; the hazard for those employed by central SOEs was lower. Within enterprises, it varied inversely with occupational skill level: Unskilled and low-skilled production workers were the most vulnerable. Similarly, the lower the level of education, the greater was the risk of retrenchment. There was an inverted U-shaped relationship with employment experience, peaking at twenty-six years of experience: Younger and older workers faced lower probabilities of being displaced. However, this would be misleading if older workers were forced into early retirement but were not reported as retrenched in the survey.[2] Relative security came with good health, male gender, and membership of the Communist Party. In summary, it appears that productivity (proxied by occupation, education, and health, but not employment experience) afforded a degree of job security, but that some of the discrimination variables (gender and party membership) did so as well.

6.4.2 The duration of unemployment

How long a spell of unemployment have the retrenched workers faced? Over half (55 per cent) of the re-employed found their new job within a year of being sacked. Among the re-employed workers, the duration of unemployment was heavily skewed: The median spell was ten months but the mean spell was eighteen months.

However, since mass unemployment is such a recent phenomenon, looking only at completed spells is likely to be misleading. The majority (63 per cent) of the retrenched workers in our sample had not found re-employment by the time of the survey. The mean spell of unemployment for the combined sample of re-employed and unemployed is twenty-four months, the median being nineteen months.

Even this statistic underestimates the expected duration of unemployment because the observed unemployment spells of the still unemployed are incomplete. To obtain a more meaningful picture, Appleton et al. (2002) allowed for the censoring of unemployment durations using the concepts of survival analysis. They estimated empirical 'hazard rates' of re-employment: The proportions of workers who found re-employment in a given month after previously being unemployed. On that basis, the expected duration of unemployment would be 47 months. The hazard rate tended to fall after the first year of unemployment and to rise at very long durations. This may reflect an initial depreciation of human capital and an eventual depletion of support and savings to such an extent that the unemployed are forced to take up any kind of work, however low-paid or unpleasant.

6.4.3   The determinants of re-employment

Table 6.2 presents the Appleton et al. estimates of the Prentice–Gloeckler model for the duration of unemployment. Positive coefficients indicate explanatory variables that raise the chances of re-employment and so lower expected duration of unemployment. Both education and health are positive and statistically significant. Each year of education increases the probability of re-employment each month by 6 per cent.[3] Workers reporting themselves to be in poor health are 40 per cent less likely to be re-employed in any given month, *ceteris paribus*.[4] Age is estimated to have a U-shaped effect on the hazard rate, with the turning point coming quite early, at 32 years of age.

Household demographic composition influences the duration of unemployment in an interesting way. Table 6.2 includes the number of children under 7, both on its own and as part of two interaction terms. The first interaction term is with a dummy for the individual worker being female. The second is with both the dummy for the individual worker being female and a variable for the number of older household members (aged 60 or over) in the household. On its own, the number of young children is not significant, implying that it does not affect the duration of unemployment for male workers. The coefficient with the dummy for being a female worker is significant and negative. Taken together with the coefficient on the number of young children, the term implies that having a young child reduces the re-employment probability of a female worker by 23 per cent if there are no older people in the household. However, the positive coefficient on the second interaction term negates this effect if there are older people in the household. It appears that older, probably retired, household members free women from the constraints of child-rearing.

TABLE 6.2 *Semiparametric model for the duration of unemployment: 1999 urban resident sample*

	Coefficient	T-ratio
Male	0.155	1.37
School years	0.057	2.40**
Age	−0.102	−1.93**
Age squared	0.002	2.22**
Minority ethnicity	−0.275	−1.28
Party member	−0.201	−1.20
In bad health	−0.507	−2.39**
Ever received unemployment benefit	−0.003	−0.03
Job search: via market	−1.015	−7.22***
Job search: using social network	−2.654	−12.97***
Job search: self employed	−1.480	−6.43
Other forms of job search	−1.476	−5.28
Beijing	−0.620	−2.55***
Jinzhou	−0.293	−1.3
Nanjing	0.250	1.09
Xuzhou	−0.406	−1.61
Zhengzhou	−0.921	−2.95***
Kaifeng	−1.188	−3.63***
Pingdingshan	−1.469	−2.77***
Chengdu	−0.530	−2.13**
Zigong	−0.672	−2.04**
Nanchong	0.548	2.11**
Lanzhou	−0.207	−0.88
Pingliang	−0.247	−1.03
No. of children under 7 × female worker	−0.540	−1.82*
No. of children under 7 × female worker × no. of oldpeople	0.417	2.51***
No. of children under 7	0.276	1.32'

Notes: The default method of job search is 'through government'. ***, **, and * denote statistical significance at the 1%, 5%, and 10% levels, respectively.

Source: Appleton et al. (2002: table 3).

The duration model contains a dummy variable indicating that the individual had received unemployment benefit, defined as institutional support on account of his or her unemployment. Just over half (56 per cent) of the retrenched workers had ever received unemployment benefit. However, this variable has a near-zero coefficient that is not at all significant. The finding that unemployment benefits do not affect the duration of unemployment in China is contrary to evidence elsewhere: In the West it is typically found that higher unemployment benefits enable workers to search for jobs, or to enjoy leisure, for longer.

There are several possible explanations for this lack of an effect on unemployment duration. First, it is possible that most unemployment is purely involuntary: Workers would take any available jobs offered, regardless of their benefits. However, the significance of household demographics casts doubt on this as a full explanation. Secondly, it may be that unemployment benefits are not sufficiently large to affect behaviour. For those who received them, the benefits averaged 210 yuan per month in 1999/2000. This can be compared to the average monthly wages of retrenched and re-employed workers of 544 yuan per month. Clearly, there remains a substantial financial incentive for unemployed workers to find jobs, even if they are fortunate enough to be among those receiving support. The finding that unemployment benefits do not affect the duration of unemployment implies that the government could help retrenched workers financially without worsening the unemployment problem. However, since the survey, the government has taken steps to reduce support because of the fiscal burden that it imposes.

The final set of determinants of unemployment duration concerns the means by which individuals sought jobs or, in the case of re-employed, found jobs. The default category is job search through the government, whether through an official employment agency or the previous work unit. The alternatives are searching through one's social network, seeking work by setting up one's own business, or searching on one's own. The alternatives all have significant negative coefficients on the re-employment hazard. Appleton et al. (2002: 269–70) show that receiving unemployment benefit increases the probability of obtaining re-employment through the government. Accordingly, they hypothesize that the government, being keen to reduce the cost of retrenched state workers, uses its administrative power to help the recipients of this state aid to regain employment.

6.5 RETRENCHMENT AND THE RE-EMPLOYMENT WAGE

Retrenched workers suffer income losses, the extent of which depends on the duration of unemployment, the level of support while unemployed, and the relative wage received on re-employment. The evidence of Section 6.4 has indicated that the expected duration of unemployment is long and that there is very incomplete coverage of unemployment benefits, which are in any case low. In this section we analyse the re-employment wage.

6.5.1 The scarring effect of retrenchment

The international literature on the effect of unemployment on subsequent wages shows a fairly consistent 'scarring': An episode of unemployment reduces the wage, and this effect can be long-lasting (e.g. Fallick 1996; Kletzer 1998; Crouch 2001). There are three main reasons why wages may fall after job separation. One is the loss of firm-specific, or non-transferable, skills which have been rewarded wholly or partly in the old job but have less value, or none, in the new job. Seniority, defined as the length of the job tenure, may be rewarded by the employer, and this premium will be lost. Secondly, the quality of the job match may be poorer, so resulting in lower pay. Here the distinction between voluntary and involuntary job separation can be important, with the latter more likely to reduce match quality, and thus the wage. Thirdly, imperfect information can be responsible for a wage penalty. Having little knowledge of the worker's productivity, the employer may screen on the basis of available signals. The worker's retrenchment may serve as a negative signal, so lowering the wage at least until the worker proves to be of higher productivity than was initially inferred. It is possible, but not inevitable, that each of these wage penalties will be reduced with the passage of time.

The relationship between retrenchment and the wage on subsequent employment will be explored at some length in Chapter 7, where we test for wage segmentation in the urban labour market among three categories of labour: Never retrenched urban workers, retrenched and re-employed urban workers, and rural-*hukou* migrant workers. We show in Table 7.6 that re-employed workers would receive 12 per cent higher wages than they actually get if they were paid in like manner to workers who had never been retrenched. This is based on ordinary least squares (OLS) estimations because the corrections for selection into unemployment and into re-employment on the basis of unobserved characteristics are not statistically significant. However, use of the selectivity-corrected wage functions would not eliminate the scarring effect of unemployment, and would indeed increase it.

6.5.2 Unemployment duration and the re-employment wage

There is international evidence that the wage is lower the longer the duration of unemployment (e.g. Pichelmann and Riedel 1993; Gregory and Jukes 2001; Nickell, Jones, and Qintini 2002). How is this result to be explained? The unemployed face difficult choices in deciding whether to accept the jobs that become available. A certain distribution of wage offers can be expected. An unemployed worker will have in mind a reservation wage—the minimum wage he or she would be prepared to accept. Those who set a high reservation wage, and stick to it, are likely to have to wait longer before a sufficiently high wage offer is received. For this reason, the re-employment wage can be expected to increase with the duration of unemployment, *ceteris paribus*.

By contrast, there are four reasons why a negative relationship might be observed. Over time a person's reservation wage is likely to fall in response to a reduction in the degree of support from family, friends, or unemployment benefit. This tends to reduce the re-employment wage as the duration of unemployment increases, *ceteris paribus*. A further consideration is the possibility that human capital will decline over time, through obsolescence or lack of use, so also giving rise to a negative relationship. Yet again, the labour market for the unemployed may become tougher over time as a redundancy programme gathers pace—of which China may provide an example. As soon as this is known or even expected, it reduces the reservation wage, and thus also the likely re-employment wage. Finally, insofar as employers offer jobs at inflexible wages, they seek the most productive worker for a job. The quality of the pool of those remaining unemployed thus declines with unemployment duration. Recognizing that the long-term unemployed are less productive, employers may lower their offered wages to such workers, who may then need to lower their reservation wages; the re-employment wage falls.

Knight and Li (2003) analyse the effect of unemployment duration on the re-employment wage, using the IE, CASS 1999 data set. They examine the group of workers who were retrenched during the period 1994–9 inclusive, and find descriptive evidence that the probability of re-employment improved over time, especially in 1999. This is consistent with the unemployed choosing to lower their reservation wages either with unemployment duration or with the passage of time.

Knight and Li (2003) estimated an earnings function for over 300 retrenched and re-employed workers, and included unemployment duration among the explanatory variables (Table 6.3). Two econometric issues had to be addressed. First, unemployment duration may be endogenous: Individuals with high reservation wages are likely to hold out longer for a high-paying job. The Hausman specification test was employed. In an equation predicting unemployment duration, the variable 'have you asked your contacts to find a job for you?' was used as the instrument. The coefficient was negative and significant at the 10 per cent level. When the predicted value of unemployment duration was introduced with the residual term in the earnings equation, the coefficient on the residual term was not significant at any level. The test suggests that endogeneity is not a problem. However, as a robustness check, the coefficients on both actual unemployment duration and its instrument are reported.[5]

Secondly, the selective nature of the re-employment group may bias the coefficients in the earnings function. Although as reported in Section 6.4, the case for selectivity-correction proved to be weak, an attempt was made to correct for selection both into retrenchment and into re-employment, using the equation 'have you asked your contacts to find a job for you?' as the exclusion restriction term. The coefficient of this variable is significant at the 5 per cent level in the probit models. Selectivity-corrected equations are reported in Table 6.3. However, the robustness of the results is checked by comparing the OLS and selectivity-corrected estimates of the coefficient on unemployment duration.

Table 6.3 presents estimates of the earnings function for re-employed workers both with (equation 1) and without (equation 2) unemployment duration as an argument. In equation 1, occupational skills and possession of training have significant positive coefficients but the coefficients on educational levels and on years of employment experience are small and not significantly different from zero. These forms of human capital are apparently not rewarded in the tough labour market facing retrenched workers. There is considerable wage discrimination against women, and the wide differences in pay among cities reflect sensitivity

T A B L E 6.3 *Estimates of earnings functions for re-employed workers:
urban resident sample, 1999*

	Equation 1	Equation 2
Intercept	7.957***	8.177***
Unemployment duration (months)		−0.0083***
Male	0.395***	0.386***
Years of work experience	0.003	0.001
Work experience squared	0.0003	0.0002
College level education	0.112	0.070
Upper-middle school education	−0.237	−0.273
Lower-middle school education	−0.500	−0.507
State-owned	0.326**	0.296**
Private or self-employed	1.677**	1.530**
Other ownership	0.857**	0.791*
Permanent contract	−0.533*	−0.458
Long-term contract	−0.568*	−0.513
Temporary or no contract	−0.580*	−0.503*
Official, manager, technician, or skilled occupation	0.488***	0.476***
Possession or training	0.420**	0.369**
Beijing	0.617***	0.595***
Jinzhou	0.677**	0.650**
Nanjing	0.585***	0.484
Xuzhou	0.763***	0.784***
Zhengzhou	0.466	0.311
Kaifeng	−1.281*	−1.165
Pingdingshan	0.202	0.203
Chengdu	0.101	−0.097
Zigong	−0.964**	−0.960**
Nanchong	−0.155	−0.204
Lanzhou	−0.484	−0.491
Pingliang	0.444	0.442*
λ_1	−0.737**	−0.666**
λ_2	1.921*	1.794*
Adj. R^2	0.118	0.140
F-value	2.430	2.690

Notes: The dependent variable is the logarithm of monthly earnings expressed in yuan per annum. In both equations the mean of the dependent variable is 8.616 and the number of observations is 306. The omitted categories in the dummy variable analysis are female sex, primary education, or below, urban collective ownership, short-term contract, unskilled occupation, no training, and Shenyang. Selectivity-corrected equations are shown because the lambda coefficients (λ_1 representing selectivity into unemployment and λ_2 selectivity into re-employment) are significant at least at the 10% level. ***, **, and * denote statistical significance at the 1%, 5%, and 10% levels, respectively.

Source: Knight and Li (2003: table 5).

to conditions in local labour markets. Wages are highest in the private sector and lowest in the urban collective sector. None of these results is altered substantively by the introduction of the unemployment duration term.

In equation 2 the coefficient on unemployment duration is negative (-0.0083) and significant at the 1 per cent level. The effect is to reduce earnings by 16 per cent over nineteen months (the mean completed duration on unemployment) and by 39 per cent over forty-seven months (the mean expected duration). The coefficient on duration is not sensitive to correction for sample selectivity, being significantly negative at the 5 per cent level (-0.0064) in the uncorrected case. Although we were unable to reject the assumption that unemployment duration is exogenous, when we instrumented duration the effect was to make the coefficient more negative (-0.1173 instead of -0.0083).

The negative relationship between unemployment duration and subsequent wage is statistically significant and quantitatively important. We offered four possible explanations—two personal and concerned with the characteristics of the workers and two impersonal and concerned with the operation of the labour market—but the evidence did not permit us to choose among them. Nevertheless, the results indicate that China's displaced workers face a tough labour market. Most have not yet been re-employed, and those who have found jobs may have succeeded because they were willing to lower their sights.

6.6 URBAN UNEMPLOYMENT VERSUS MIGRANT EMPLOYMENT

City governments have pursued active policies of regulating the inflow of migrants in order to protect their residents. For instance, a particular city labour bureau was reported to classify jobs into three types: urban-*hukou* jobs, rural migrant jobs, and jobs open to all but with urban workers receiving preference. It also imposes quotas on the number of migrants that each enterprise can employ; these are enforced by inspection teams. The restrictions are sensitive to the state of the city labour market, being tightened if unemployment rises. Some city governments make price as well as quantity interventions. Enterprises must pay for their quotas, and they must pay an extra charge in order to exceed their quotas. Similarly, enterprises receive subsidies, in the form of tax relief, if they recruit *xia gang* employees. It is clear that migrant workers are frequently treated as the residual supply which should be adjusted to match the excess demand for urban labour.

Province-level data from the *Labour Statistics Yearbook* of the Ministry of Labour and Social Security enable us to estimate a regression equation predicting provincial variations in migrant employment. The explanatory variables are the registered unemployment rate, the *xia gang* employment rate, average earnings, and the recent growth of formal sector employment. The data are gathered administratively and have to be interpreted with caution. For instance, the migrant employment rate relates only to employment in the formal sector, that is, urban registered work units; and the unemployment rates relate only to those eligible to register as unemployed or as *xia gang* employees. In principle, both registered unemployment and *xia gang* employment should encourage city governments to restrict the employment of migrants. Insofar as urban workers are substitutes for migrants, we expect more urban unemployment and redundancies to reduce migration. Both average earnings and recent growth of employment represent pressure of demand in the labour market, which can be met by employing more migrants. We therefore expect their effects to be positive.

The equation is estimated for the years 1995 and 1996 (Table 6.4). All the coefficients have expected signs and most are significantly different from zero. There is a roughly one-to-one inverse relationship between *xia gang* employment rate and the migrant employment rate (columns (1) and (3)). The effect is weaker in the case of the registered unemployment rate: Its impact on the migrant

TABLE 6.4 *The determinants of migrant employment in urban enterprises: province analysis, 1995 and 1996*

	1995		1996	
Column (1)	(1)	(2)	(3)	(4)
Intercept	−47.368	−41.616	−21.185	−18.460
Xia gang employment rate	−1.293**		−0.825*	
Registered unemployment rate	−0.463		−0.498	
Total unemployment rate		−0.908**		−0.728*
Ln annual average earnings	6.643*	6.020*	3.526	3.249
Annual percentage employment growth	0.855**	0.815*	0.818*	0.794*
Adj. R^2	0.413	0.365	0.297	0.311
F-value	6.091**	6.557**	4.064**	5.358**
Mean dependent variable	7.748	7.748	6.845	6.845
Number of observations	30	30	30	30

Notes: The dependent variable is rural migrants employed in urban enterprises expressed as a percentage of formal sector employment. The explanatory variables are: *xia gang* employment as a percentage of total urban employment; registered unemployment as a percentage of the urban labour force; total unemployment rate, being the *xia gang* employment rate plus the registered unemployment rate; the logarithm of annual average earnings from employment; and the annual average percentage employment growth 1993–5 or 1993–6. ** denotes statistical significance at the 1% and * at the 5% level.

Source: PRC, MOL (1996, 1999).

employment rate is roughly a half. When the two forms of unemployment are combined (columns (2) and (4)), the average effect of a 1 per cent increase in (open plus disguised) unemployment is to reduce migrant employment by 0.8 percentage points. The variables representing pressure of labour demand also work well. In 1995, when migrant employment was 7.75 per cent of the total, an increase in provincial average earnings by one standard deviation (22 per cent) would raise the province's migrant employment rate by 1.30 percentage points. Moreover, a 1 per cent faster growth of employment would raise the migrant employment rate by over 0.8 percentage points.

Any conclusions from this analysis have to be qualified because of the cross-section nature of the data set: It has not been possible to standardize for unobserved heterogeneity among the provinces. For instance, there could be unobserved characteristics of a province which are responsible for both high unemployment and low migrant employment, with the implication that an exogenous rise in unemployment need not itself cause migrant employment to fall. Our first conclusion is therefore tentative: Although urban and rural employees often do different jobs, it seems that the growth of unemployment and redundancy among urban workers reduces the employment of migrants, probably on account of the policies of city governments. Second, the growth of urban employment has a strong, positive effect on the employment of migrants.

6.7 CONCLUSIONS

This chapter has been concerned to understand the remarkable change in government policy that took place in the mid-1990s: A reform of the state sector that had at its centrepiece a programme of mass redundancies which was intended to eliminate or reduce surplus labour in the state sector. This difficult and dangerous policy was forced on government by the declining competitiveness and profitability of the SOE sector, which threatened to curb economic growth and government revenues. It was difficult because of the sheer size of the unemployment problem that resulted, given the absence of a comprehensive institutional framework of unemployment insurance. It was dangerous because it threatened urban workers, who had previously enjoyed much preferential treatment and protection by the state. Urban workers are relatively well informed and geographically concentrated, and thus are more capable than rural people of protesting and organizing opposition to government policies.

A representative urban household survey, conducted at the start of 2000 specifically to investigate the redundancy programme, yielded insights into its implementation and consequences. The incidence of job loss was widespread: 19 per cent of households had experienced a retrenchment, and 11 per cent of workers. The majority (63 per cent) of the displaced workers had not yet found re-employment. The application of survival analysis suggested that the average expected duration of unemployment was almost four years.

The incidence of both retrenchment and re-employment was uneven. The highest risks of retrenchment were borne by employees of urban collectives and of local SOEs and, within enterprises, by workers with low educational and occupational skills and in poor health. Thus, the more productive workers enjoyed a degree of job security. Discriminatory behaviour is suggested by the relative protection afforded also to male workers and party members.

Personal productivity, in the form of possessing education and good health, improves the chances of finding another job, as does age beyond thirty-two years. On the one hand, the sensitivity of re-employment to household demographics implies that unemployment is partly voluntary for some people. On the other hand, the fact that over half of the unemployed did not receive unemployment benefit and the low level of benefit for those who did receive it both suggest that many are involuntarily unemployed. It appears that receiving government financial support also means receiving government assistance in job search, so improving the chances of re-employment.

Workers who are made redundant suffer a 'scarring' effect: Their re-employment wages are lower than the wages they could be earning if they had never been retrenched. Moreover, the longer the duration of unemployment, the lower the subsequent wage. There are four possible explanations for this negative relationship. Loss of income support, or of human capital, as unemployment continues, an escalating redundancy programme, and screening on the basis of unemployment duration can each reduce the reservation wage, and hence the likely re-employment wage. Most of the laid-off workers remained unemployed, and they could expect to remain unemployed for a long time. Those who found new jobs had to accept lower wages, especially if they had been unemployed for long, and their new jobs did not reward education and experience. Retrenched workers appeared to face a tough labour market.

Our analysis of the relationship between urban unemployment and migrant employment suggests that the rise in redundancy and unemployment among urban workers reduces the employment of migrants in the urban formal sector. This probably occurs through the policies of city governments to secure employment for their residents and to protect them against competition from migrants. It is urban employment outpacing the natural increase in the urban-*hukou* labour force that permits and encourages the increased employment of migrants.

Our study of the redundancy programme has thrown much light on the labour market dilemmas facing the Chinese government, and its bold response to those dilemmas. This episode illustrates the advantage of having a strong government able to take a long-term view. The urban workers who suffered in the short term may be disadvantaged in the long term as well if—as in other countries—the scarring effect of unemployment on wages proves to be long-lasting. Nevertheless, the long-term benefits—in terms of continued rapid growth of output, employment, and government revenue—may well eventually justify the radical surgery on the state sector that was performed from the mid-1990s onwards.

NOTES

1. This discrepancy is not the result of oversampling households with retrenched workers: over-sampling is corrected for by estimating the probit with weights. It is partly because of the non-linearity of the probit model and partly because the rates of individual worker retrenchment are higher in the additional sample of 503 households experiencing retrenchment than in the 747 similar households in the representative sample of 4,000 households.
2. We fear that this may have been the case although the questionnaire required them to be reported as retrenched.
3. This result mirrors the finding of Zhang, Huang, and Rozelle (2002) that education increases the probability of re-employment in rural China.
4. The percentage effect of a unit change in the explanatory variable on the hazard rate is $100 [\exp(\beta) - 1]$, where β is the relevant coefficient.
5. An exhaustive search for other instruments was made but none was significant in the duration equation but not in the earnings equation.

REFERENCES

Appleton, Simon, John Knight, Lina Song, and Qingjie Xia (2002). 'Labour retrenchment in China: determinants and consequences', *China Economic Review*, 13: 252–75.

Byrd, W. and G. Tidrick (1987). 'Factor allocation and enterprise incentives', in G. Tidrick and J. Chen (eds) *China's Industrial Reform*, New York: World Bank and Oxford University Press.

Crouch, Kenneth A. (2001). 'Earnings losses and unemployment of displaced workers in Germany', *Industrial and Labor Relations Review*, 54, 3: 559–72.

Fallick, B.C. (1996). 'A review of recent empirical literature on displaced workers', *Industrial and Labor Relations Review*, 50, 1: 5–16.

Gregory, Mary and Robert Jukes (2001). 'Unemployment and subsequent earnings: estimating scarring among British men 1984–94', *Economic Journal*, 111, 475: F607–25.

Groves, T., Y. Hong, J. McMillan, and B. Naughton (1994). 'Autonomy and incentives in Chinese state enterprises', *Quarterly Journal of Economics*, cix: 183–209.

Hay, D., D. Morris, G. Liu, and S. Yao (1994). *Economic Reform and State-Owned Enterprises in China, 1979–87*, Oxford: Clarendon Press.

Hussain, A. and J. Zhuang (1994). 'Impact of reforms on wages and employment determination in Chinese state enterprises, 1986–1991', Discussion Paper EF No. 12, STICERD, London School of Economics.

Jefferson, G.H. and W. Xu (1991). 'The impact of reform on socialist enterprises in transition: structure, conduct and performance in Chinese industry', *Journal of Comparative Economics*, 15: 45–64.

Kletzer, L.G. (1998). 'Job displacement', *Journal of Economic Perspectives*, 12, 1: 115–36.

Knight, John and Xue Jinjun (2003). 'How high is urban unemployment in China?', Department of Economics, University of Oxford, mimeo.

—— and Li Shi (2003). 'Unemployment duration and earnings of re-employed workers in urban China', Department of Economics, University of Oxford, mimeo.

Nickell, S.J., P. Jones, and G. Qintini (2002). 'A picture of job insecurity facing British men', *Economic Journal*, 112, 476: 1–27.

People's Republic of China, Ministry of Labour (PRC, MOL) (various years). *China Labour Statistics Yearbook*.

People's Republic of China, State Statistical Bureau (PRC, SSB) (1997). *China Statistical Yearbook*, Beijing: China Statistical Publishing House.

Pichelmann, K. and M. Riedel (1993). 'Unemployment duration and relative change in individualised earnings: evidence from Austrian panel data', Research Memorandum No. 317, Vienna: Institute for Advanced Studies.

World Bank (1993). *China. New Skills for Economic Development. The Employment and Training Implications of Urban Enterprise Reform*, Washington DC: World Bank.

Zhang, L., J. Huang, and S. Rozelle (2002). 'Employment, emerging labour markets, and the role of education in rural China', *China Economic Review*, 13, 2–3: 316–31.

7

Immobility and Segmentation of Labour

The introduction of market forces to the urban labour market in China was selective. For some urban residents—those who were made redundant—'the iron rice bowl' was shattered. For others, the iron rice bowl may have cracked but they retained their *danwei* jobs and many of the privileges that were attached. Only rural–urban migrants—who had never enjoyed the same rights and protection—experienced the chill wind of market forces throughout the reform period. One source of labour market segmentation, therefore, was the emergence of these distinct types of workers.

Although involuntary job mobility was thrust upon a substantial minority of urban residents from the mid-1990s onwards, voluntary job mobility remained low throughout the 1990s. The underlying problem was that *danwei* members stood to lose a great deal from quitting their *danwei* because it continued to provide important benefits that might otherwise be lost. While the *danwei* remained a social institution, members expected its success to be shared within the *danwei* community. The resultant tendency for profit-sharing, combined with lack of job mobility, gave rise to another form of labour market segmentation—segmentation among firms.

In this chapter we explore these two forms of labour market segmentation. We draw on three papers that analyse data sets which we helped to design, and of which one or both of us was a joint author. Section 7.2 provides estimates of the extent of job mobility in the urban labour market, both for urban residents and for rural migrants, using the IES, CASS 1999 urban survey. Section 7.3 uses the same survey to look for and measure wage segmentation among the three types of workers: urban workers who have never been retrenched, retrenched and re-employed urban workers, and rural–urban migrants. In Section 7.4 we use the IE, CASS 1995 and IE, CASS 1999 urban surveys to examine the relationship between wages and firm profitability, thus both illuminating the nature of the Chinese *danwei* and measuring the extent of segmentation among firms. Section 7.5 concludes.

7.2 IMMOBILITY AMONG JOBS

In this section we examine the extent of worker mobility among employers, for both urban residents and rural–urban migrants. We draw on Knight and Yueh (2004), which conducted a systematic study of this issue. Under the planning system the mobility of urban-*hukou* workers was very seriously restricted. During the subsequent period of rapid economic growth and structural transformation, we might have expected many job changes as some firms and sectors declined and others expanded, and as goods and factors were reallocated in response to market forces. The inherent productivity of some jobs rose and that of others fell. Nevertheless, involuntary mobility was negligible until the labour retrenchment policy was introduced in the mid-1990s. Moreover, voluntary mobility remained low throughout the 1990s, being impeded by the relatively high wages of non-retrenched workers, seniority payments, and employer-specific provisions of social welfare.

There are two possible variables for analysis: Labour turnover (in which the employer is the unit) and labour mobility (in which the employee is the unit). Having a household-based data set, we concentrate on labour mobility. This can be measured as the number of job quits per period made by a worker. An inverse measure of mobility from one job to another is the length of tenure of workers, that is, job duration, whether complete or incomplete.

There is evidence that urban residents in China have relatively long job duration by international standards, whereas the job duration of rural–urban migrants is relatively short. The average length of tenure of the former is 19.9 years and that of the latter is 4.5 years (Knight and Yueh 2004: table 1, using IE, CASS 1999). By contrast, in 1995 the average tenure in Poland (another transition economy) was 17.5 years, in Japan (noted for its powerful internal labour markets) 11.3 years, and in the United States (with its flexible labour markets) 7.4 years (OECD 1997).

A common reason for studying labour mobility concerns the normative issue: How much mobility is socially optimal? Mobility can lead to loss of firm-specific human capital or to unemployment hardship, but it can also lead to improved matching of workers to jobs, and thus higher productivity, or to the allocative gains that market forces generate. There can be no presumption that economic agents, in pursuing their own interests, will produce the degree of mobility that is optimal for society: Mobility can create externalities by imposing costs or benefits on the other party to an employment relationship or on third parties. Nor can there be a presumption that the optimal degree of mobility is similar in different economies, as it is likely to depend on the institutions and conventions of the labour market. Our concern in this section, however, is narrow: Is there enough mobility to create a functioning labour market?

7.2.1 *Job mobility of urban residents*

To our knowledge, the IE, CASS 1999 representative survey of urban resident households is the first data set that permits an analysis of inter-firm mobility in urban China. In addition to the more standard socio-economic questions, it obtained considerable information on the employment history of each worker. For instance, it asked those in the labour force how many jobs they had held since entering the labour market.

The most notable feature of the sample was the lack of mobility between employers. As many as 78 per cent of respondents had held only one job, and a further 16 per cent two jobs. Thus, only 6 per cent had been in three jobs or more. No less than 74 per cent of current employees with thirty or more years of employment experience were still in their first jobs. For the select minority of workers who had changed jobs, their average length of completed tenure was 5.5 years. However, this is not representative of the urban sample as a whole. The average length of first job tenure, including incomplete tenure, was 21.3 years. Considering only current job tenure, that is, omitting completed jobs, the average length was 16.6 years. Allowing for the future tenure in continuing jobs, the predicted duration of completed tenure for the sample as a whole would be extremely long.

We have information on the previous (i.e. most recent) job change, which we can date. Table 7.1, drawn from Knight and Yueh (2004: table 3), is created accordingly. For each entry cohort, we show the percentage who have never changed jobs, the percentage who have done so more than once, and the percentage who have made one job change. These last are in turn broken down according to the five-year period in which the single job change was made.[1] It is thus possible to obtain a period-specific, first-job mobility rate, by entry cohort. Our concern is to discover the extent to which mobility rose as labour market reforms progressed. The Western literature would suggest that job separations are highest in the first years of employment and decrease thereafter (Farber 1999). We need, therefore, to allow for this possible effect.

The table can be viewed down the columns (standardizing for the period in which separation occurred), across the rows (standardizing for entry cohort), or down the diagonals (standardizing for duration of tenure). Examining the columns, we observe the familiar tendency for mobility to decline with employment experience. By contrast, the rows indicate that, for post-1970 entrants, separation rates uniformly rise with time. The Western pattern is obscured by the increasing flexibility of the labour market over time. This explanation is verified from the diagonals, which show an almost monotonic increase in mobility over time, standardizing for the duration of employment. For instance, whereas the 1965–9 cohort had a 1.4 per cent separation rate over the subsequent five-year period, 1970–4, the 1990–4 entry cohort had a 12.1 per cent separation rate in the corresponding five-year period, 1995–9.

We go on to conduct the same exercise distinguishing between voluntary and involuntary mobility (Table 7.2). This is not an easy distinction to make, relying as it does on the reason for leaving a job that the worker reports.[2] There is a general tendency for the voluntary mobility rate to be higher the more recent the cohort, and when we standardize for duration of employment, the more recent the period. Involuntary separations were far higher in 1995–9 than in the previous five-year periods. The iron rice bowl became increasingly fragile over time, and indeed it was effectively broken in the period 1995–9.

TABLE 7.1 *Percentage of job separations by period of entry into the labour market and by period of job separation, for those with one job change, 1999 (number of observations in parentheses)*

Period of entry	Period of job separation								Never changed	Multiple changes
	1960–4	1965–9	1970–4	1975–9	1980–4	1985–9	1990–4	1995–9		
1960–4 (724)	1.5 (11)	2.8 (20)	1.1 (8)	1.5 (11)	2.3 (17)	1.5 (11)	1.1 (8)	1.0 (7)	71.4 (517)	15.5 (112)
1965–9 (1,472)	—	1.8 (26)	1.4 (21)	2.9 (42)	3.2 (47)	3.3 (49)	1.9 (28)	2.2 (32)	72.1 (1,061)	10.4 (153)
1970–4 (1,256)	—	—	2.2 (28)	2.9 (37)	2.9 (36)	3.0 (38)	3.6 (45)	6.0 (75)	67.5 (848)	9.7 (122)
1975–9 (1,517)	—	—	—	3.6 (54)	3.2 (48)	3.9 (59)	4.2 (64)	8.6 (130)	68.6 (1,040)	4.9 (74)
1980–4 (1,198)	—	—	—	—	3.4 (41)	4.9 (59)	5.7 (68)	8.8 (105)	70.0 (839)	3.5 (42)
1985–9 (897)	—	—	—	—	—	4.2 (38)	5.1 (46)	10.5 (94)	71.3 (640)	3.1 (28)
1990–4 (626)	—	—	—	—	—	—	5.4 (34)	12.1 (76)	72.8 (456)	4.2 (26)
1995–9 (532)	—	—	—	—	—	—	—	7.7 (41)	82.1 (437)	6.8 (36)

Note: The rows do not sum up to 100 because there are those with one job change for whom we do not have information on the year of separation.

Source: Knight and Yueh (2004: table 3).

The Urban Labour Market

TABLE 7.2 *Percentage of voluntary, and of involuntary, separations by period of entry into the labour market and by period of job separation, for those with one job change: urban resident sample, 1999 (number of observations in parentheses)*

Period of entry	Period of job separation							
	1960–4	1965–9	1970–4	1975–9	1980–4	1985–9	1990–4	1995–9
Voluntary separations								
1960–4	0.1	0.3	0.1	0.3	0.6	0.3	0.4	0.0
(724)	(1)	(2)	(1)	(2)	(4)	(2)	(3)	(0)
1965–9	—	0.5	0.2	1.0	0.7	0.8	0.3	0.4
(1,472)		(8)	(3)	(14)	(10)	(12)	(5)	(6)
1970–4	—	—	0.5	0.6	0.8	0.6	0.7	0.7
(1,256)			(6)	(8)	(10)	(8)	(9)	(9)
1975–9	—	—	—	0.5	0.6	1.5	1.3	1.3
(1,517)				(8)	(9)	(22)	(20)	(20)
1980–4	—	—	—	—	0.8	2.1	2.1	1.3
(1,198)					(10)	(25)	(25)	(15)
1985–9	—	—	—	—	—	0.8	1.8	1.6
(897)						(7)	(16)	(14)
1990–4	—	—	—	—	—	—	1.8	3.8
(626)							(11)	(24)
1995–9	—	—	—	—	—	—	—	3.2
(532)								(17)
Involuntary separations								
1960–4	0.1	0.0	0.0	0.0	0.0	0.0	0.1	0.7
(724)	(1)	(0)	(0)	(0)	(0)	(0)	(0)	(5)
1965–9	—	0.2	0.1	0.0	0.0	0.0	0.3	1.2
(1,472)		(3)	(2)	(0)	(0)	(0)	(4)	(18)
1970–4	—	—	0.3	0.2	0.0	0.1	0.6	4.4
(1,256)			(4)	(2)	(0)	(1)	(7)	(55)
1975–9	—	—	—	1.0	0.3	0.3	1.6	5.7
(1,517)				(15)	(5)	(4)	(25)	(86)
1980–4	—	—	—	—	0.8	0.3	1.8	6.0
(1,198)					(10)	(3)	(22)	(72)
1985–9	—	—	—	—	—	1.0	1.7	6.9
(897)						(9)	(15)	(62)
1990–4	—	—	—	—	—	—	1.4	7.2
(626)							(9)	(45)
1995–9	—	—	—	—	—	—	—	2.6
(532)								(14)

Notes: 'Voluntary separation' comprises the following answers to the question 'Why did you leave your previous job?': low income; lack of job security; unsatisfactory work conditions; insufficient benefits; to start own business. 'Involuntary separation' comprises the following answers: contract expired; laid-off by work unit; became *xia gang*; and 'other' if the worker is currently unemployed. Not all responses could be classified.

Source: IE, CASS 1999, Urban resident sample.

TABLE 7.3 *Transition matrix for those who had changed jobs once, row percentage in each ownership category, by ownership category of previous sector: urban resident sample, 1999 (number of observations in parentheses)*

Previous sector	Current sector				
	SOEs	UCEs	Self-employed	Private sector	Total
SOEs	84	3	4	9	100
	(555)	(22)	(27)	(61)	(665)
UCEs	41	33	14	12	100
	(38)	(31)	(13)	(11)	(93)
Self-employed	33	8	42	17	100
	(4)	(1)	(5)	(2)	(12)
Private sector	65	5	0	30	100
	(28)	(2)	(0)	(13)	(43)
Total	77	7	6	11	100
	(625)	(56)	(45)	(87)	(813)

Notes: SOEs are central, provincial, and local state-owned enterprises. UCEs are urban collective enterprises. Self-employed are individual or household businesses. The private sector comprises all private firms, including partnership, Chinese–foreign joint venture, foreign company, state share-holding company, other share-holding company, rural individual enterprise, and 'other' enterprise.

Source: Knight and Yueh (2004: table 5).

Table 7.3 presents the transition matrix for those who had changed jobs once. Four ownership categories are distinguished—state, urban collective, self-employed, and private—for both destination and origin. The table shows combined voluntary and involuntary mobility. Of those who moved from one employment to another, 84 per cent moved from one state-sector job to another. Only 13 per cent of those leaving the state sector, and 26 per cent of those leaving the urban collective sector, entered the self-employed or private sectors. Whereas 73 per cent of the voluntary movers went to the state sector, only 33 per cent of the involuntary movers did so (table not shown). The state sector appears to be the preferred destination.

Although overall mobility was low, the two mobility rates could nevertheless be fairly well predicted. An analysis of their determinants showed that home-ownership, human capital, and social capital all tend to increase voluntary mobility, the first because it diminishes the potential cost of job change and the last two because they improve opportunities for beneficial job change. The factors that reduce the involuntary mobility rate are being a non-manual worker, working in the state sector, and being a Communist Party member (Knight and Yueh 2004: table 2). Each of these characteristics might provide, or have provided, relative protection against job loss.

An earnings function analysis yielded two relevant results (Knight and Yueh 2004: table 6). First, seniority is highly rewarded: Ten years of tenure add

22 per cent to earnings, whereas ten years of schooling add 34 per cent. The many urban workers with long tenure receive a substantial reward for seniority—the earnings premium being 32 per cent for those with average current tenure (16.6 years)—and this discourages them from engaging in job search. Secondly, when the voluntary and the involuntary mobility rates are included as explanatory variables in the earnings function, the former has a positive and the latter a negative coefficient, both as expected, although neither is significantly different from zero (Knight and Yueh 2004: table 6).

7.2.2 Job mobility of rural–urban migrants

The analysis of migrants is based on workers in a sample of rural–urban migrant households, that is, households resident in the survey cities in 1999 but retaining their rural *hukou*. As they live in resident households, these migrants are unlikely to be representative of rural–urban migrants as a whole. Migrants who leave their rural homesteads and come to the cities on their own to work temporarily, often living with other migrants at their workplace or in dormitories, are likely to be under-represented in this sample. Their mobility rate is likely to be higher than that of migrants putting down urban roots.

In some respects, the migrants appear similar to urban workers. As many as 77 per cent had been in only one job, another 10 per cent had been in two, 7 per cent in three, and only 6 per cent in more than three jobs. However, these similarities are misleading. For urban workers, we are analysing the period since entry to the labour force, but for migrants the analysis refers to the period since entry to the city labour market—at which point they become comparable to urban workers. Thus, the average length of employment experience of urban workers is 22.8 years, whereas the average length of city employment experience of migrants is 5.9 years. The difference is partly because migrants are younger (28.6 years of age, compared with 38.4 years) and partly because most migrants did not come immediately to the city when they entered the labour force: Most had previously been engaged in rural household economic activities.

The average completed duration of employment of migrants is 2.2 years. It is lowest (1.3 years) for migrants in their twenties and highest (4.1 years) for those in their fifties. The first job tenure, including incomplete spells, averages 5.0 years; the average length of current job tenure is 4.5 years. Each of these tenure figures is fraught with problems of interpretation. On the one hand, briefly employed migrants—more likely to be unsuccessful—may have returned to the village. On the other hand, it is difficult to predict the length of incomplete spells. For instance, it could be misleading to double the average current tenure (from 4.5 to 9.0 years), as would be appropriate if the process were in steady state. A more welcoming policy towards migrant urban settlement would encourage migrants to continue at the workplace much longer than in the past. Nevertheless, even the figure of 4.5 years is high by comparison with the conventional wisdom about migrant employment.

For those migrants who changed jobs, a high proportion (72 per cent) had done so voluntarily. This is much higher than in the case of urban workers. Knight and Yueh (2004: tables 4–6) show that private-sector employment is the preferred state for migrants, as is borne out by the significantly higher standardized pay of migrants in the private than in the state sector. The mobility rate also figures in the earnings function for migrants. The coefficient is positive and significant at the 5 per cent level. It implies that, by comparison with remaining in the same job, a move every four years involves an 8 per cent rise in earnings (Knight and Yueh 2004: table 6). The coefficient on a year of tenure (0.027) is positive and significant at the 5 per cent level. It implies that the earnings premium of migrants with the mean years of current tenure (4.5 years) is 13 per cent. This is much smaller than for urban residents: Migrants have less incentive to remain with their employer. The premium could represent either skill formation, or improved matching within the firm, or a process of good workers selecting or being selected to stay on. On the other hand, the actual return to tenure is likely to understate the potential return. Firms are deterred from investing in migrants by the institutional favouring of migrants for the more skilled jobs. There can be a vicious circle: Short tenure discourages investment in skills but lack of skills and thus of reward encourages short tenure.

7.3 SEGMENTATION AMONG WORKERS

The extent of labour market competition by status of workers has been examined by Appleton et al. (2004), using IE, CASS 1999. In the 1990s, employed urban residents were brought into potential competition with two emerging groups of workers: Rural–urban migrants prepared to work for low wages, and retrenched urban workers seeking re-employment. Retrenchment creates an opportunity for firms to renegotiate old contracts, both formal and implicit, with their remaining employees, and it may force the displaced urban workers to compete with migrants for work. On this view, labour market forces grew stronger as competition among the groups intensified. On the alternative view, this development simply created a three-tier labour market. Urban residents who keep their jobs may continue to be employed on preferential terms, and displaced urban workers may suffer prolonged unemployment or enter a secondary labour market. The retrenchment policy and the consequent rise in urban unemployment has led to tighter controls on migrants, aimed at restricting their numbers and in this way assisting the laid-off. Those migrants who are allowed to enter or stay in the cities may be left to make a living from self-employment or to take marginal jobs that even the retrenched urban residents would reject.

Our study in Chapter 5 of the labour market in the mid-1990s, just prior to the redundancy policy, found evidence of sharp segmentation between urban residents and migrants. This, we argued, arose from the political and institutional arrangements which gave urban residents privileged access to secure employment at above market-clearing wages and which controlled the flow of peasants to the cities, allowing rural migrants to fill only the jobs that urban dwellers did not want. Did this situation change as a result of the dramatic redundancy programme of the late 1990s?

Appleton et al. (2004) analyse wages by means of IE, CASS 1999, distinguishing three subgroups in the urban labour force. One division is between those with urban residential (*hukou*) status—henceforth termed 'urban workers'—and rural–urban migrants, retaining their rural-*hukou* status. Migrants are usually excluded from official counts of the Chinese urban labour force because they lack urban-*hukou* status, although they may live and work in the urban sector and wish to retain urban jobs. However, the survey contains a separate subsample representative of rural-*hukou* households residing in the surveyed cities and registered with neighbourhood committees. The survey also makes possible a subdivision between urban workers who have been retrenched and those who have not. Although there is a large literature on the effect of retrenchment on wages in Western countries, the impact on wages of the recent mass redundancies in urban China has not previously been studied.

This section compares wage levels and structures across these three groups of workers. It poses the question: Are there wage differences among workers who share the same characteristics? However, the presence of residual wage differences does not necessarily imply segmentation. Even if we establish that the three groups are rewarded differently, the underlying reasons may remain unclear.

Consider the comparison of non-retrenched and re-employed urban workers. A standardized wage difference favouring the former might reflect the distinction between a non-competitive primary labour market and a competitive secondary labour market. However, the literature on displaced workers in Western countries shows that they normally experience earnings losses after being retrenched and unemployed, and that these losses can last for many years (Gregory and Jukes 2002; Nickell, Jones, and Qintini 2002). Many hypotheses for this phenomenon have been proposed (Fallick 1996). For example, individuals who are retrenched may have lost their firm-specific human capital by the time they become re-employed, they may have lost some of their general labour market experience, and re-employment may have involved poorer matching of workers to jobs. These explanations do not reflect a lack of labour market competition. Nevertheless, the scale of the mass retrenchment in urban China means that it is important to explore its impact on wages, whatever the causal mechanism involved.

It is not clear a priori what one should expect about the wages of migrants relative to those of re-employed urban workers. On the one hand, institutional factors favour the re-employed: They benefit from the labour market restrictions imposed on migrants. Moreover, after 1997, the Chinese Government instructed local agencies to give priority to laid-off urban workers in allocating vacant jobs. Migrants may also suffer from the productive disadvantage—unobserved by the researcher—that they lack the experience and skills acquired from being brought up and living in the city. On the other hand, migrants have not experienced the 'scarring' effect of retrenchment that has been noted in the empirical literature on Western economies. Migrants may be more established in their current jobs than are retrenched and re-employed urban residents, both because we focus on those who have established urban households—the more settled migrants—and because the mass displacement of urban workers is a recent phenomenon.

7.3.1 Wage functions for different types of workers

Of the employed workers in the sample, 5,770 are non-retrenched urban workers, 433 are re-employed, and 1,065 are rural–urban migrants. There are also 726 workers who have been retrenched since 1992 but were unemployed at the time of the survey. This fourth category of workers is used in controlling for selectivity of retrenchment and of re-employment. The dependent variable in the wage function analysis is the logarithm of wage per eight-hour day.[3]

It was necessary to address the issue of possible selection into retrenchment and, if retrenched, into re-employment on the basis of unobserved characteristics such as laziness or ability: Unless corrected, this could bias the estimated coefficients in the wage functions. A multinomial logit model was used to estimate the probability of an urban worker being in each of the three categories: Non-retrenched, retrenched and unemployed, and retrenched and re-employed. A selectivity correction term (the inverse Mills ratio) was then included in the wage function for each category. Valid instruments—satisfactory on both a priori and empirical grounds—were found which could predict the category but did not directly affect wages. However, it was not possible to reject the hypothesis of no selectivity bias. The analysis therefore relies on ordinary least squares (OLS) estimates of the wage functions.

Table 7.4 sets out the variable definitions and Table 7.5 presents estimates of the three wage functions. A common set of human capital, discrimination, and segmentation explanatory variables is employed. Wald tests established that no two wage functions could be pooled, and that many of the corresponding coefficients in different wage functions were significantly different. We begin with the potential discrimination variables. The wage premium for men is distinctly higher for the retrenched and for migrants, who are more subject to managerial autonomy, than for the non-retrenched, who are more subject to institutional protection. Communist Party membership is rewarded among the non-retrenched but not among the retrenched.

Turning to the human capital characteristics: The returns to a year of education are distinctly higher for non-retrenched and migrant workers than for retrenched workers. The full returns to education are best seen in Mincerian earnings functions that exclude such variables as occupation and ownership, which are likely to be influenced by education. In that case the returns are 6.0, 5.7, and 0.2 per cent, respectively. The low return for retrenched workers suggests that they have been absorbed into low-skill jobs in which education is not productive, and the high return for migrants implies a more efficient matching process. On the other hand, migrants receive the lowest returns to employment experience.

TABLE 7.4 *Variable definitions used for the analysis of worker categories*

Variable name	Definition
Male	1 if male, 0 otherwise
Education	Years of education
Experience	Years of potential experience (age–education–six)
Experience squared	Experience squared
Ethnic minority	1 if not Han Chinese, 0 otherwise
Party member	1 if member of Communist Party, 0 otherwise
Poor health	1 if self-described as in 'bad health', 0 otherwise
Sectoral variables (default is employment by local government, including locally controlled SOE)	
Central SOE	1 if employed by central government, including centrally controlled SOE
Urban collective	1 if employed by urban collective
Urban private	1 if employed by urban private company
Urban individual	1 if self-employed
Foreign invested	1 if employed by a company with foreign investment
State listed	1 if employed by a state enterprise listed in the stock market
Other listed	1 if employed by non-state enterprise listed in the stock market
Rural enterprises	1 if employed by rural enterprise
Other ownership	1 if employed in type of enterprise not listed above
Occupation variables (default is professional or technical)	
Administrative	1 if employed in an administrative or managerial position
Clerical	1 if employed in a clerical position
Industrial worker	1 if employed as an industrial worker
Commercial worker	1 if employed as a commercial worker
Service worker	1 if employed as a service worker
Other occupation	1 if employed in another occupation
Low-skill industrial	1 if employed as a low-skilled industrial worker
High-skill industrial	1 if employed as a high-skilled industrial worker
Unskilled industrial	1 if employed as a unskilled industrial worker
City dummy variables (default is Beijing)	
Shenyang, Liaoning	1 if in Shenyang
Jinzhou, Liaoning	1 if in Jinzhou
Nanjing, Jiangsu	1 if in Nanjing
Xuzhou, Jiangsu	1 if in Xuzhou
Zhengzhou, Henan	1 if in Zhengzhou
Kaifeng, Henan	1 if in Kaifeng

TABLE 7.4 (*continued*)

Variable name	Definition
Pingdingshan, Henan	1 if in Pingdingshan
Chengdu, Sichuan	1 if in Chengdu
Zigong, Sichuan	1 if in Zigong
Nanchong, Sichuan	1 if in Nanchong
Lanzhou, Gansu	1 if in Lanzhou
Pingliang, Gansu	1 if in Pingliang
Fixed effects model	
Variable name * 96 etc.	Denotes interaction between variable and a year dummy for 1996 etc.

Source: Appleton et al. (2004: table 1), using the IE, CASS 1999 survey.

There are significant differences also in occupational wage structure. There is a clear three-way division for the non-retrenched, apparently based on skill levels: Administrative, technical, and professional workers receive the highest wages, *ceteris paribus*, followed by clerical workers, with commercial, industrial, and service occupations forming a relatively undifferentiated group. By contrast, clerical workers are particularly hard-hit by retrenchment. The many migrant workers in service occupations receive lower wages relative to other occupations than do urban residents.

Finally, consider the segmentation variables. The controls added for ownership sector generally matter more for non-retrenched workers than for the less secure categories. For the non-retrenched, there is a clear hierarchy of sectors in terms of the wages they offer. Foreign enterprises are the highest paying, followed by centrally run SOEs, and those listed on the stock market. Urban collectives and rural enterprises pay least. These patterns are generally not repeated for retrenched and for migrant workers. Few of their wage differences between ownership sectors are statistically significant. For instance, neither category receives a wage premium for being employed in a centrally run SOE, suggesting that these firms hire retrenched workers and migrants on more competitive terms than those given currently to the non-retrenched. The generally negative and significant city dummy variables imply that workers in the default city, Beijing, receive a wage premium. However, the premium does vary across the three categories of workers. The pattern of city dummies is also significantly different for the non-retrenched workers, who are the least subject to labour market competition.

Overall, therefore, the comparison of wage functions suggests that workers in urban China are rewarded differently according to whether or not they have been retrenched and whether they are migrants possessing rural *hukous*. Actual wages differ across the three groups. Non-retrenched workers are the highest paid, with mean wages of 33 yuan per day. The comparison between migrant and retrenched workers is rather nuanced. Whereas they have the same arithmetic

TABLE 7.5 *Wage functions for the non-retrenched, re-employed, and migrant workers, 1999*

	Non-retrenched urban workers		Re-employed urban workers		Migrant workers	
	Coefficient	T-ratio	Coefficient	T-ratio	Coefficient	T-ratio
Constant	2.850	44.42***	2.778	8.72***	2.498	14.49***
Male	0.135	9.75***	0.313	5.11***	0.210	5.12***
Education (in years)	0.034	10.61***	0.007	0.44	0.045	4.64***
Experience (in years)	0.037	12.13***	0.052	3.99***	0.024	3.21***
Experience squared	-0.001	-9.40***	-0.001	-3.67***	0.000	-2.83***
Ethnic minority	0.051	1.54	-0.131	-1.24	0.112	1.22
Party member	0.074	4.68***	-0.038	-0.23	0.178	0.88
Poor health	-0.085	-2.05**	-0.056	-0.55	-0.219	-1.49
Central SOE	0.156	10.77***	0.057	0.60	0.029	0.23
Urban collective	-0.169	-6.86***	-0.129	-1.83*	0.124	1.11
Urban private	0.104	1.26	-0.117	-0.55	0.074	0.81
Urban individual	-0.031	-0.59	0.125	1.42	0.094	1.14
Foreign invested	0.347	6.35***	-0.380	-3.09***	0.490	2.47**
State listed	0.085	2.35**	0.000	0.00	-0.169	-0.92
Other listed	0.064	1.21	0.187	0.83	0.342	2.21**
Rural enterprises	-0.257	-2.40**	-0.624	-6.50***	0.115	1.21
Other ownership	-0.023	-0.36	-0.181	-1.04	0.064	0.57
Administrative	0.000	-0.02	0.016	0.12	-0.052	-0.58
Clerical	-0.068	-3.43***	-0.327	-2.34**	0.059	0.53
Industrial worker	-0.239	-12.68***	-0.173	-1.72*	-0.199	-2.00**
Commercial worker	-0.226	-6.57***	-0.123	-1.04	-0.340	-3.47***

	(1)	(2)	(3)	(4)	(5)	(6)
Service worker	−0.254	−7.46***	−0.346	−2.18**	−0.422	−4.74***
Other occupation	−0.346	−5.24***	0.124	0.56	−0.233	−2.40**
Shenyang, Liaoning	−0.477	−17.64***	−0.252	−1.61	−0.121	−1.39
Jinzhou, Liaoning	−0.445	−11.80***	−0.520	−4.12***	−0.238	−2.47**
Nanjing, Jiangsu	−0.136	−5.23***	−0.162	−1.21	−0.324	−3.73***
Xuzhou, Jiangsu	−0.341	−10.67***	−0.207	−1.46	−0.149	−1.21
Zhengzhou, Henan	−0.431	−14.09***	−0.478	−2.47**	−0.537	−4.66***
Kaifeng, Henan	−0.692	−19.88***	−0.636	−3.32***	−0.444	−4.48***
Pingdingshan, Henan	−0.477	−15.69***	−0.379	−1.55	−0.706	−7.31***
Chengdu, Sichuan	−0.404	−14.86***	−0.231	−1.70*	−0.197	−2.08**
Zigong, Sichuan	−0.527	−15.53***	−0.754	−4.41***	−0.566	−5.40***
Nanchong, Sichuan	−0.585	−17.31***	−0.511	−3.90***	−0.400	−4.06***
Lanzhou, Gansu	−0.456	−16.08***	−0.336	−2.54**	−0.304	−2.83***
Pingliang, Gansu	−0.642	−21.16***	−0.691	−4.53***	−0.824	−9.44***
Number of observations	5,770		433		1,065	
Mean of dependent variable	3.340		3.009		2.824	
Adj. R^2	0.330		0.151		0.199	
Standard error of equation	0.486		0.595		0.672	

Notes: Dummy variables for year of employment are included but not reported. Default dummy variables in these models are female, Han ethnicity, healthy, non-party member, professional or technical, local SOE, and Beijing. ***, **, and * denote statistical significance at the 1%, 5%, and 10% levels, respectively.

Source: IE, CASS 1999.

mean wages (25 yuan per day), median wages are higher for retrenched workers than for migrants (19 compared to 16 yuan per day), reflecting higher variation in migrant wages.

Differences in wages among categories of workers may be consistent with a competitive labour market if they can be explained by differences in the productive characteristics of workers. Appleton et al. (2004) went on to conduct simulations using their estimated wage functions. The following counterfactual question was posed: What is the predicted log wage of a worker with the mean characteristics of workers in group i if they are paid according to the wage function of group j? It was thus possible to predict the extent to which differences in wage structure explain differences in mean log wages. The difference in the predicted log wages can be interpreted as the percentage difference in predicted geometric mean wages. Mincerian wage functions were used because occupation and ownership categories may standardize inappropriately. Migrants tend to be crowded into certain occupations—often self-employment—and retrenched workers are likely to find re-employment in disadvantageous ownership categories. Controlling for these factors may understate the full effects on wages of impediments to competition between groups of workers.

The simulations imply that workers of given mean characteristics are predicted to be paid considerably more if paid like non-retrenched workers (Table 7.6). The differences imply that the non-retrenched wage function carries a premium of some 20–25 per cent over the other two functions. Moreover, this premium does not apparently reflect selectivity on the basis of unobserved characteristics—as it might, for instance, if less able workers are more likely to have been sacked. Whereas a retrenched worker is predicted to receive 7 per cent more if paid like a migrant, a migrant would earn 15 per cent more if paid like a retrenched worker. These results imply that, even if the retrenched and migrants are not competing

TABLE 7.6. *Predicted mean log wage from the wage functions, 1999 (standard error in brackets)*

	If paid like non-retrenched workers	If paid like re-employed urban workers	If paid like migrants
Non-retrenched urban workers	3.340 (0.485)	3.097 (0.593)	3.042 (0.678)
Re-employed urban workers	3.125 (0.485)	3.010 (0.591)	2.905 (0.676)
Migrants	3.091 (0.485)	3.105 (0.598)	2.817 (0.672)

Note: Wages are predicted using actual mean characteristics and the coefficients of the relevant wage function.

Source: Appleton et al. (2004: table 3).

with each other on equal terms, they occupy segments of the labour market that are close to each other. Retrenchment has led urban residents to lose most of the wage premium that might have derived from their urban-*hukou* status.

7.3.2 Wages over time

As well as asking about current wages, IE, CASS 1999 sought information on the wage of each urban resident over the previous four years. Appleton et al. (2004) combined the data to create a five-year (unbalanced) panel of wage information. Wages are converted into 1999 prices using the urban consumer price index. Although most of the explanatory variables (excluding experience) contained in the cross-sectional wage function are time-invariant, the panel could be used to explore whether there are changes in the effects of these variables over time. A fixed effects estimator was used to remove potential biases caused by correlations between the explanatory variables and the time-invariant unobserved characteristics of the individual.

The fixed effects estimates, estimated separately for the non-retrenched and the retrenched, are shown in Table 7.7. The year dummy variables measure the rise in real wages over time. The terms interacting each explanatory variable with each year dummy shows how the coefficient on that variable changed over time. The re-employment interaction terms relate to retrenched workers who had been re-employed. A parsimonious Mincerian specification of the wage function is used.

Consider the non-retrenched workers (the first column of Table 7.7). The year dummies in the wage function imply substantial wage growth over the period. For example, the year dummy for 1999 indicates a 45 per cent higher wage in that year than in the base year of 1995 for a worker with the default characteristics. This real wage growth of 8 per cent per annum during a time of retrenchment and high unemployment suggests a weakness of competition. In a competitive labour market one would expect a fall in the demand for labour to depress real wages. Even if capital accumulation and technological change had increased the marginal product of labour, this should have raised employment rather than wages given an elastic supply of labour. That the real wage rose is more consistent with rent-sharing theory, whereby the retrenchment of excess labour raises the surplus available to firms and some of this rise is shared with the remaining workers through higher pay. We examine this hypothesis in Section 7.4.

Some non-retrenched workers have enjoyed higher wage increases than others. The positive and statistically significant interactions between the year dummy for 1999 and a number of personal characteristics indicate that those characteristics are more highly rewarded in 1999 than they were in 1995. For example, the coefficients on the interaction terms between years of education and the year dummies rise with the year. The term for 1999 is statistically significant at the one per cent level and implies that the return to education is one per cent higher in 1999 than in 1995. This change sounds modest, but the corresponding return to education in 1999 was

TABLE 7.7. *Fixed effects estimates of changes in wage function coefficients for urban workers, 1995–9*

	Non-retrenched		Retrenched	
	Coefficient	T-ratio	Coefficient	T-ratio
Male*99	−0.003	−0.26	0.113	1.52
Male*98	−0.008	−0.65	0.037	0.94
Male*97	−0.005	−0.45	0.035	0.91
Male*96	−0.005	−0.38	0.021	0.56
Experience*99	−2.07E-02	−7.48***	1.41E-02	0.69
Experience*98	−1.92E-02	−7.19***	−7.92E-03	−0.75
Experience*97	−1.13E-02	−4.34***	−7.49E-04	−0.08
Experience*96	−1.65E-03	−0.65	−8.78E-03	−0.94
Experience squared*99	3.60E-04	6.00***	−4.43E-04	−0.96
Experience squared*98	3.76E-04	6.22***	−2.83E-05	−0.12
Experience squared*97	2.33E-04	3.80***	−1.46E-04	−0.64
Experience squared*96	4.32E-05	0.69	1.38E-04	0.61
Education in years*99	0.012	4.61***	−0.012	−0.69
Education in years*98	0.006	2.21**	−0.012	−1.25
Education in years*97	0.003	1.11	−0.014	−1.50
Education in years*96	0.000	0.11	−0.001	−0.09
Minority ethnicity*99	0.088	2.84***	0.020	0.11
Minority ethnicity*98	0.047	1.50	−0.032	−0.32
Minority ethnicity*97	0.043	1.38	0.024	0.25
Minority ethnicity*96	0.028	0.88	−0.002	−0.03
Party member*99	0.059	4.25***	0.122	0.94
Party member*98	0.055	3.95***	−0.001	−0.02
Party member*97	0.039	2.76***	0.066	1.01
Party member*96	0.010	0.70	−0.013	−0.21
Year dummy for 1999	0.370	7.84***	0.037	0.12
Year dummy for 1998	0.283	6.20***	0.177	1.06
Year dummy for 1997	0.129	2.91***	0.113	0.73
Year dummy for 1996	0.000	−0.00	0.055	0.37
Dummy variable for re-employment (time-varying)			0.842	2.93***
Interactions with a time-varying dummy variable for re-employment				
Male*re-employment			0.169	2.62***
Experience*re-employment			−3.35E-02	−1.75*
Experience squared*re-employment			5.79E-04	1.34
School years*re-employment			−0.041	−2.54***
Minority*re-employment			0.150	1.06
Communist Party member* re-employment			−0.319	−2.83***
Year dummy for 1999*re-employment			−0.131	−1.19
Year dummy for 1998*re-employment			0.204	2.16**
Year dummy for 1997*re-employment			0.066	0.70
Year dummy for 1996*re-employment			−0.018	−0.19
Constant	3.089	724.54***	2.710	206.89***
Number of observations	26,938		4,639	
R^2 across individuals	0.1421		0.0675	

Note: ***, **, and * denote statistical significance at the 1%, 5%, and 10% levels, respectively.

Source: Appleton et al. (2004: table 4).

6 per cent—implying that the return increased by a fifth over the four years. This finding is consistent with a greater rewarding of productive characteristics, and thus with the hypothesis of an increasingly competitive labour market. However, it could also arise for other reasons such as an increase in the demand for skilled labour relative to the supply, for instance, on account of skill-biased technological change. In other words, the increase could represent a rise in the market equilibrium rate rather than a move from a wage-compressed disequilibrium towards the market equilibrium.

By contrast, the returns to employment experience of the non-retrenched workers appear to have fallen. The experience terms interacted with the dummy variable for 1999 imply a U-shaped curve, with a turning point at 29 years of experience. Because most workers occupy the downward-sloping section of the U-shape, the returns to experience generally fell between the base year, 1995, and 1999. Employment experience is probably a less good measure of human capital than schooling. Under central planning, seniority was a central aspect of China's administered wage system. We showed in Chapter 3 that in 1988 the earnings of workers peaked only in their fifties, *ceteris paribus*. Given the extreme weakness of labour market forces at that time, it is unlikely that these payments reflected productivity benefits. Indeed, seniority was probably overpaid prior to reform.

It is not clear that non-productive characteristics came to matter less in the late 1990s. Indeed, the premium paid to Communist Party members rose by 6 percentage points between 1995 and 1999, a statistically significant increase. It appears that party members who avoided retrenchment did particularly well on pay. This is in addition to the fact, documented with the same data set in Chapter 6, that party membership afforded some protection against retrenchment.

For workers who were ever retrenched after 1992 (the second column of Table 7.7), all the year dummies are insignificant and, in 1998 and 1999, have much smaller coefficients than in the case of the non-retrenched. Thus, soon-to-be-retrenched workers did not receive the wage increases enjoyed by their never-retrenched colleagues. This may be because the enterprises in which they worked were in financial difficulties and thus unable to fund wage increases. From the terms interacting re-employment and year, we learn that the 1999 wage of re-employed workers was no higher than in 1995. The re-employed workers—like the retrenched in their old jobs—did not experience real wage growth over this period.

The dummy variable for re-employment of the retrenched has a statistically significant positive coefficient. This means that the retrenched were paid more on re-employment than they were paid on losing their jobs, both (artificially) expressed in the wages of 1995. Thereafter, however, the re-employed lost out increasingly over time relative to other workers. The rise in the returns to education of the never retrenched was not observed among the workers who would become retrenched, and when they eventually found new jobs they suffered a substantial and significant fall in the returns to education. It is clear that the urban workers who lost their iron rice bowls were thrown onto a tough labour market. Especially if they possessed human capital, they were re-employed on less favourable terms than their protected colleagues.

7.4 SEGMENTATION AMONG FIRMS

During the period of economic reform, increased market competition from various sources squeezed the profits of state-owned enterprises (SOEs). The budgetary implications of rising subsidies to loss-making firms and falling revenues from profit-making firms, together with the prospect of entry to the World Trade Organization, forced the Chinese Government to initiate, and later to accelerate, the reform of the SOE sector. One of the principal elements in the reform was to accord more autonomy to the SOEs, for instance in terms of prices and products, so allowing them greater freedom to engage with the market. As a result, some enterprises have been successful in making profits and others have failed.

Management has also acquired greater powers to determine the wages of employees. The various pressures on managers may well have caused the wage level to be linked to the profitability of the enterprise. At the same time, governments have reduced the subsidies to enterprises incurring losses, so making it difficult for loss-makers to pay even contracted wages. These changes can be expected to have created or strengthened a linkage between the wages of workers and the performance and profitability of their firms.

In a competitive labour market workers can be expected to move, whenever possible, from low-paying to high-paying employers. Wage differences, whether based on the profitability of firms, the employment status of workers, or spatial differences in labour markets, should be ironed out by labour mobility and labour market competition. However, we have shown in Section 7.2 that the mobility of urban workers from one employer to another, whether in different localities or the same, remains extremely low. Thus large and persistent wage segmentation across firms is possible, and it may even have grown as enterprise reform progressed.

In this section we examine how enterprise profitability affects the wages of workers, and how the relationship has changed during the period of most rapid enterprise reform in the late 1990s. We are reporting the work of Knight and Li (2004).

7.4.1 Hypotheses

There is a growing literature on the relationship between a firm's profitability and its workers' wage level. Krueger and Summers (1987, 1988), Blanchflower, Oswald, and Garrett (1990), Nickell and Wadhwani (1990), Christophides and Oswald (1992), Blanchflower, Oswald, and Sanfrey (1996), and Teal (1996) have all suggested that rent-sharing takes place. Their evidence is drawn from various countries. The causal explanation of the relationship between wages and profits could be either rent-sharing or efficiency wage-setting. The standard efficiency wage argument is that profit-maximizing firms increase the wage in order to raise productivity by inducing greater effort, normally because a higher wage improves the morale of workers or because it serves to discipline workers now keener to retain their jobs. Whereas a rise in profits does not alter the efficiency wage in the standard efficiency wage model, the payment of an efficiency wage can be expected to raise profits. However, Krueger and Summers (1988) argue that rent-sharing cannot be separated from efficiency wages, for two reasons. First, if a firm generates rents, then a failure to share them with its employees may result in their withdrawal of cooperation. Secondly, in an efficiency wage environment, rent-sharing is less expensive for firms if an increase in the efficiency wage above the optimum is partly offset by an efficiency gain. Thus, the possibility of rent-sharing may increase the efficiency wage and the possibility of efficiency wage gains may increase rent-sharing.

The potential endogeneity of the profits variable in the wage equation thus poses a problem of identifying the causal effect of profits on wages. The problem is generally solved in the literature by instrumenting the profits variable with one that is exogenous to wages but is well correlated with profits. In the absence of efficiency wage effects—given that an increase in the wage decreases profits, *ceteris paribus*—simultaneity bias reduces the estimated coefficient on profits; in the presence of efficiency wage effects, the direction of bias depends on the relative slopes of the two curves (see Maddala 2001: 369–71).

In China the association between enterprise reform and wages has been examined at an early stage of economic reform. In the 1980s, basic wages were strictly laid down but enterprises had some discretion in the payment of bonuses from their retained profits. Using enterprise-level data for that period, Hay et al. (1994) obtained a significant positive coefficient on firm profitability in their wage equation, Groves et al. (1994) found that profit retention increased the bonus per employee, and Hussain and Zhuang (1994) similarly found that the bonus rose with profitability in profit-making enterprises (PMEs). These results are consistent with profit-sharing behaviour. However, Groves et al. (1994) also estimated bonus payments to raise firm productivity, and Zhuang and Xu (1996) obtained a positive coefficient on the bonus in their profit equation: these results were interpreted as evidence of efficiency wage-setting. Jefferson et al. (1999), using a slightly later data set, found evidence both that the bonus increased profits and that profits increased labour productivity. Thus the evidence from these early enterprise-level surveys—with their panel data generally enabling instrumenting by means of lagged variables—is consistent with there being two-way causation in the initial reform period, when managers lacked sticks and held only one carrot, in the form of the bonus.

In the early stages of Chinese SOE reform there was little managerial autonomy. Under the initial contract system, in the late 1980s and the early 1990s, the contract was made between the *danwei* as a whole—both workers and managers—and the government. The enterprise was like a cooperative, and managers had little autonomy, for example, over the level of employment or the dismissal of workers. It was therefore pointless to pay wages as a disciplinary device. However, relating wages to profits would have provided a group incentive to workers. Later, as the contract became one made between managers and the government, managers acquired rather more autonomy. The environment now provided some incentive for worker effort, especially under the redundancy programme of the late 1990s. Nevertheless, it remained plausible that workers would expect to share *danwei* profits and would lose some motivation if this did not happen, that is, the efficiency wage may well have remained a positive function of enterprise profitability.

We sought a theoretical framework for our analysis. It was not to be found in the standard bargaining game in which the firm maximizes profits and workers value the wage and employment (e.g. Nickell and Wadhwani 1990): In China managers need not maximize profits and may instead promote the interests of their workers. Nor was it to be found in a model of the cooperative enterprise, with its prediction that collective firms restrict employment in the interests of their worker members (Ward 1958). The State was a crucial player in the game, and effectively took the employment decision. The authorities preferred unemployment to be shared and disguised within the enterprise rather than selective, open, and on the streets. It is generally acknowledged that until the late 1990s enterprises contained surplus labour.

A more promising framework is provided by an adaptation of the standard efficiency wage model. We start with the standard model. Assume that the output per head (y) responds as follows to the relative wage ($\pi - w$):

$$y = (\pi - w)^\lambda \tag{7.1}$$

where π is the efficiency wage, w the wage in the absence of efficiency wage effects, and λ represents the elasticity of output per worker in response to the relative wage. Using the equilibrium efficiency wage property for minimum wage cost per unit of output, and thus setting $\partial\pi/\pi = \partial y/y$, we derive the efficiency wage mark-up as:

$$(\pi - w)/\pi = \lambda \tag{7.2}$$

The higher is λ, the elasticity of response, the higher the firm's chosen wage mark-up.

Departing from the standard model, we introduce the assumption that the efficiency wage is responsive to the profit per worker of the firm in the absence of efficiency wage setting, denoted by s. Workers expect to be paid more when the firm is profitable, and apply less effort if they are not paid more:

$$y = (\pi - w)^{\lambda s} \tag{7.3}$$

It follows that

$$(\pi - w)/\pi = \lambda s \qquad (7.4)$$

Thus, the wage mark-up depends positively on the firm's profitability.[4] This provides a rationale for profit-sharing.

Consider a simple profit-sharing model. Assume that income per worker (π) is made up of the wage in the absence of profit-sharing and of efficiency wage-setting, and a fraction (α) of the firm's profit per worker (s):

$$\pi = w + \alpha s \qquad (7.5)$$

In an enterprise making a profit, $\alpha s > 0$, so that $\pi > w$, that is, employees of the enterprise share the profit. In one making a loss, $\alpha s < 0$, so that $\pi < w$, implying that its employees share the loss. Differences in income per worker depend on the levels of profits and losses per worker and on the profit-sharing rate. The value of α may differ according to whether a profit or loss is made. The presence of surplus workers implies that more workers have to share the profit available for distribution. It also means that laying-off surplus workers raises the income of each worker who remains. Given this mechanism, it is understandable that the enterprises with redundant workers may not experience resistance from the majority of their workers in implementing a redundancy policy, at least once it is known, or can be predicted, who will be laid-off. The majority can expect benefits from this policy, at the expense of the minority being laid-off.

7.4.2 The data

The data used in this section are from the two urban household surveys of IE, CASS 1995 and IE, CASS 1999. These were not enterprise-based surveys, and so only a little information is available on the employers of the sampled workers. However, workers were questioned, inter alia, about the sector, ownership status, and the profitability of their employer. There were slightly different questions regarding the profitability of the work unit in the 1995 and 1999 surveys. In the former, the question is: 'Was your enterprise making a loss in 1995?'. We can thus group workers into loss-making enterprises (LMEs) and profit-making enterprises (PMEs). In the 1999 survey the question offers three answers, that is, '(1) making a loss (or on the edge of bankruptcy), (2) making marginal profit, and (3) making high profit'. We can thus group workers into two, as we do for the 1995 sample, or into three, according to their answers.

One could argue that a worker's perception of profitability may be a misleading guide to the actual state of the firm. This argument is not valid because of the special nature of Chinese SOEs, whose employees account for nearly 80 per cent of the sample. On the one hand, SOE managers have no incentive to block information on profitability from their workers, and on the other hand, they are required by governments to provide open financial information to their workers. It is laid down that 'Managers must provide a financial report to the annual conference of workers' representatives in the enterprise'.[5]

Whereas 30 per cent of workers reported working in LMEs in 1995, the figure reached 38 per cent in 1999. The average wage in 1995 was 27 per cent higher in PMEs than in LMEs, and in 1999, 56 per cent higher. Over the four years the average LME wage increased by only 15 per cent in real terms, whereas the average PME wage was up by 41 per cent. There was very little difference in mean characteristics between the two groups of workers other than in wages. Table 7.8 defines and labels the variables, and provides descriptive statistics.

7.4.3 How do profits affect the wage level?

In order to standardize the wage difference between the two groups of workers, we estimate wage functions in which PME and LME are treated as dummy variables (LME being the omitted category). There are two specifications for the 1999 wage function. In the first, two dummies regarding profitability are introduced to make a comparison with the 1995 wage function, and in the second, three dummies are introduced to examine the effect of the size of profits.

Although we explained above why workers are unlikely to misunderstand the profitability of their enterprises, we cannot rule out the possibility that workers will judge profitability by their own wages, nor that efficiency wage setting will raise profits. Accordingly, we need to test for the endogeneity of the dummy variables, PME and LME. The Hausman specification test is used here. The instruments chosen are whether the father is a party member and whether he is in a professional or managerial occupation. The results show that the residual term is not statistically significant, and thus cannot reject the null hypothesis that the profit variables are exogenous in the wage functions.[6]

Table 7.9 shows the estimated wage functions for 1995 and 1999. The dependent variable is the logarithm of monthly wages (expressed annually). The control variables include gender, work experience (in years), educational attainment, ownership of work unit, occupation, Communist Party membership, employment sector, and province. The results from the 1995 wage function show that the workers in PMEs on average earned wages 21 per cent more than those in LMEs,[7] *ceteris paribus*. The difference is striking. However, it is even more striking in 1999, being as large as 41 per cent. Furthermore, when profitability is specified as three dummies, we see a notable difference between workers in enterprises with marginal profit (with wages 37 per cent higher than in LMEs) and those in enterprises with high profit (with wages 78 per cent higher than in LMEs). The average standardized wage of the latter is thus 30 per cent higher than that of the former.

In order to explore the mechanisms by which profits affect wages, we estimated the equations of Table 7.9 for different province pairs and for different components of pay. We combined Beijing and Jiangsu to represent provinces in which economic reform had gone far, and we took Henan and Gansu to be provinces in which reform had lagged.[8] Our hypothesis was that wages are more sensitive to profits in the

TABLE 7.8. *Notation and descriptive statistics of the variables used for the analysis of profit-sharing, 1995 and 1999*

Name of variable	Notation	1995		1999	
		Mean	Standard deviation	Mean	Standard deviation
Firm making loss*	*ent1*	0.307	0.461	0.384	0.486
Firm making profits	*ent2*	0.693	0.461	0.616	0.486
Firm making marginal profits	*ent3*			0.527	0.499
Firm making large profits	*ent4*			0.089	0.284
Male	*sex1*	0.531	0.499	0.548	0.498
Female*	*sex2*	0.469	0.499	0.452	0.498
Years of work experience	*we*	19.760	9.414	20.139	8.742
Work experience squared	we^2	479.058	379.653	481.970	349.585
Four-year college education	*ed1*	0.039	0.194	0.053	0.224
2–3-year college education	*ed2*	0.116	0.320	0.175	0.380
Professional school education	*ed3*	0.143	0.351	0.138	0.345
Upper middle school education*	*ed4*	0.272	0.445	0.289	0.453
Lower middle school education	*ed5*	0.367	0.482	0.324	0.468
Primary school education or less	*ed6*	0.062	0.242	0.021	0.143
SOE	*own1*	0.779	0.415	0.774	0.419
UCE*	*own2*	0.190	0.392	0.139	0.346
Private enterprise or other	*own3*	0.014	0.119	0.086	0.281
Professional or technician	*occ1*	0.179	0.383	0.195	0.396
Enterprise manager	*occ2*	0.025	0.155	0.018	0.133
Division head	*occ3*	0.063	0.243	0.078	0.269
Clerk	*occ4*	0.166	0.372	0.141	0.348
Skilled	*occ5*	0.287	0.453	0.315	0.465
Unskilled*	*occ6*	0.211	0.408	0.236	0.425
Other	*occ7*	0.046	0.209	0.011	0.105
Party member	*par1*	0.199	0.399	0.258	0.438
Non-party member*	*par2*	0.801	0.399	0.741	0.438
Agricultural sector	*sec1*	0.024	0.154	0.051	0.219
Manufacturing*	*sec2*	0.574	0.494	0.459	0.498
Construction	*sec3*	0.041	0.198	0.063	0.242
Transportation and communication	*sec4*	0.059	0.235	0.122	0.327
Wholesale, retail, and food services	*sec5*	0.178	0.383	0.109	0.312
Real estate and social services	*sec6*	0.029	0.168	0.108	0.311
Health, education, culture, and public services	*sec7*	0.031	0.174	0.035	0.183
Finance and insurance	*sec8*	0.011	0.105	0.015	0.121
Government, party, and social organizations	*sec9*	0.012	0.109	0.007	0.086
Other sectors	*sec10*	0.040	0.195	0.032	0.177
Beijing	*prov1*	0.073	0.260	0.135	0.342
Liaoning*	*prov2*	0.121	0.326	0.200	0.400
Jiangsu	*prov3*	0.123	0.328	0.172	0.377
Henan	*prov4*	0.080	0.271	0.183	0.387
Sichuan	*prov5*	0.135	0.342	0.182	0.386
Gansu	*prov6*	0.044	0.206	0.128	0.334

Note: * Denotes the default dummy category in the wage function analysis.

Source: Knight and Li (2004: table 1), using the IE, CASS 1995 and IE, CASS 1999 surveys.

The Urban Labour Market

TABLE 7.9. *Earnings functions for urban residents, 1995 and 1999*

Independent variable	1995		1999			
			Specification I		Specification II	
	Estimate	*t*-value	Estimate	*t*-value	Estimate	*t*-value
Intercept	7.407	179.05***	7.370	134.74***	7.351	135.51***
ent2	0.187	12.33***	0.345	18.16***		
ent3					0.316	16.45***
ent4					0.576	16.79***
sex1	0.135	9.27***	0.117	6.25***	0.115	6.19***
we	0.058	21.29***	0.047	12.19***	0.049	12.81***
we^2	−0.001	−16.25***	−0.001	−8.46***	−0.001	−8.90***
ed1	0.137	3.60***	0.314	6.91***	0.297	6.57***
ed2	0.081	3.13***	0.147	4.98***	0.147	5.02***
ed3	0.029	1.22	0.069	2.29**	0.069	2.34**
ed5	−0.066	−3.64***	−0.049	−2.09**	−0.046	−1.97**
ed6	−0.210	−6.55***	−0.161	−2.54**	−0.164	−2.60***
own1	0.149	8.37***	0.214	8.03***	0.206	7.80***
own3	0.300	4.97***	0.331	8.41***	0.305	7.79***
occ1	0.147	5.81***	0.214	6.92***	0.206	6.72***
occ2	0.167	3.37***	0.121	1.68*	0.125	1.75**
occ3	0.164	4.80***	0.150	3.63***	0.136	3.32***
occ4	0.027	1.15	0.128	4.04***	0.127	4.04***
occ5	0.073	3.70***	0.107	4.26***	0.105	4.20***
occ7	0.000	−0.01	0.050	0.57	0.061	0.70
par1	0.067	3.44***	0.080	3.40***	0.080	3.46***
sec1	0.016	0.35	0.097	2.32*	0.101	2.43**
sec3	−0.032	−0.90	−0.002	−0.04	0.004	0.11
sec4	0.035	1.18	0.245	8.40***	0.222	7.65***
sec5	−0.052	−2.64**	0.068	2.17**	0.062	2.02**
sec6	−0.029	−0.69	0.246	8.06***	0.228	7.53***
sec7	−0.018	−0.43	0.122	2.43**	0.103	2.08**
sec8	0.223	3.38***	0.361	4.83***	0.350	4.73***
sec9	−0.064	−1.02	0.058	0.560	0.010	0.090
sec10	−0.330	−9.15***	−0.028	−0.540	−0.037	−0.710
Adj. R^2	0.290		0.361		0.373	
F-value	75.60		62.20		63.40	
Mean of dependent variable	8.539		8.881		8.881	
No. of observations	6,748		3,466		3,466	

Notes: The dependent variable is the logarithm of (annualized) monthly wages, expressed in 1995 prices. The earnings functions include a set of province dummy variables among the explanatory variables, but these are not reported. ***, **, and * denote statistical significance at 1%, 5%, and 10% levels, respectively. The omitted dummy variable categories are enterprise making a loss, female, upper middle school, urban collective sector, unskilled, non-party member, and manufacturing.

Source: Knight and Li (2004: table 3).

TABLE 7.10. *Coefficients on the profit variables in earnings functions for various components of earnings of urban residents, 1995 and 1999*

Earnings component	1995	1999		
		Specification I	Specification II	
	ent2	ent2	ent3	ent4
	(1)	(2)	(3)	(4)
Basic wage	0.080***	0.745***	0.714***	0.984***
Other income, *of which*:	0.384***	0.384***	0.316***	0.917***
Bonus	1.010***	0.737***	0.658***	1.350***
Subsidy	0.307***	0.267***	0.287***	0.113
Other	0.311***	−0.134	−0.166	0.117

Notes: The dependent variable is the logarithm of the relevant component of earnings, expressed in 1995 prices. The equation specification is the same as for Table 7.9. The omitted category is *ent1* (LMEs), columns (1) and (2) show the coefficients on *ent2* (PMEs), and columns (3) and (4) the coefficients on the dummies for firms making marginal profits and firms making large profits, respectively. *** Denotes statistical significance at the 1% level.

Source: Knight and Li (2004: table 4).

more reformed parts of the Chinese economy. However, there is no substantial or significant difference between the two pairs.

It is clear that in 1995 the profit-sensitive component of pay was not the basic wage but 'other income', especially the bonus (Table 7.10). Employers had more control over the bonus than over the basic wage. However, we find a different pattern for 1999. The basic wage was then highly sensitive to profit-making (the coefficient of PME), and more so than 'other income'. This is partly because employers had greater discretion than before over the basic wage, and partly because some LMEs were unable to pay even their contracted basic wages. Consistent with this interpretation, the difference in basic wages between loss-making firms and those making marginal profits was greater than the difference between marginally and highly profitable firms. There was a wider disparity in other income between high and marginal profit-making than between the latter and loss-making. This suggests that a rise in profits encourages profitable firms to increase the most discretionary form of remuneration—the bonus—rather than basic pay.

It is arguable that our use of the (annualized) monthly wage as the dependent variable instead of the hourly wage might exaggerate the difference in pay between PMEs and LMEs. For instance, it is plausible that longer hours are worked in more profitable firms. It was not possible either to standardize for hours worked or to predict wage per hour in the wage equations owing to the lack of data on hours in 1999. However, the information is available for 1995, and this is used as a check. In fact, workers in PMEs were employed for 2,200 h on average in that year, and those in LMEs for 2,199 h—only one hour less. The introduction of hours worked into the wage equation produced a positive and significant coefficient on hours, as expected. However, the coefficient on *ent2* (the premium on employment in a profitable enterprise) was barely altered, being 0.186 ($t = 11.67$) compared with 0.187 ($t = 12.33$) in Table 7.9. Similarly, when the wage per hour was made the dependent variable, the coefficient was 0.190 ($t = 11.39$). Our results are robust.

7.4.4 How are profits distributed among workers?

To explore how profits are allocated to workers, Knight and Li (2004) introduced interaction terms between the profitability variable and the other explanatory variables. Among all the interaction terms attempted, only two sets have significant coefficients in the 1995 function. These are interaction with work experience, *ent2.we*, and its squared term, *ent2.we*^{2}, and with ownership, *ent2.own$_i$*. From Table 7.11 it can be observed that the introduction of the interaction terms dramatically changes the coefficient on the profit variable in 1995. The coefficient becomes negative and insignificant, which implies that the interaction terms are crucial. The interaction coefficients indicate that profits in PMEs were distributed to reward work experience in 1995. Since years of employment experience are the same as years of tenure for the great majority of workers, it seems that tenure, that is, length of service in the firm, was the major criterion for profit-sharing. The other interaction terms suggest that, for workers in SOEs and private enterprises, the profitability of the enterprise made a greater difference (6 and 32 per cent more, respectively) than for workers in the omitted ownership category, urban collective enterprises (UCEs). Although these coefficients are significant only at the 10 per cent level, they hint that profit-sharing was more important in SOEs and private enterprises than in collectives.

Looking at the coefficients of the interaction terms in the 1999 wage function, we find a different pattern. None of the coefficients is statistically significant, neither in specification I nor in specification II. Seniority was no longer important to profit distribution in 1999, nor was ownership. As a result, the coefficients on the profitability variables alone remain very similar to those in Table 7.9: They are highly significant and large in size. The effect of profits on wages is uncorrelated with any of the other determinants of wages. These results suggest that the profits being shared by PMEs were more equally distributed among their employees in 1999 than in 1995.

7.4.5 Does profit-sharing affect wage inequalities?

Does profit-sharing tend to widen wage inequalities? Knight and Li (2004) decomposed the difference between the two types of workers in average wage growth over the four years. This decomposition requires the estimation of wage functions for the two groups separately. This can involve a selectivity problem, implying that the coefficients in the wage equations are biased. The Heckman selection model

TABLE 7.11. *Earnings functions for urban residents, containing interaction terms, 1995 and 1999*

Independent variable	1995		1999			
			Specification I		Specification II	
	Estimate	*t*-value	Estimate	*t*-value	Estimate	*t*-value
Intercept	7.577	123.87***	7.403	92.13***	7.402	92.95***
ent2	−0.049	−0.77	0.423	4.466***		
ent3					0.382	4.09***
ent4					0.511	2.99***
sex1	0.135	9.26***	0.115	6.16***	0.114	6.16***
we	0.043	8.32***	0.054	8.42***	0.054	8.46***
we^2	−0.001	−6.00***	−0.001	−6.12***	−0.001	−6.13***
ed1	0.147	3.72***	0.312	6.85***	0.295	6.52***
ed2	0.082	3.18***	0.149	5.03***	0.148	5.05***
ed3	0.031	1.33	0.069	2.31**	0.068	2.29**
ed5	−0.063	−3.50***	−0.050	−2.11**	−0.047	−2.01**
ed6	−0.211	−6.57***	−0.164	−2.58**	−0.169	−2.67***
own1	0.107	3.66***	0.189	4.98***	0.188	4.99***
own3	0.075	0.47	0.239	3.53***	0.239	3.55***
occ1	0.146	5.76***	0.211	6.82***	0.206	6.72***
occ2	0.163	3.30***	0.120	1.68*	0.124	1.74*
occ3	0.162	4.75***	0.151	3.66***	0.137	3.34***
occ4	0.025	1.09	0.126	4.00***	0.124	3.97***
occ5	0.072	3.66***	0.105	4.19***	0.103	4.13***
occ7	−0.003	−0.07	0.046	0.53	0.062	0.71
par1	0.068	3.346***	0.079	3.37***	0.079	3.39***
sec1	0.013	0.29	0.097	2.31**	0.100	2.40**
sec3	−0.032	−0.92	−0.001	−0.02	0.004	0.10
sec4	0.037	1.24	0.244	8.36***	0.225	7.69***
sec5	−0.051	−2.58**	0.061	1.94**	0.057	1.82*
sec6	−0.028	−0.68	0.241	7.89***	0.228	7.51***
sec7	−0.014	−0.35	0.119	2.38**	0.102	2.05**
sec8	0.226	3.42***	0.353	4.72***	0.343	4.63***
sec9	−0.060	−0.95	0.055	0.53	0.018	0.17
sec10	−0.328	−9.09***	−0.034	−0.64	−0.043	−0.83
ent2.we	0.021	3.56***	−0.010	−1.27		
ent2.we^2	0.000	−3.38***	0.000	0.85		
ent2.own1	0.062	1.73*	0.050	0.97		
ent2.own3	0.280	1.63*	0.141	1.70		
ent3.we					−0.008	−0.95
ent3.we^2					0.000	0.64
ent3.own1					0.037	0.72
ent3.own3					0.057	0.68
ent4.we					0.002	0.17
ent4.we^2					0.000	−0.33

TABLE 7.11. (*continued*)

Independent variable	1995		1999			
			Specification I		Specification II	
	Estimate	*t*-value	Estimate	*t*-value	Estimate	*t*-value
ent4.own1					0.052	0.38
ent4.own3					0.291	1.82*
Adj. R^2	0.296		0.362		0.373	
F-value	68.70		55.50		51.30	
Mean of dependent variable	8.539		8.881		8.881	
No. of observations	6,748		3,466		3,466	

Notes: The dependent variable is the logarithm of the annualized monthly wages, expressed in 1999 prices. ***, **, and * denote statistical significance at the 1%, 5%, and 10% levels, respectively. The omitted dummy variable categories are enterprise making loss, female, upper middle school, urban collective sector, unskilled, non-party member, manufacturing, Liaoning province, and interaction terms *ent2.own2* and *ent3.own2*.

Source: Knight and Li (2004: table 5).

was used to test for selectivity bias. The channel of finding the job (*jobc* = 1 if job was assigned by the government, and *jobc* = 0 if job was obtained through other channels) was chosen as the exclusion restriction variable. This exclusion restriction variable was valid for 1995, being significant in the selection model but not in the wage equations. A probit equation was estimated to predict whether a worker was employed in a profit-making or loss-making firm. The inverse Mills ratio (λ) so obtained was then included in the wage functions. However, the estimation did not yield statistically significant coefficients on the λ terms. This implies that selectivity was not a problem. When the same exclusion restriction variable was applied in the 1999 estimation, its coefficient was not significant in the selection model. Other variables were experimented with as exclusion restriction variables but none proved to be valid.

The possibility of sample selection bias was investigated in further ways. First, we restricted the sample to workers who had been employed in their enterprises for more than five years in the 1995 survey and for more than ten years in the 1999 survey. Before the 1990s, jobs were mainly assigned through official channels and there was little freedom for workers to find jobs for themselves. The wage functions showed that the coefficient of the profitability variable fell slightly, from 0.345 to 0.327 in the 1999 equation (specification I) but rose slightly, from 0.187 to 0.205, in the 1995 equation. The second test was to examine the extent of mobility in the urban labour market. Only 18.5 per cent of workers in the 1999 survey had changed their jobs since first entering wage employment, and this proportion does not differ significantly between workers in PMEs and LMEs

(19.1 versus 17.3 per cent). Mobility is likely to be even lower in 1995 but there is no equivalent question in the 1995 survey. The extreme immobility of workers helps to explain why sample selectivity appears not to be a problem, that is, the sorting of workers into profitable and non-profitable firms by unobserved 'ability' is negligible.

7.5 CONCLUSIONS

Enterprise reform in urban China had involved greater managerial autonomy, including more decentralized wage-setting. In principle this could have produced a more competitive labour market, in which the 'law of one price' increasingly prevailed. However, the process was hampered by several factors. One was the lack of labour mobility from one employer to another by urban workers, which we examined in Section 7.2. Had employees in jobs with low wages been willing and able to move to jobs with high wages, the resultant adjustments in labour supply should have generated market forces bringing wages closer together. Yet another factor was the differences in employment rights and obstacles among different groups of workers, which we examined in Section 7.3. Greater equality in access to and competition for jobs would have reduced this wage segmentation by employment status. Yet another factor was the structure of managerial incentives. Even in the late 1990s, it was not necessary for firms to be profit-maximizing, and they were apparently willing to hand over some of their profits to their workers. This profit-sharing, associated with the nature of the *danwei*, contributed to growing wage segmentation among firms, as shown in Section 7.4.

Urban residents have relatively long job duration by international standards: The average job duration was 19.9 years and as many as 78 per cent of workers had only one job. However, that situation was changing as economic reform proceeded: We found an almost monotonic increase in mobility standardizing for duration of employment. The voluntary mobility rate rose over time, and the involuntary mobility rate was far higher in 1995–9 than in the previous five-year periods. Most of the mobility, especially if it was voluntary, took place within the, preferred, state sector. Such voluntary mobility as occurred appeared to raise wages. The evidence suggests that home ownership, human capital, and social capital are the characteristics that permit or encourage voluntary mobility and thus facilitate the emergence of a market for labour. By contrast, the high returns to seniority is one of the factors that deter job search.

The extreme immobility of most urban workers is the outstanding feature of our analysis. This presents an obstacle to the achievement of a functioning labour market in urban China. Job stickiness begets wage stickiness. The extent of job mobility, or of expected job mobility, from one employer to another has not been sufficient to iron out wage differences among firms or sectors of the economy. By contrast, the relatively high mobility observed among rural–urban migrants suggests that market forces can function in this segment of the urban labour market.

However, that degree of mobility—to some extent artificially imposed on migrants from the rural areas by urban institutions and rules—may well be inimical to human capital formation.

The relatively privileged position of urban workers in China was challenged in the 1990s first by a great wave of migrants and then by a programme of mass lay-offs within the state sector. Both developments might be expected to act as restraining forces on wages for urban workers and possibly to usher in an era of labour market competition. However, the evidence was more consistent with the creation of a 'three-tier' labour market. The highest-paid tier—corresponding to labour economists' concept of a 'primary' labour market—consists of those urban workers who were not made redundant during the 1990s. Even after standardizing for their personal characteristics, the group are paid more than either migrants or urban workers who have been re-employed after having been made redundant. It is less clear how migrants and re-employed urban workers stand in relation to each other. Their average wage rates—both standardized and unstandardized— are quite similar. However, they appear to be paid according to rather different wage structures, making it unlikely that they can be regarded as jointly forming a single 'secondary' labour market.

The wage structure for non-retrenched urban workers, estimated using the 1999 urban household survey, corresponds well in most respects with the wage structure estimated from the 1995 urban household survey (Chapter 3). However, the wage structures for migrants and for retrenched urban workers differ both from that of non-retrenched urban workers and from each other. For instance, for both these tiers, there are no wage premia for Communist Party membership or for employment in central SOEs. One might be tempted to ascribe this to the effect of greater competition in eroding wage differentials not related to productivity. However, exposure to greater competition has not prevented the emergence of increased gender discrimination. Where the migrants and the re-employed workers differ, however, is in wage structure by education and occupation. For the re-employed there appear to be no returns to education and limited occupational differentials, suggesting that the market they face is a tough one that is not working well for them. Despite the difficulty of interpreting residual differences—which we acknowledged—the evidence suggests that the urban labour market in 1999 comprised three tiers, created because the three groups of workers differ in the institutional arrangements that they face and thus in the extent to which they are open to market forces.

The combination of low labour mobility and profit-sharing may explain why we found a considerable difference in (standardized) mean wages between profit-making and loss-making firms. Despite the loosening of labour market policies and the redundancy programme of the late 1990s, it is evident that labour market segmentation among firms became stronger over the period. The relationship between profits and wages also contributed to a widening of wage inequalities over the late 1990s. Not only were employees of loss-making firms paid less than those of profit-making firms in 1995 but also their wages grew less rapidly over the subsequent four years, and among them it was particularly the unskilled workers with low-paying characteristics who fell behind.

Our interpretation of the wage–profit nexus is that managers, if they have profits, are willing to share them with their workers, and that some loss-making firms are unable to pay even contracted wages. We favour the rent-sharing, as opposed to the conventional efficiency wage, explanation for two reasons. First, we were unable to reject the exogeneity of profits in the wage equation. Secondly, the lay-offs of the late 1990s should have acted as a disciplinary device for employees, so reducing the equilibrium efficiency wage, whereas the sensitivity of the wage to profits actually rose. In any case, it is plausible in Chinese conditions that failure to share profits can lead to the withdrawal of cooperation by workers. Given this threat, the efficiency wage is a positive function of profits: Profit-sharing and efficiency wage effects are intertwined, and their separation would be artificial. This intertwining reflects the distinctive characteristics of the Chinese *danwei*. To some extent it remains a social institution with a set of managerial objectives and worker attitudes that set it apart from an enterprise in the Western sense.

To summarize this chapter: What has held back progress towards a functioning labour market? At the conceptual level, the underlying problem is that market-equilibrating wage movements have been impeded. Where there is excess supply, the undercutting of wages does not generally happen. Subject to a profit constraint, enterprises support their (generally long-standing) employees. Indeed, arrangements and incentives within the *danwei* encourage managers to share profits with their workers. Real wages rose rapidly during the period of retrenchment policy and high urban unemployment, and only the workers who lost their jobs felt the forces of competition. In the case of excess demand, there is too little voluntary mobility of labour for employers generally to use wage policy as a recruitment device. A reason for the lack of voluntary mobility has been the high private cost of changing jobs, associated with the social welfare provision—such as housing, healthcare, and pensions—that have been tied to the employer. Thus a fully functioning labour market waits on continuing enterprise and social welfare reforms.

NOTES

1. It is necessary to confine the analysis to those who changed jobs once as we have information only on the last job move. The last job of those who changed jobs more than once would have been the most recent. If these workers were included the results would be biased towards more recent periods. Fortunately, of those who moved at all, more than two-thirds had done so only once.
2. For instance, a worker expecting to be dismissed may leave voluntarily beforehand, and a worker wanting to leave may take advantage of a redundancy programme.
3. Data on hours worked are available for migrants but not for urban residents, whose hours are generally standard: their monthly wage is calculated on the basis of 22 eight-hour days.
4. This account of the efficiency wage model is adapted from Layard, Nickell, and Jackman (1991: 151–61).
5. See *The Outline of Enterprise Management in the Ninth Five-year Plan*, issued by the State Economic Trade Commission, February 1996.

6. The instrument is significant at the 5% level in the first-stage equation and the first-stage residual has a *t*-value of under 0.5 in the second. A systematic search for identifying instruments was made but—the (past) allocation of workers to (current) profit-making or loss-making firms being a fairly random process—no other variables could be found.
7. Derived as $\exp(\beta) - 1$, where β is the coefficient.
8. Beijing and Jiangsu average sixth and Henan and Gansu seventeenth in the marketization index for China's provinces created by Fan, Wang, and Zhang (2001).

REFERENCES

Appleton, Simon, John Knight, Lina Song, and Qingjie Xia (2004). 'Contrasting paradigms: segmentation and competitiveness in the formation of the Chinese labour market', *Journal of Chinese Economics and Business Studies*, 2, 3: 185–205.

Blanchflower, D., A. Oswald, and M. Garrett (1990). 'Insider power in wage determination', *Economica*, 57, 226: 143–70.

——————, and P. Sanfrey (1996). 'Wages, profits and rent-sharing', *Quarterly Journal of Economics*, 111, 1: 227–51.

Christophides, L. and A. Oswald (1992). 'Real wage determination and rent-sharing in collective bargaining agreements', *Quarterly Journal of Economics*, 107, 3: 985–1002.

Fallick, Bruce C. (1996). 'A review of recent empirical literature on displaced workers', *Industrial and Labor Relations Review*, 50, 1: 5–16.

Fan Gang, Xiaolu Wang, and Liwen Zhang (2001). 'Marketization index for China's provinces', Beijing: National Economic Research Institute, mimeo.

Farber, Henry S. (1999). 'Mobility and stability: the dynamics of job change in labor markets', in Ashenfelter, Orley and David Card (eds) *Handbook of Labor Economics*, vol. 3B, ch. 37, Amsterdam: North Holland.

Gregory, M. and R. Jukes (2002). 'Unemployment and subsequent earnings: estimating scarring among British men 1984–94' *Economic Journal*, 111, 475: 607–25.

Groves, Theodore, Y. Hong, J. McMillen, and B. Naughton (1994). 'Autonomy and incentives in Chinese state enterprises', *The Quarterly Journal of Economics*, 109, 1: 183–209.

Hay, Donald, Derek Morris, Guy Liu, and Shujie Yao (1994). *Economic Reform and State-owned Enterprises in China, 1979–1987*. Oxford and New York: Oxford University Press.

Hussain, Athar and Juzhong Zhuang (1994). 'Impact of reform on wage and employment determination in Chinese state enterprises, 1986–1991', Programme of Research into Economic Transformation and Public Finance, London School of Economics, EF/12, November.

Jefferson, G., I. Singh, A. Hu, and B. Wang (1999). 'Wage and employment behavior in Chinese industry', in Jefferson, Gary and Inderjit Singh (eds), *Enterprise Reform in China: Ownership, Transition, and Performance*, Oxford and New York: Oxford University Press for the World Bank, 171–96.

Knight, John and Shi Li (2004). 'Wages, profitability and labour market segmentation in China', *China Economic Review*, forthcoming.

—— and Linda Yueh (2004). 'Job mobility of residents and migrants in urban China', *Journal of Comparative Economics*, 32: 637–60.

Krueger, Alan and Lawerence Summers (1987). 'Reflections on the inter-industry wage structure', in Kevin Lang and Jonathan S. Leonard (eds), *Unemployment and the Structure of the Labor Market*, New York: Basil Backwell Inc.

———— (1988). 'Efficiency wages and the inter-industry wage structure', *Econometrica*, 56, 2: 259–93.

Layard, Richard, Stephen Nickell, and Richard Jackman (1991). *Unemployment. Macroeconomic Performance and the Labour Market*, Oxford: Oxford University Press.

Maddala, G.S. (2001). *Introduction to Econometrics*, 3rd edn, Chichester: Wiley.

Nickell, Stephen and Sushil Wadhwani (1990). 'Insider forces and wage determination', *Economic Journal*, 100 (June) 496–509.

———, P. Jones, and G. Quintini (2002). 'A picture of job insecurity facing British men', *Economic Journal*, 112, 476: 1–27.

Organisation for Economic Co-operation and Development (OECD) (1997). *Employment Outlook*, Paris: OECD.

Teal, Francis (1996). 'The size and sources of economic rents in a developing country manufacturing labour market', *Economic Journal*, 106, 437: 963–76.

Ward, Benjamin (1958). 'The firm in Illyria: market syndicalism', *American Economic Review*, 48, 4: 566–89.

Zhuang, Juzhong and Chenggang Xu (1996). 'Profit-sharing and financial performance in the Chinese state enterprises: evidence from panel data', *Economics of Planning*, 29, 3: 205–22.

PART III

THE RURAL LABOUR MARKET

8

Rural Labour Allocation

The process of economic development brings a transfer from agricultural to non-agricultural activities. However, the nature of this transfer can take various forms. One is permanent rural–urban migration. A second is the temporary migration of rural people to urban work, while keeping their rural households. A third is the development of local rural industry and services. In another dimension, agricultural households can either become specialist non-agricultural households or diversify into non-agricultural activities. Different developing countries display different forms. Some are characterized by the rapid urbanization of rural people, as in Latin American countries. In many African countries a process of circular migration for wage employment developed, but in recent years it has given way to more permanent urban settlement. In few countries has rural industrialization played a major role.

China may be unusual. During the commune and planning period, the population was sharply divided into rural peasants and urban workers. There was little scope for peasants to enter non-farm activities except to meet commune needs. Migration to the urban areas, whether temporary or permanent, was rigidly controlled and severely restricted. This situation changed after 1978, when the economic reforms were initiated. Alternatives to farming do, therefore, exist for China's 500 million rural workers.

One alternative is local non-farm employment, often referred to as 'rural industry', much of it taking the form of employment in township and village enterprises (TVEs). Under central planning, industry had been dominated by the state sector and confined to the urban areas. The state had used a policy of 'price scissors'—high manufacturing prices and low food procurement prices—to finance urban industrialization. During the period of rural economic reform, China experienced a remarkable growth of rural industry, which now employs more than 130 million workers. This development reflected market disequilibrium: Super-normal profits were there to be earned by competing against the inefficient, high price, state-owned enterprises (SOEs). With rural restrictions lifted, township and village cooperatives and private entrepreneurs responded to these opportunities. However, differences in initial resource endowments, in proximity to markets, and in access to capital and skills meant that the development of non-farm activities is very unevenly spread across the provinces, counties, and villages of rural China.

The second alternative to farming is migration for work away from home, normally in the towns and cities. Although severe restrictions on permanent urban settlement remain to this day, the rural and—after 1984—urban economic reforms brought some lifting of restrictions on the temporary migration of rural people for urban wage- and self-employment. City governments regulated the inflow of migrant labour to protect their residents. Nevertheless, the rapid growth of the urban economy compared to the slow growth of the urban-based labour force meant that there was an increasing urban demand for rural workers. Temporary migration expanded to meet that need. The 'floating population' of urban China cannot be measured accurately. However, on the basis of a nationally representative rural household survey contemporaneous with our own 1994 rural labour force survey, rural household members working in urban areas numbered about 40 million (Knight and Song 1999: 273).

The rural sector is generally considered to be characterized by surplus labour in relation to scarce land. China reached the limits of its land availability decades ago. The growth of population thus threatened to reduce the marginal product of labour and to depress rural living standards. Over the commune and planning period (1952–78) the area under cultivation rose by only 3 per cent, and cultivated land per rural worker fell by more than half. Over the period of economic reform (1978–2000) this trend continued, the fall exceeding a third. The rate at which labour could move away from farming was crucial for rural development. In fact the amount of cultivated land per farm worker continued to fall, by over a tenth, during the reform period.

How good are the opportunities for households, or their members, to enter non-farm activities? We shall present evidence suggesting that the average and marginal returns to rural labour differ greatly among activities, with the returns to non-farm activities exceeding those to farming. What prevents the further transfer of labour that would equalize returns at the margin? Is it a matter of preference, for instance the consequence of taste or of risk-spreading behaviour, or are there costs of transfer, or is there rationing of non-farm employment? How and why do the characteristics of workers in the various activities differ? Do these differences reveal whether workers, or their households, are freely able to choose their activities, or whether there is labour market segmentation? If there is segmentation, and rationing of non-farm employment, which workers, and households, are the fortunate ones? These questions are important for understanding rural development in China.

Our analysis is based on a rural labour force survey designed jointly by the authors and the Ministry of Labour, and conducted by the Ministry of Labour. We refer to it in Chapter 1 as MOL 1994. It covers 4,000 households in eight provinces, selected to be representative of the thirty-one provinces in China. The 500 households selected in each province were drawn from ten villages spread over three counties, the counties being the 25th, 50th, and 75th percentiles for the province in terms of income per capita. Within each county, villages were chosen by a stratified random procedure, the criteria for stratification being income per capita and distance from the county town. The survey gathered detailed information on each household and each of its workers, including data on income, economic activity, and time use. To obtain a representative national picture it is necessary to weight the sample in deriving sample means and proportions;[1] the unweighted sample is used in the econometric analyses.

Much of the information, including that on income, related to the year 1994. Households were defined according to *hukou*, that is, residence registration: The difficulty of changing one's place of *hukou* means that even workers who migrated regularly remained part of the household. The labour force was defined as those aged 16–65 and not in full-time education, and migrants those who worked outside the 'township' (a collection of villages) for more than 60 days. Income information related to the individual if the recipient could be identified but otherwise to the household. Income was categorized into farm and non-farm sources. Land was measured as land used, but the absence of land markets and the paucity of rental markets means that this was frequently the same as land allocated to the household, which was normally done by the village on a per-capita or per-worker basis.

This chapter draws on Knight and Song (2003). In Section 8.2 we present the basic facts about labour allocation by rural workers and their households. Section 8.3 contains attitudinal evidence from the survey suggesting that rural people perceive higher returns outside farming but face restricted opportunities to pursue non-farming activities. Our first test of segmentation involves the estimation of household income functions: In Section 8.4 we examine evidence on the returns to labour in different activities. The second test of segmentation is by means of the analysis of activity choice, exploring the determinants of non-farm employment (Section 8.5). An analysis of days worked on and off the farm— their interaction and their determinants—constitutes the third test (Section 8.6). Section 8.7 concludes.

8.2 LABOUR ALLOCATION BY WORKERS AND HOUSEHOLDS

In this section we describe the degree of labour specialization, diversification, and utilization by rural workers and households. We examine the number of days worked in farm and non-farm activities by workers and by households where, in this case, days are expressed per household worker (Table 8.1). Workers are generally more specialized than households: More than half the workers, but less than a third of the households, do no non-farm work. Since all rural households are allocated village land, 96 per cent of the households work the land; by contrast, 15 per cent of workers perform no farm work at all. Households and workers also differ in their degree of labour diversification. Only one-third of workers do both farm and non-farm work but two-thirds of households combine both activities. A third of households work more days off the farm than on it. With regard to labour utilization, the mean labour input by workers and by households (expressed per worker) is the same: 267 days a year. However, their frequency distributions

TABLE 8.1 *Degrees of labour specialization, diversification, and utilization, households and workers: weighted sample*

Percentage with	Household (per worker)	Worker
Degrees of labour specialization		
Non-farm work		
None	29	53
<30 days	35	55
<60 days	43	58
<90 days	51	60
Farm work		
None	4	15
<30 days	7	20
<60 days	14	27
<90 days	24	35
Degrees of labour diversification		
Both farm and non-farm work		
Any of each	67	33
>30 days	58	27
>60 days	43	18
>90 days	25	10
More farm than non-farm days worked	65	63
Less farm than non-farm days worked	35	37
Degrees of labour utilization		
≤90 days	1	5
91–180 days	10	14
181–270 days	39	27
271–330 days	32	30
>330 days	18	25
Mean days	267	267

Note: The number of farm days is calculated as $(D_b H_b + D_s H_s)/8$, where D_b, D_s are the number of days worked in the busy and the slack periods and H_b, H_s the number of hours worked per day in the busy and the slack periods.

Source: Of this and other tables in the chapter, Knight and Song (2003), using the MOL 1994 survey of the rural labour force.

are rather different. More workers than households put in few (<180) days, and many (>330) days, a year, that is, there is variation in labour inputs among the workers of a household. When households are classified according to sources of income, we see that almost all households (97 per cent) have some farming income. However, two-thirds (66 per cent) combine farm and non-farm sources of income. No less than 37 per cent of households obtained some income from migration, and 43 per cent from some form of village non-farm activity.

We conclude from this description that households are more diversified and less specialized than workers in their allocation of labour. This result is not surprising: It could arise even if households comprise randomly assorted individuals each making their own choices, as the variability of averages is always smaller than that of individual observations. However, there are two possible additional interpretations. First, the household may choose to spread risks: Income variability as well as income level can enter its utility function. If there is a corner solution, which would otherwise imply complete specialization by the household, risk-spreading means that this may no longer occur; and if there is not a corner solution, marginal products may remain apart if greater diversity reduces risks. Even if the household chooses to diversify, a worker can specialize, being insured against risk by household income-pooling. A worker will choose to be fully specialized if he has a preference for one activity, for instance if it pays more. Even if indifferent among activities, he may prefer specialization itself or experience increasing returns to labour in an activity, or be required to work full-time in it. The second additional explanation is that the greater specialization of workers than of households reflects the rationing of opportunities. Some working members of the household who want to enter non-farm activities may be unable to do so. If we were to assume that six days per week were available for work, the average surplus labour, on this arbitrary definition, would be 46 days, or 15 per cent of the time available. The fact that the average labour input represents only three-quarters of a full year, and the considerable dispersion of workers around that mean, suggest that there are limited opportunities for productive use of labour.

8.3 PERCEPTIONS OF THE RURAL PREDICAMENT

The survey contained various attitudinal questions, designed to discover the perceived aspirations of, and constraints on, rural households.[2] The answers have to be interpreted with caution because responses may contain different implicit assumptions and respondents may be poorly informed. They nevertheless provide pointers to the interpretation of quantitative evidence (Table 8.2).

A high proportion of households (75 per cent) considered that household labour was being fully used. This is of course consistent with the marginal product of labour being very low. Among those households whose labour was not fully used, the average time put in by a worker was 240 days; for the rest it was 265 days. Less than a third of households (31 per cent) wanted to increase the size of their farms. Yet even fewer households (25 per cent) reported that their farm income could be raised without an increase in farm land. Among the majority who did not want a larger farm, the major problems cited were the low profitability of farming (41 per cent) and the low returns to marginal farm inputs (29 per cent). It seems that farming was simply not an attractive activity.

Households were generally in favour (71 per cent) of having various sources of income, largely (79 per cent) because it would provide higher income rather

TABLE 8.2 *Worker preferences and opportunities for labour allocation: weighted sample*

1 Was household labour fully used in 1994?	
Yes (%)	74.9
2 How many days worked per worker?	
If no to (1)	240
If yes to (1)	265
3 Is the household hoping to increase its farmland?	
Yes (%)	31.2
4 Can household farm income be raised without increasing land?	
Yes (%)	25.8
Possible but difficult (%)	19.8
No (%)	41.7
Do not know (%)	12.7
5 *If no to (3)*, why not?	
No profit in farming (%)	41.2
Low returns to marginal inputs (%)	29.1
Other	29.7
6 Should the household have various sources of income?	
Yes (%)	70.8
7 *If yes*, why?	
Higher income (%)	79.4
Less risk (%)	19.0
Other (%)	1.6
8 Is the non-farm income of your household too low?	
Yes (%)	66.1
9 *If yes to (8)*, why?	
Lack of capital (%)	59.8
Lack of skills (%)	14.8
Lack of opportunities (%)	15.4
Lack of social contacts (%)	5.7
Other (%)	4.2
10 Does your household plan to increase its *local* non-farm income?	
Yes (%)	32.3
11 *If yes to (10)*, how?	
Seek local wage employment (%)	29.6
Open new business (%)	27.3
Expand existing business (%)	25.7
Other (%)	
12 Does your household want to increase migration activity?	
Yes (%)	35.3
No (%)	54.7
Do not know (%)	9.0

TABLE 8.2 *(continued)*

13 *If yes to (12)*, why have you not done so?	
No contacts (%)	35.5
Lack of information (%)	25.0
Too much farm work (%)	21.5
No jobs despite contacts (%)	13.4
Other (%)	4.6
14 *If no to (12)*, why not?	
Have not considered migration (%)	44.8
Migration is too insecure (%)	16.8
Limited net gain (%)	14.6
Costs and difficulties of travel (%)	8.9
Migrant work is too hard (%)	7.8
Other (%)	7.1
15 What are the main difficulties you face in trying to improve household income and employment?	
Lack of capital (%)	50.3
Lack of labour (%)	15.8
Lack of skills (%)	9.9
Lack of jobs (%)	8.3
Policy constraints (%)	7.3
Lack of information (%)	5.8
Other (%)	2.6
16 Do you wish to receive training in new skills?	
Yes (%)	71.2
17 *If yes to (16)*, which skills?	
Farming (%)	27.4
Artisan (%)	47.1
Service (%)	13.9
Non-manual service (%)	11.5
18 Is it difficult to get training?	
Yes (%)	62.4
19 *If yes to (18)*, what are the difficulties?	
Cannot afford training (%)	42.8
No suitable training courses (%)	22.4
No time to learn (%)	18.3
Not educated enough (%)	10.4
Other (%)	6.1

than spread risk (19 per cent). The great majority (66 per cent) reported that the non-farm income of the household was too low. The main obstacle cited by these households was lack of capital (60 per cent), followed by lack of opportunities and of skills (each 15 per cent). A third of households (32 per cent) aspired to increase their local non-farm income, mainly by seeking local wage employment (mentioned by 30 per cent of these), opening new businesses (27 per cent), or expanding existing businesses (26 per cent). Migration is the other possible source of non-farm income: 36 per cent of households wanted to increase migration activity. The reasons they gave for not yet having done so were lack of contacts (36 per cent), of information (25 per cent), and of jobs even when they had the necessary contacts (13 per cent). However, 22 per cent of the would-be migrant households could not spare the farm labour—suggesting that indivisibilities are important for some households. Most households did not want to enter or expand migration. Among the reasons cited were the insecurity of migration (17 per cent), the costs and difficulties of travel (9 per cent), and the hard work (8 per cent). Many (45 per cent) had simply not considered migration—suggesting a lack either of interest or of information. Only a few (15 per cent) gave as their reason the limited net gain.

When households were asked for the main constraint on improving their income and employment, they stressed lack of capital (50 per cent), of labour (16 per cent), and of skills (10 per cent). The skills most in demand were artisanal, such as electrician, driver, and builder (47 per cent) and new farming skills (27 per cent). The great majority of respondents (71 per cent) wanted to receive training but many (62 per cent) felt it was hard to get. The most commonly cited difficulties were inability to pay (43 per cent)—suggesting that skill formation is limited by its high price or by imperfect capital markets—and lack of suitable training courses (22 per cent)—implying missing markets.

Households were divided into four quarters according to income per capita and into three activity types (farming-only, with migrants, and with village industry workers). The most interesting differences are shown in Table 8.3. As expected, there is a monotonic rise with income in the percentage of households that were satisfied or very satisfied with their production structure, their income level and their employment, and a lower percentage of farming-only households were in this category than those with non-farm activities. The poorest households were the least likely to use their household labour fully, and the most likely to want to increase their farm land, and by more mu on average; as were the farming-only households. It is interesting that the farming-only households particularly wanted additional farming activities, that households containing migrants were keenest on more migration, and that households with local non-farm activities were keenest on more of such employment. These results may reflect revealed preference, albeit constrained; but aspirations may well be influenced by what people know about and what they think is feasible. It was the poorest, and the non-farm, households that most commonly complained of too little non-farm income and attributed this to the lack of capital. Desire for more migration was most common among the poorest households and those that already possessed migrants. These two groups were also held back by lack of contacts for migration. The poorest households were the keenest to learn more skills, and the most likely to want farming skills. However, they were the least willing to pay for training, and the most likely to cite the cost of training as their reason for this.

TABLE 8.3 *Attitudinal response, according to household income and activity type: weighted sample*

Percentage of households	Income quartile				Activity type		
	Poorest	Second	Third	Richest	Farming only	With migrants	With local non-farm workers
Satisfied or very satisfied with:							
Household production structure	46	62	64	68	60	68	73
Household income level	39	43	47	51	42	47	58
Household employment	52	59	61	61	56	67	69
Household labour not fully used	22	17	20	21	21	16	20
Hopes to increase farmland	44	35	26	26	33	27	25
If yes, size of increase (mu)	1.9	1.6	0.7	0.8	1.4	0.7	0.6
Households should have various sources of income	76	70	70	69	71	68	75
If yes, which additional source?							
Farming	46	35	27	28	37	25	23
Own business	9	13	16	17	13	17	21
Village industry employment	7	5	6	6	6	4	8
Migration	6	9	7	7	6	12	4
Household non-farm income is too small	75	67	62	64	71	58	54
If yes, due to lack of capital	53	40	38	34	43	34	29
Household wants more migration	41	40	34	34	34	52	27
If yes, prevented by lack of contacts	18	14	12	11	12	18	11
Difficulty in raising income and employment							
Lack of capital	55	49	51	45	52	43	46
Wants to learn more skills	56	50	44	51	49	54	51
If yes, in farming	32	24	14	19	24	13	10
Would be willing to pay for training	45	51	46	59	48	56	63
If not, cannot afford training	36	30	23	19	26	28	21

The picture that emerges from the attitudinal evidence is imprecise but suggestive. Households generally want to diversify their economic activities further. However, migration is restricted by lack of contacts, information, and opportunities, and local non-farm activities by lack of capital, skills, contacts, and opportunities. The limited opportunities which many rural households face can be interpreted within a private cost–benefit framework, in which imperfect information, risk-aversion, transaction costs, opportunity costs, and capital market imperfections all figure. Nevertheless, some of the evidence is also consistent with the rationing of opportunities at existing prices.

8.4 THE RETURNS TO FARMING AND NON-FARMING ACTIVITIES

We wish to test the hypothesis that labour markets within the activity set facing rural workers are segmented. Our direct test is to compare the returns to labour across activities: Are there higher returns in non-farming than in farming? In an economy characterized by competitive labour markets the marginal returns to each activity tend to be equalized. They may differ in equilibrium, however, because of compensating payments for differences in the attractiveness of activities or because there are costs of transferring between activities.

It is possible to estimate the number of days worked in agricultural activities (broadly defined) and in non-agricultural activities by each household, and the income derived from them. The resultant income per day is no less than 49 per cent higher in non-farm than in farm activities (Table 8.5). Non-farm activities are clearly much more remunerative on average. However, the more relevant concept for labour allocation is the marginal returns to household labour in the two economic activities.

We estimate separate household income functions for income from agriculture (Y_a) and income from non-agriculture (Y_{na}). Y_a is the value added from agriculture and Y_{na} the sum of value added from non-farm household businesses and the wage income earned from non-farm employment by household members. To estimate Y_a we distinguish three factors of production: Labour, land, and capital. Labour is the days worked in agriculture by household members, land is the cultivable land used by the household, and capital is the accumulated fixed agricultural assets. To estimate Y_{na} we distinguish two factors: Labour and capital. Labour is the days worked by household members in non-farm activities, and capital is the current value of assets used in non-agricultural production. To allow for flexibility in the effects of the factors of production, we use a translog production function:

$$\ln Y_i = a + \sum_{j=1\ldots n} b_j \ln X_i + \sum_{j=1\ldots n} \sum_{k=1\ldots n} c_{jk} \ln X_{ij} \ln X_{ik} + \sum_{s=1\ldots m} d_s Z_{is} + \epsilon_i \quad (8.1)$$

where $n = 3$ for Y_a and $n = 2$ for Y_{na}.[3]

Individual coefficients are difficult to interpret in a translog model because of the second-order terms. The problem can be overcome by substituting ($\ln X_{ij} - \ln \bar{X}_j$) for $\ln X_{ij}$, where $\bar{X}_j$ is the sample mean of input X_{ij}. This transformation allows the coefficients on the scaled factors of production to be interpreted as the elasticities evaluated at the sample means. Z_{is} stands for a set of other explanatory variables representing human capital (average years in education), social capital (contacts), and location (village characteristics and province). Although most of the Z_{is} coefficients are statistically significant and economically substantive, their contribution is to improve the estimated equation: We concentrate on the returns to factors. Because farming land is generally allocated among the households of the village according to the number of household members or workers and—land rental markets being rare—land used normally equals land allocated, we can treat land as exogenous. Labour inputs into farming and non-farming are instrumented to correct for endogeneity, the valid instrument being the ratio of young dependants to workers. Capital inputs should ideally be instrumented as well but our potential instruments were too closely related to household production.

In the case of farming the elasticities in Table 8.4 indicate the importance of land (0.12), then labour (0.08), and capital (0.06). The sum of these elasticities

T A B L E 8.4 *Production functions for farming and non-farming activities: translog model*

	Farm income	Non-farm income
Constant term	7.1890 (21.9)***	−2.6134 (0.6)***
Ln labour	0.0768 (3.0)***	0.5050 (2.6)***
Ln labour squared	0.0338 (2.1)**	0.6435 (8.1)***
Ln land	0.1224 (4.1)***	
Ln land squared	−0.1288 (5.6)***	
Ln capital	0.0605 (5.3)***	1.6435 (2.6)***
Ln capital squared	−0.0010 (0.4)	−0.0819 (2.4)**
Ln land * ln labour	−0.0542 (1.8)*	
Ln land * ln capital	0.0465 (4.2)***	
Ln labour * ln capital	−0.0118 (1.7)*	0.0422 (0.4)
F-value	32.400	23.241
Adj. R^2	0.187	0.238
Dependent mean	7.894	6.355
Number of observations	3,404	1,492

Notes: The dependent variables are $\ln Y_a$ and $\ln Y_{na}$. The former equation includes all households with farm income and the latter all those with non-farm income. The bracketed figures are *t*-ratios. *** Denotes significance at the 1%, ** at the 5%, and * at the 10% level. The logs of the factors of production are scaled by subtracting the logs of their means. A number of human capital, social capital, and location variables are included but are not reported in the table.

T A B L E 8.5 *Average and marginal returns to the factors of production*

	Return (yuan)	
	Average	Marginal
Farm income		
Farm labour (day)	10.7	0.82
Farm land (mu)	776.17	94.92
Farm capital (yuan)	1.33	0.08
Non-farm income		
Non-farm labour (day)	15.9	8.02
Non-farm capital (yuan)	1.59	1.02

Notes: The marginal returns are derived from the coefficient estimates of Table 8.4. The marginal return is calculated as the elasticity multiplied by the average product. As with the elasticity, the return is shown at the mean of the explanatory variable.

indicates the returns to scale: Since it is much less than one, sharply decreasing returns are implied. The elasticities are considerably higher in the case of non-farm incomes, being 0.64 for capital and 0.51 for labour. Their sum indicates increasing returns to scale. These results suggest that households would benefit by transferring resources from agriculture to non-agriculture.

The elasticities of Table 8.4 can be multiplied by the average products to yield marginal returns to labour in farming and non-farming (Table 8.5). The marginal product of a day of farm labour is less than 1 yuan (0.82 yuan) whereas that of non-farm labour is 8.02 yuan: their ratio is a factor of 10. It is also notable that the marginal products are considerably lower than the average products, especially in the farm sector, implying that there are diminishing returns to labour. The same patterns are to be found for capital.

It is helpful to distinguish between non-farm activities within the township (which we refer to loosely as rural industry) and activities beyond the township (essentially from migrant labour). The survey does not permit a precise allocation of non-farm activities by days worked locally and non-locally, but it is possible to identify specialist workers and their location of employment. Table 8.6 indicates that there is considerable specialization by some workers. Those who worked at least 60 days in a non-farm activity averaged over 300 days in it. This group constituted 12.3 per cent of workers and contributed 14.3 per cent of days worked, 8.3 per cent in migrant work and 6.0 per cent in rural industry. We see that the non-farming specialists were willing and able to work more days during the year than the specialist farmers. The table also shows, for each specialist activity, the number of days worked in that activity and the average specialist income per worker, and hence derives the average income per day. Farming yields the lowest number of days per annum and also the lowest income per day. Migration provides

TABLE 8.6 *Allocation and mean income of specialist workers according to specialization: weighted sample*

| | Specialist activity | | | |
	Farming	Village industry	Migration	Total
Workers (percentage of total)	86.7	5.6	7.7	100.0
Mean days worked				
Farming	194	5	3	169
Non-farming	65	300	305	97
Total	259	305	308	265
Specialist activity	194	300	305	208
Mean income per worker in specialist activity				
Per day				
Yuan	9.4	12.7	17.4	
Farming = 100	100	135	185	
Per annum				
yuan	1,827	3,809	5,298	
Farming = 100	100	208	290	

Notes: As we lack precise information on the number of days worked outside the township, we classified specialist non-farm workers (i.e. those with more than sixty days of non-farming activity) into village industry and migrant workers according to the location of the current (January 1995) employment. Specialist farmers are those who worked on the farm for more than thirty days and were not engaged in non-farm activity for more than sixty days. Non-specialist workers are those not included in any of the above categories; they represented 7.4% of all workers.

the highest number of days worked and the highest daily rate, so generating a much higher total income for the specialist migrants than for the specialist farmers. The advantages of non-farm activities are twofold: They provide more work and more remunerative work.

We distinguish the marginal returns to rural industry and migration in Table 8.7 by estimating a household income function. The dependent variable is household net income (ln Y), and labour is measured as the days worked by household members classified into the specialist categories and the residual non-specialist category of Table 8.6. Land quantity and quality (proxied by province) and productive assets are also included as arguments. The average rural household obviously works far longer on the farm (381 days) than in non-farm activities (14 and 13 days in village industry and migration, respectively). The coefficient on farm labour days is actually negative, and significantly so. It implies that an extra day worked on the farm reduces household income by 1.2 yuan. The negative relationship may reflect inadequate standardization for land quality: Fertile areas support more people and therefore have smaller farms. The coefficients on labour specialized in non-farm activities are positive. They imply that an extra day worked in the township raises

TABLE 8.7 *Marginal income per worker day from household specialist activities: coefficient in regression analysis*

	Mean	Coefficient	Absolute effect at the mean values of variables (per day)
Farming labour days	381	−0.0003**	−1.2
Rural industry labour days	14	0.0005	2.1
Migrant labour days	13	0.0007*	3.1

Notes: ** Denotes statistical significance at the 1% and * at the 5% level. The dependent variable is $y = \ln Y$ where Y is household income (yuan per annum). The independent variables are number of days of specialist farming labour, rural industry labour, and specialist migrant labour and non-specialist labour, as well as land size, household productive assets, and province. Household income includes migrant remittances but not the unremitted income of migrants. The equation has adj. $R^2 = 0.143$, F-value $= 48.33$, mean of dependent variable $= 8.354$, and $N = 3965$.

household income by 2.1 yuan, and outside the township by 3.1 yuan. These marginal returns to employment are much lower than the average returns shown in Table 8.7. Nevertheless, they yield the same pattern: Non-farm activities are more rewarding than farm activities, both on average and at the margin.[4]

Could the large differences in marginal returns to labour represent compensating differentials for the more arduous, unpleasant, or risky nature of non-farm work? On the contrary, we would expect local non-farm activities to be more attractive than farming, and thus to yield a lower return. In the case of migration, compensation may be required for the psychic costs of separation from home, the financial costs of moving, searching and acquiring various permits, and the risks of migration. However, it is dubious that there is a need for compensation on the scale required by the differences in returns (see Knight, Song, and Jia 1999; Knight and Song 1999: ch. 9, on the costs, benefits, and attitudes of migrants). The implication, therefore, is that labour may be misallocated between farming and non-farming.

Misallocation could be the result of labour restrictions or wage rigidities. It remains extremely difficult for a rural person or household to become permanently urbanized and, although temporary migration is now permitted, city governments impose restrictions on the employment of migrants by enterprises under their jurisdiction in order to minimize unemployment and maintain social order (Knight, Song, and Jia 1999). Such restrictions both ration opportunities and help to keep up the market-determined wages of rural–urban migrants. In the case of self-employment, high returns may reflect barriers to entry resulting from failure in the markets for credit and skills.

There are plausible reasons why the wages of many rural workers exceed their market-determined levels: Institutional wage determination, efficiency wage setting, and rent-sharing. In Chapter 5, we analysed the wages of migrants employed in urban enterprises. The migrants were found to be at a disadvantage by comparison with urban residents with regard to housing, pension, and medical subsidies. Although the rate for the job often prevailed, they also received lower cash wages, largely because they were given inferior jobs. It appeared that many migrant wages were set institutionally, and were above their market-clearing levels. An indication that wages in rural areas are not set competitively is provided by an inter-province analysis for the twenty-eight provinces in 1988, using a national household survey (Knight and Song 1993). When the wage per employee was explained by income per worker in households not receiving wage income, the relationship was positive but very weak: The wage/income ratio was much higher in poor than in rich provinces. The insensitivity of local non-farm wages to local labour market conditions could represent efficiency wage payments (in private enterprises), profit-sharing (in community-owned enterprises), or the use of state urban wage scales (in the larger, township enterprises).

If wage rigidities were the only problem, it is likely that in equilibrium rural workers would be indifferent about migration. It is an equilibrium condition of probabilistic rural–urban migration models that, in aggregate, migration takes place up to the point at which the urban 'expected wage' equals the rural supply price (Harris and Todaro 1970). The rate of urban unemployment is the equilibrating variable, adjusting the expected wage downwards by reducing the probability of getting a job. Put another way, the search costs of migrants rise so as to equate the rural supply price—including compensation for the risks involved in search—to the urban wage. However, only the exogenous element of transaction costs is relevant in judging whether apparent segmentation in reality represents compensating payments: The endogenous increase in the urban unemployment of migrants implies that urban jobs are rationed for them. In any case, the restrictive controls on rural–urban migration in China—intended to protect urban workers and residents—appear to maintain a migration disequilibrium.

8.5 THE DETERMINANTS OF PEASANT CHOICES

The evidence of Section 8.4 suggests that the labour market facing rural workers is segmented. Our second, indirect, test of segmentation is to look for the predictable consequences of segmentation. Formal tests of labour market segmentation have been developed, and these have influenced our approach. Dickens and Lang (1985) investigated dual labour markets in the United States, using an unobservable (in the sense that the sectors emerged from the estimation) endogenous switching model. Their test was whether the sectorial earnings functions differed, and whether the coefficient differences corresponded to the coefficients in the sectorial choice function. Magnac (1991) used an observable endogenous switching model to choose between labour market competition and segmentation in urban Colombia. He compared the differences in the coefficients of the formal and informal sector earnings functions with the coefficients in the switching equation: Correspondence would imply freedom of activity choice and a competitive market. Yao (1999) followed Magnac in testing for segmentation between wage- and self-employment in a rural county of Zhejiang province, China, and found little correspondence between the relevant coefficients.

In a competitive labour market, with farm production being subject to diminishing returns, incomplete household specialization may be required to equate the marginal product on the farm with that in other activities and with the market wage. However, homogeneous workers within the household should be indifferent as to which activity within that set they choose. It is the heterogeneity of workers that gives rise to preferences among activities. There can be heterogeneity in tastes, transaction costs, and productive characteristics. Among the factors governing taste for an activity might be age and gender (for instance, young men are keener to migrate than others). In equilibrium, the market sets a value on taste, in the form of a compensating wage differential, but those with a relatively strong taste for migration will derive rent from migrant labour, and so will prefer it to other activities. Transaction costs might be reflected in the local availability or otherwise of rural industry and the cost of migration (workers with non-farm opportunities at hand have an advantage). If a particular productive characteristic (say, education) is more highly rewarded in a particular activity (say, rural industry) than elsewhere, a higher proportion of the educated will be engaged in it than would be the case if workers were randomly allocated. Unless productive characteristics are bundled, their rents are competed away. In equilibrium, the market returns to education are the same in each activity: Workers are indifferent among activities irrespective of their productive characteristics. Characteristic prices may differ across activities, however, if tastes are correlated with characteristics. For instance, a taste for non-farm work by the educated may reduce the equilibrium relative return to education in that activity. It is heterogeneity not of productive characteristics but of tastes and transaction costs, therefore, that gives rise to worker preferences for one activity rather than another in competitive equilibrium.

If the returns to labour in non-farm activities exceed those in farming, non-farm jobs may be rationed. How, then, are the scarce opportunities allocated? There are two types of criterion: Those which determine demand for and those which determine supply of jobs. The former concerns transaction costs and tastes, for instance, workers with a strong taste for farming will not demand alternatives, despite the higher income that they would receive. Employers select workers from the pool of those who do. Their recruitment criteria concern productive or other personal characteristics that employers value. These might include human capital variables such as education, training, and employment experience, and discriminatory variables such as gender and ethnicity. Workers with capital and relevant skills might be better able to enter non-farm self-employment.

The nature of employer preferences depends on the nature of the labour market imperfection, for instance, on whether the wage premium is across-the-board or only at the minimum. Workers offer themselves if their potential wages exceed their supply prices; employers recruit from among such workers those whose productive characteristics are most valuable in relation to their wages. There is thus no reason why the workers who stand to gain the largest economic rents will be recruited. If wages are not proportional to productivity, recruitment is likely to be based on productive characteristics. However, if the profit motive ensures that wages are proportional to productivity, recruitment may depend on chance, contacts, or employers' tastes.

This discussion of worker and firm preferences yields a testable model of activity choice. Let P_i represent the unobserved value placed by the worker on activity i and V_i represent the unobserved value of the worker to employers in activity i. Then we postulate the index functions

$$P_i = a'X + u \tag{8.2}$$
$$V_i = b'Z + v \tag{8.3}$$

where X is a vector of individual characteristics influencing worker preferences, Z is a vector of worker characteristics, and u and v are error terms. X may contain characteristics representing productivity as well as tastes insofar as productive characteristics are differently rewarded in different sectors. Similarly, Z may contain personal as well as productive characteristics if employers have a taste for discrimination. Let P_i^*, V_i^* indicate the utility placed on the net value of P_i, V_i, respectively after deduction of the relevant opportunity costs. In the case of workers, the opportunity costs correspond to the 'reservation wage', subjectively interpreted; and in the case of employers, they represent the cost of employing the worker.

If P_i^* is positive, the worker selects activity i, and if V_i^* is positive, employers select the worker for activity i. Where E_i is a dummy variable indicating the sector of economic activity, the decision rule is:

$$\begin{aligned} E_i &= 1 \quad \text{iff} \quad P_i^* > 0 \quad \text{and} \quad V_i^* > 0 \\ E_i &= 0 \quad \text{iff} \quad P_i^* < 0 \quad \text{or} \quad V_i^* < 0 \end{aligned} \tag{8.4}$$

Only one of the four outcomes is known: There is partial observability, the methodology for which was developed by Poirier (1980).

If u and v have the standard properties, the probability of a worker choosing activity i is $F(a'X)$ and the conditional probability of being chosen for activity i is $F(b'Z)$, where $F(.)$ is the standard normal cumulative frequency distribution. On the assumption of independence between the worker's choice and the employer's conditional choice, the probability of observing a worker in activity i is $F(a'X)F(b'Z)$ (Heywood and Mohanty 1994). In the absence of rationing, only $F(a'X)$ is relevant: All the parameters in $b'Z$ except the constant term are zero. Identification of the separate equations is problematic because both decisions are influenced by largely the same set of variables. We shall examine the significant coefficients in the estimated equation for consistency with a labour supply and a labour demand interpretation.

We examine the determinants of the economic activities of rural workers. The underlying question concerns the extent to which their choices are rationed. Are there determinants of non-farm activities which can be interpreted only as labour supply decisions or only as labour demand decisions? The former implies that the worker can choose freely and the latter that the firm chooses among workers. Table 8.8 reports the results of the multinomial logit estimation. The omitted category is specialist farming, and the results (making a comparison with this category) relate to specialist migrants and specialist local non-farm workers. Coefficients are presented in order to provide tests of statistical significance. We also show standardized probabilities, that is, estimating the effect on the probabilities of altering one explanatory variable at a time while holding others at their mean values (if continuous variables) or omitted categories (if dummy variables). Only a small proportion of the unweighted sample being used in the analysis specialize in non-farm activities: 6.1 per cent are specialist migrants and 4.9 per cent are specialist village workers. The predicted probabilities are accordingly low, whatever the worker characteristics being considered. We therefore show the probabilities in more helpful, relative, form, with the lower or the lowest probability in each case being expressed as 100.

Poor health may discourage migration but it actually improves the chances of a local non-farm job. Being female lowers the probability of non-farm work, especially migration, whereas being single raises both probabilities. The responsibilities associated with household headship reduce the chances of migration. The most important personal variables are age and education. Age has a powerful deterrent effect, particularly on migration. The chances of a twenty-year old migrating are 3.5 times greater than those of a forty-year old. Education encourages both migration and village industry employment: The coefficients rise monotonically in the latter case and almost so in the former. The chances of an upper-middle school graduate migrating or obtaining a village industry job are more than three times higher than those of an uneducated worker. Membership of the Communist Party is an advantage in obtaining local non-farm employment. Previous visits to a large- or middle-size city are associated with current migration but not with village industry employment. However, a visit could be either the cause of a decision to migrate or the result of a predisposition to migrate. Similarly, possession of good urban contacts may facilitate migration and deter village industry employment, but may reflect predisposition.

Various household characteristics are also potentially relevant to choices or opportunities. The coefficients indicate that having more workers in the household reduces the odds of being a specialist migrant or local non-farm worker rather than a specialist farmer, but the effect is not statistically significant.[5] If choices were unrationed, we might expect a significantly positive relationship: Additional workers relative to land should seek non-farm income. Household wealth serves to encourage both migration and village industry employment, the

TABLE 8.8 *Multinomial logit analysis of peasant choices*

	Coefficients		Probabilities (lower probability = 100)	
	Migrant worker	Village industry worker	Migrant worker	Village industry worker
Intercept	−1.4701	0.9102		
In good health	0	0	880	100
Not in good health	−0.4180	1.7068**	100	107
Male	0	0	182	123
Female	−0.7139**	−0.2838*	100	100
Married	0	0	100	100
Single	0.9912**	0		159
Household head	0	0		
Not household head	0.7358**	0.2030	164	100
Education				
Higher	0.7584	1.5124*	389	718
Professional high	−0.2562	0.6512	189	418
Upper middle	0.0869	0.3046	311	336
Lower middle	0	0	311	336
Primary 4–6	−0.1734	−0.2531*	267	218
Primary 1–3	−0.5481*	−0.6634**	200	145
No education	−0.2350**	−1.0625**	100	100
Communist Party member	0	0	100	181
Not Communist Party member	0.3936	−0.6271	150	100
Has previously been to big city	0	0	338	100
Has previously not been to big city	−0.8105**	0.1492	100	152
Has previously been to middle-sized city	0	0	338	100
Has not previously been to middle-sized city	−0.7911**	0.1492	100	152
Without urban contacts	0	0	100	133
With good urban contacts	0.0524	−0.3286*	109	100
Household workers	−0.0189	−0.0609		
1			100	100
2			107	115
4			117	147
Wealth of households (000)	0.0133*	0.0096		
Wealth squared	−0.0000	−0.0000		

TABLE 8.8 (*continued*)

	Coefficients		Probabilities (lower probability = 100)	
	Migrant worker	Village industry worker	Migrant worker	Village industry worker
Wealth (yuan)				
5,000			100	100
17,700 (mean)			115	110
25,000			123	115
Land per capita (mu)	−0.0259	−0.5723**		
1			107	100
5			107	200
10			100	100
Proportion of village industry workers in village labour force	−0.1796	1.3710		
0.25			107	100
0.50			100	131
Proportion of migrants in village labour force	0.0110	−0.4511**		
0.25			100	110
0.50			107	100
Distance from city (li)	0.0013	−0.0049**		
20			100	189
100			133	146
200			175	100
Province				
Sichuan	0.6655**	0.5166*	314	493
Guangdong	1.4673**	0.7954	443	393
Hubei	0.4673**	−0.3408	271	207
Jiangsu	0	0	214	373
Anhui	−0.7815*	0.2463	100	487
Shangdong	−0.1913	−1.6691*	186	207
Hebei	−0.5450*	−1.2419	114	100
Gansu	−0.1094	−0.5175	157	173

Notes: The categories specialist farmer, specialist migrant, and specialist village worker are as defined in Table 8.6. The omitted category is specialist farmer. The fourth category, non-specialist worker, is also included in the estimation for completeness but the coefficients are not operated. Log-likelihood = −6,079.0, pseudo-R^2 = 0.249, and the number of observations = 9,343.

former significantly. It may help to provide the funds and the security needed for migration, and it may provide the resources for non-farm self-employment or provide the deposit sometimes required for a village industry job. Lack of land adds little to the probability of migrating but greatly to the probability of working in village industry: It is nine times higher when the household has only 1 mu per capita than when there are 5 mu per capita. However, the direction of causation is ambiguous as households in industrialized suburban rural areas possess little land.

The characteristics of the village and its location are important for non-farm employment opportunities. The proportion of village industry workers in the village work force raises the chances of being employed in village enterprises—reflecting the greater local opportunities. By contrast, the existence of many migrants in the village has the opposite effect. In a village without local industry, workers have to migrate to get non-farm employment, and the existence of migrant networks in the village reduces the transaction costs of migration. Distance from a city—reflecting remoteness—reduces local non-farm employment and increases migration. Finally, the province dummy variables have powerful effects on the probabilities. Migration from the township is highest in prosperous Guangdong (where it is mainly within the province, reflecting opportunities in Guangdong) and in heavily populated Sichuan (where it is mainly outside the province).

In summary, it is clear that the various personal characteristics have an effect on peasant choices of activities. Some of these are likely to represent preferences, which in turn reflect tastes or perceived needs. Thus gender, marital status, position within the household, and health are influential, and probably show the division of household duties. Age and education might also stand for worker preferences—the young and the educated dislike farming and like to travel—but they might equally reflect employer preferences when employment opportunities are limited. Some of the evidence suggests that the opportunities for non-farm employment are limited. Experience of cities, city contacts, and household wealth all reduce the costs and risks of migration which might otherwise act as a deterrent: Those lacking these resources seem to be at a disadvantage. Having more workers in the household might be expected to push people out into non-farm activities, but it appears not to do so. The activities of the village are important for the individual, because they increase opportunities for local non-farm employment and because they can ease the path out of the village for migrants. Moreover, the location of the village provides very different opportunities for non-farm employment, suggesting that the transaction costs of leaving the farm are important for some workers.

How do those who become specialist non-farm workers choose between local and distant non-farm work? A binomial logit analysis shows the following factors to be significant in that choice (Table 8.9). Migration rather than local non-farm work is encouraged by having a high proportion of migrants in the village, having been a soldier, and having visited a city. All these suggest the importance of possessing the opportunity or information to migrate. Local rather than distant non-farm employment is encouraged by there being a high proportion of non-farm

TABLE 8.9 *The choice between non-farm local and migrant work: binomial logit analysis and the interaction terms in an earnings function, with non-farm local work as the omitted category*

	Coefficient for	
	Logit analysis of worker choice	OLS analysis of ln earnings (interaction terms)
Intercept	2.053*	0.450
Female	−0.345**	0.105
Age	−0.046***	0.005
Single	0.441**	0.034
Ill-health	−1.746*	−0.697
Not a member of the party	1.694***	0.007
Never a soldier	−1.399**	−0.146
Never a teacher	2.013**	−0.176
Agricultural skills	−1.373**	0.522*
Never visited a big city	−0.867***	0.080
Never visited a middle-sized city	−1.218***	0.020
Proportion of migrants in village	0.575***	0.050
Proportion of TVE workers in village	−0.959***	−0.341**
Sichuan	−0.019	−0.005
Guangdong	1.328**	0.026
Hubei	1.048**	−0.431*
Anhui	−1.368***	−0.211
Shandong	0.513*	0.064
Hebei	−0.345	−0.402*
Gansu	0.138	0.478
College education	−0.528	−1.348*
Professional school	−0.318	0.424
Upper middle school	−0.084	−0.219
Primary school, 4–6 years	0.109	−0.197*
Primary school, 1–3 years	−0.082	0.016
No education	−0.383	0.405
−2 log-likelihood	1043.915***	
Pseudo-R^2	0.330	
Percentage of correct predictions	77.2	
Adj. R^2		0.255
F-value		7.157***
Number of observations	1,144	1,026

Notes: The dependent variables are migrant work in the logit activity function and migrant work × characteristic interaction terms in the earnings function. * Denotes statistical significance at the 10%, ** at the 5%, and *** at the 1% level. The omitted categories in the dummy variable analysis are male, married, health, party member, soldier, teacher, no agricultural skills, visited a big city, visited a middle-sized city, Jiangsu, and the lower middle school.

workers in the village, Communist Party membership, and being a teacher—all of which could represent local opportunities. In addition to age, being female or married, being in ill-health and possessing agricultural skills tend to tie people to local non-farm employment: Migrant supply prices are likely to be raised. It is interesting that education has no significant effect on the choice between the two activities.

If workers could choose between local and distant non-farm work, their choices would be based on the respective wage offers in relation to the respective reservation wages. In Table 8.9 we also examine whether the determinants of labour allocation are related to the relative earnings with which those determinants are associated. An ordinary least squares (OLS) earnings function is estimated for the combined sample of migrant and local non-farm workers, with a full set of interaction terms (the products of the dummy variable denoting migrant and the other explanatory variables). The sign and the significance of their coefficients denotes how and whether the effect on earnings of each independent variable is different for migrants and local workers. For instance, we can examine whether the positive influence on migration of residence in Hubei province is associated with a positive effect on the migrant (relative to the local) wage for Hubei. We see that, contrary to the hypothesis, the coefficient is significantly negative. In fact, the interaction term coefficient has the right sign and is significant (along with the logit coefficient) in only one case. A higher proportion of local non-farm workers in the village increases both the probability of being a local non-farm worker and local non-farm pay in relation to migrant pay. However, given village barriers to the employment of outsiders, causation may well run from job to pay rather than in the hypothesized direction. The general lack of correlation between the determinants of allocation and their effects on relative earnings suggests that workers cannot make free choices.

8.6 THE IMPORTANCE OF EMPLOYMENT OPPORTUNITIES

We found that both the type of work done and the amount of time worked are important determinants of household and individual incomes (Table 8.6). Moreover, the composition of employment and its level appeared to be related. This section explores that relationship further: It provides our third test of segmentation. If those employed in non-farm activities work longer, this suggests that those confined to the farm are discouraged from working by diminishing returns to farm labour and that the higher returns to non-farm employment elicit a greater labour supply. It indicates that those with access to non-farm employment have both an opportunity and an incentive to work longer. However, it also suggests that the others have an incentive to diversify into non-farm activities—offering not only higher marginal returns but also additional net employment—yet cannot do so.

Yao (1999) distinguished two forms of rationing in his Chinese case study: Entry rationing and time rationing. Entry rationing takes the form of restrictions on entry to local non-farm activities, and time rationing restrictions on days worked in those activities. The former can arise where villages differ in their non-farm employment opportunities and protect residents against outsiders; the latter can arise where village leaderships intervene to equalize household incomes in the village by spreading non-farm employment opportunities. In his small and homogenous sample he found evidence of the latter. Insofar as they were concerned with choice of activities, Sections 8.4 and 8.5 above tested for entry rationing. Section 8.6, being concerned with days worked, provides a test that is also consistent with time rationing.

We estimated regression models of the time opportunity cost of non-farm employment for both workers and households. The number of days worked on the farm (L_f) was regressed on days worked off the farm (L_n), the latter being instrumented to correct for endogeneity.[6] The effect of non-farm employment on farm employment could be seen from the coefficients on L_n. The coefficients are -0.77 for workers and -0.10 for households, both significant at the 1 per cent level. When a worker works an extra day away from the farm, this reduces his farm work by three-quarters of a day; when a household does so, its time on the farm is reduced by only one-tenth. Although an individual cuts back sharply on his own farm work when he becomes a migrant or a village industry worker, his household can normally find the labour resources largely to replace his work on the farm. Non-farm employment benefits a rural household in two ways: Not only by increasing its marginal income per day but also by increasing its number of days worked.

Table 8.10 presents regression analyses of the number of days worked in total, in farming, and in non-farming activities by the sample of 9,343 workers. The mean working time is 266 days and the standard deviation is 93 days. Of the total days, 161 are worked in farming and 104 in non-farming. Non-farming days are very unequally distributed: Their coefficient of variation is no less than 125 per cent. The explanatory variables include personal and household characteristics, household resources, locational and activity variables. By interpreting the role of the influential determinants of days worked, we hope to discover whether workers are free to choose their work intensity. It will become apparent that the determinants of farm and non-farm days are distinctly different, so that the coefficients in the total days equation, being a weighted average, are less interesting than their components. A tobit regression model is estimated in the case of the dependent variables farm days and non-farm days, on account of left-censoring (the proportion of zero observations being 15 and 53 per cent, respectively). The reported coefficients show the effect on the latent variable rather than the actual variable. The reported multiplicative factors can be used to show the marginal effect of a regressor on observed days worked, either without condition or given that some work is done.[7]

Consider first the variables relating to the individual. Gender and marital status play a role but they interact; moreover, they interact differently for farm and non-farm activities. For men, marriage increases time worked on the farm. Unmarried women work longer than unmarried men on the farm but shorter off the farm. Women reduce their income-earning activities on marriage and tend to restrict them to the farm, presumably because of their additional household duties. Being a household head adds to farm days worked and subtracts from non-farm days. This may reflect domestic responsibilities. These results show an intra-household labour allocation that is predictable from the conventional roles within Chinese peasant families.

Work increases with age up to 37 years (when 23 more days are worked than at age 20), and then it declines. This pattern is true not only of total days but also of farm days worked. The inverse U-shaped relationship is likely to reflect worker preferences and responsibilities that influence labour allocation within the household. By contrast, non-farm days decline slowly after fifteen years of age. Here employer preferences may also be relevant. Health is important: Those reporting good health work thirty-six days more than those reporting poor health. Education has quite different effects on and off the farm. The number of farm days worked generally falls as education increases, whereas the number of non-farm days rises strongly. This may be a matter of preferences, but it may alternatively reflect the better opportunities that the educated have for non-farm employment.

Now consider whether the household variables influence the amount of aggregate and disaggregate employment. The number of workers in the household has only a small effect on the total days put in by a worker but reduces them over the range 1–3 workers (accounting for over 75 per cent of households). The number of farm days declines strongly and monotonically, and the number of non-farm days shows a U-shaped relationship, turning at the most common household type (containing two workers). This may reflect either the extent of underemployment on the farm when the household has more than two workers or the presence of young adults who are willing to migrate or who receive preference in recruitment to village industry. The fact that the number of workers in the household was not significant in the analysis of the activity choice (Table 8.8) but has a significant positive effect (beyond three workers) here suggests that village leaders may ration time spent in village industry employment so as to favour households with more workers than normal. An increase in household farming land, from one standard deviation below the mean to one standard deviation above it, has the effect of raising farm work by 62 days and lowering non-farm work by 69 days. There are alternative explanations: The lack of adequate land may propel workers into non-farm activities or the more industrialized suburban rural areas may suffer from land shortage.

Location is important in providing opportunities for employment. As expected, distance from town and city increases days worked on the farm and decreases days worked off the farm. Province makes a huge difference to days worked: Heavily populated Sichuan workers average fifty days less than the workers in the omitted province, prosperous Jiangsu. Two other poor provinces with limited work are Gansu (with very low farm days) and Anhui (with very low non-farm days).

TABLE 8.10 *The determinants of total, farm, and non-farm days worked by workers in 1994: regression analysis*

	Mean value, or proportion	Total days (OLS)	Farm days (tobit)	Non-farm days (tobit)
Intercept	1.000	156.039**	−152.935**	265.882**
Female	0.479	−8.371*	19.690**	−40.942**
Married	0.818	3.137	20.589**	4.601
Married, female	0.402	−42.297**	28.202**	−163.398**
Household head	0.397	−2.992	17.419**	−13.514
Age (years)	36.070	6.075**	6.925**	2.412
Age squared		−0.083**	−0.066**	−0.080**
Good health	0.953	36.417**	38.282**	12.855
Number of workers in household				
1	0.040	7.215	5.110	18.979
3	0.193	−5.205*	−15.701**	10.506
4	0.166	2.878	−23.263**	33.216**
5–	0.075	2.158	−41.981**	56.246**
Educational level				
College or above	0.002	−10.873	−97.070**	76.668*
Professional high	0.006	−3.361	−15.403	9.488
Upper middle school	0.075	0.067	−20.749**	29.417**
4–6 years primary school	0.271	−8.591**	14.181**	−32.702**
1–3 years primary school	0.115	−5.035	35.711**	−67.580**
No education	0.158	−4.344	28.435**	−90.293**

Farming land of household (mu)	5.678	−1.220**	6.728**	−14.500**
Farming land squared		0.065**	−0.083**	0.234**
No urban contacts	8.851	14.184**	2.313	20.583**
Distance to town (li)	5.474	1.482**	1.448**	−0.406
Distance to county town (li)	20.681	−0.200**	0.325**	−0.936**
Distance to city (li)	74.318	0.168**	0.425**	−0.411**
Province				
Sichuan	0.127	−51.957**	−30.910**	−54.052**
Guangdong	0.128	−30.082**	−42.801**	−22.917*
Hubei	0.114	−31.609**	−6.537	−55.103**
Anhui	0.133	−43.119**	10.145	−105.602**
Shandong	0.122	−21.628**	−5.567	−26.090**
Hebei	0.114	−19.032**	40.043**	−113.532**
Gansu	0.127	−41.678**	−39.836**	−10.894
Adj. R^2		0.148		
F-value		55.122**	161.325	104.515
Mean of dependent variable		265.841	120.239	130.615
Standard deviation of dependent variable		92.543		
Number of observations	9,343	9,343	9,343	9,343

Notes: ** Denotes statistical significance at the 1% and * at the 5% level. The omitted categories for the dummy variables are male, unmarried, unmarried male, poor health, two workers in household, lower middle school education, with urban contacts, Jiangsu province, and specialist farming worker. Total days, not being censored, is estimated by OLS whereas farm and non-farm days, being censored, are estimated by means of the tobit regression model. The multiplicative factors for derivatives are: For observed y, 0.908 for farm and 0.495 for non-farm; for observed $y | y > 0$, 0.726 for farm, and 0.361 for non-farm.

The differences reflect better resource endowments or a more developed rural economy in some provinces.

To summarize the results of this section, the role of some of the personal variables suggest that the extent to which people want to work does influence how much they do work: Supply factors governing the reservation wage, such as the need for the person to remain at home, are clearly relevant. To a considerable extent they reflect the allocation of household employment among its members. However, some of the evidence is consistent with the presence of labour market segmentation. Household non-farm employment appears to have little opportunity cost in terms of farm work. Although having more workers in the household decreases the time a worker spends on, and increases the time he spends off, the land, this does not necessarily imply that non-farm work is readily available: It may instead reflect egalitarian time rationing by village leaderships or the demand of employers for the (relatively educated) young who normally comprise the additional workers (beyond two) in the household. The disadvantages of remoteness and the role of the province suggest that the absence of local opportunities, and thus higher transaction costs, for non-farm employment is important.

8.7 CONCLUSIONS

In this chapter we have explored how Chinese peasant households allocate their labour among migration, rural industry, and farming. Underlying our approach was the hypothesis that many rural households are rationed in their non-farm activities. We adduced a number of pieces of supporting evidence from a nationally representative survey:

1. Attitudinal responses suggest that many rural people wish to diversify their economic activities but feel prevented in various ways.
2. Rural workers work on average for less than a full working year, and the estimated marginal product of labour in farming appears to be extremely low.
3. The average and marginal returns to rural labour are far higher in non-farm than in farm activities.
4. Additional days worked off the farm appear to increase the total number of days worked by households.
5. Some of the determinants of workers' economic activities, and of the time spent in them, suggest demand-side explanations.

Our most striking evidence was the large differences in marginal returns among activities. However, these differences are not necessarily evidence of non-price rationing. They could at least partly represent compensating differentials for the risks, the psychic costs and the financial costs of migration. For instance, the role of location in the models of activity choice and of days worked implies that the transaction costs of migration can be important. In the case of local non-farm activities, the differences in marginal returns could result from market imperfec-tions in the supply of capital and skills. Differential returns might also reflect the inertia of economic agents when information is poor.

Nor were any of our other tests conclusive. Attitudinal responses can be mislead-ing. Surplus labour is a perilous concept, both empirically and conceptually. The endogeneity of farm and non-farm employment makes it difficult to establish the causal relationship between them. Our attempt to distinguish between demand and supply constraints on employment was hindered by the fact that most explanatory variables could be given either demand or supply interpretations. Nor should we expect to find a simple dichotomy: Even if employment opportunities were tightly rationed, they could still be somewhat elastic to search effort. Nevertheless, taken as a whole our evidence suggests that many Chinese peasant households have limited opportunities to expand their non-farm activities, and that an important reason for this is the rationing of employment that results from labour market segmentation.

The issues addressed in this chapter have also been investigated by Bowlus and Sicular (2003). They test for 'separability' between rural households' labour demand and labour supply. The test is whether farm labour demand, that is, the quantity of labour used on the farm, depends only on the factors that determine production or whether it also depends on factors that determine consumption—specifically, on labour supply. Non-separability suggests that there is surplus labour in the household. The authors find evidence of non-separability: Having more household members, and especially more adult males, increases work on the farm. The explanation may well lie in the immobility of labour among villages: Separability is rejected not only in land-scarce but also in land-abundant villages, in the latter possibly because of labour shortage. This is consistent with their find-ing of separability in townships with much non-agricultural employment—creating conditions for inter-village movement within the township and so permitting households unconstrainedly to optimize their farm labour inputs. One cannot gen-eralize from 259 households in 16 villages in only one of more than 2,300 counties! Nevertheless, the study supports our view that many rural households are unable freely to choose alternatives to farming, and that the unevenness of rural develop-ment and the immobility of rural labour retard the process of eliminating surplus labour in the Chinese countryside.

Bearing in mind the qualifications that call for more research, consider the implications of our interpretation. The most important way of raising household income in rural China is by diversifying away from farming. Households that suc-ceed in diversifying nevertheless hold onto their land and their farming activities. This is partly because of the system of allocating land, that is, land is leased out to all households within the village on a formula basis. It may also be because a combination of activities reduces income variability and so provides security for the household. Moreover, it is often not possible for all workers of the household to secure non-farm employment. Fortunate individuals derive the benefits of non-farm specialization while their households retain the advantages of diversification, including both risk-spreading and the higher income resultant from fuller and better remunerated employment.

Consider local non-farm employment as a means of diversification. Of crucial concern here is whether the village, or the township, has developed industrial enterprises. This is a matter of having a good agricultural or natural resource base, a favourable location or transport facilities, funds for investment, and relevant business and technical skills, partly acquired through learning-by-doing. A study of seven villages in the Handan prefecture of Hebei province showed how mechanisms of cumulative causation can launch some villages into rapid local industrialization (Knight and Li 1997). Capital market imperfections and the favouring of village members then make it possible for villages that are geographically close together to be economically far apart. Such processes give rise to unequal opportunities for non-farm employment. Within the village we saw that it was the educated young who tended to obtain the available non-farm jobs. However, productive characteristics may not be the only recruitment criterion used by village industries. Means of access to village wage-employment can differ from one community to another. For instance, in a study of three counties, Wu, Wang, and Xu (1990: 326) reported that, at one extreme (Wuxi), most employees had been designated by local government, at the other (Nanhai), there was a well-developed local labour market, and in an intermediate case (Jieshou) the labour market was governed less by the authorities and market forces and more by social networks, that is, many workers had been recruited through their relatives and friends.

If non-farm employment is not available, there is still the possibility of migrating to find non-farm employment elsewhere. However, migration opportunities can also be limited. This stems partly from the institutional protection which urban and village 'insiders' are accorded against rural 'outsiders'. Rural migrants can aspire only to the residual jobs not wanted by incumbents or insider entrants. The limitations on migration arise also from the risks and costs involved. Both can be reduced by having a network of contacts, which can provide information, opportunities, and support. Formal recruitment methods, such as those provided by Ministry of Labour employment bureaux or village labour contract companies, can also ease the paths of migrants. There is much evidence of the importance of networks and contacts in facilitating migration. For instance, in a companion survey of rural migrants employed in urban enterprises in 1996, 61 per cent gained the job through an introduction by friends or relatives, 30 per cent were formally recruited, and 9 per cent succeeded through their own efforts (Knight, Song, and Jia 1999). Moreover, networks have a sound theoretical basis in that they can reduce risks and costs for both migrants and employers.

The model underlying our description of the Chinese peasant labour allocation is a modified version of the probabilistic model of rural–urban migration. This posits a rural–urban income differential and rationed urban employment opportunities, and predicts urban open or disguised search unemployment. So far the process of rural–urban migration in China has been adequately restricted and sufficiently orderly to avoid serious urban unemployment, owing partly to government controls and restrictions and partly to the relative lack of migrant networks for what is only a recent phenomenon. Nevertheless, the incentives to seek non-farm employment are powerful. They will increase if inequalities between rural and urban China, or within rural China, continue to grow. Moreover, the slower growth of rural industry as urban restrictions on non-state activity have been and continue to be relaxed, and the predictable depressing effect of entry to the World Trade Organization on the land-intensive sectors of Chinese agriculture, are both likely to spur migration. Because migration is a cumulative process, facilitated by networks, these pressures could in time lead to great and potentially excessive movements of labour.

NOTES

1. To avoid under-representation of the larger provinces and of the median county in each province.
2. Respondents were asked to choose from a list of possible answers to a question, including an open-ended answer to be specified.
3. See Berndt and Christensen (1973) and Appleton and Balihuta (1996). The restriction of the translog to a Cobb–Douglas specification is rejected owing to the significance of most of the second-order terms.
4. Similar patterns have been obtained in other, more localized, studies of rural household income functions. For instance, Zhao (1996: table 5) estimated the marginal income for an additional farm worker, local non-farm worker, and migrant worker to be 5%, 19%, and 55%, respectively in Sichuan Province; and Hare, and Zhao (1996: app. A) estimated the marginal income from an extra 1,000 hours (say 125 days) in farming, local non-farming, and migration to be 1%, 17%, and 8%, respectively in one county of Henan Province.
5. The fact that the probabilities rise with number of household workers despite the negative coefficients reflects the strongly negative coefficient on the fourth, unreported, activity (non-specialist worker).
6. The instruments in the worker sample are the education dummies, province dummies, and possession of urban contacts, and in the household sample the village dummies and the number of workers in the household.
7. The coefficient answers the question: What is the effect on the days worked of someone who is already working some days? The multiplicative factors are needed to answer the respective questions: What is the effect on the average days worked of the sample as a whole, and of those with positive days (comparing those who work some days before and those who work some days after)?

REFERENCES

Appleton, S.M. and A. Balihuta (1996). 'Education and agricultural productivity: evidence from Uganda', *Journal of International Development*, 8, 3: 415–44.

Berndt, E. and L. Christensen (1973). 'The translog function and the substitution of equipment, structures, and labour in U.S. manufacturing, 1929–1968', *Journal of Econometrics*, 1: 81–114.

Bowlus, Audra J. and Terry Sicular (2003). 'Moving towards markets? Labor allocation in rural China', *Journal of Development Economics*, 71: 561–83.

Dickens, William T. and Kevin Lang (1985). 'A test of dual labor market theory', *American Economic Review*, 75, 4: 792–805.

Hare, Denise and Shukai Zhao (1996). 'Labor migration as a rural development strategy: a view from the migration origin', paper presented at the International Conference on the Flow of Rural Labor in China, Beijing, 25–27 June, typescript.

Harris, John and Michael Todaro (1970). 'Migration, unemployment and development', *American Economic Review*, 60, 1: 126–42.

Heywood, John S. and Madhu S. Mohanty (1994). 'The role of the employer and workplace size in the US federal sector job queue', *Oxford Bulletin of Economics and Statistics*, 56, 2: 171–88.

Knight, John and Lina Song (1993). 'Workers in China's rural industries', in Keith Griffin and Zhao Renwei (eds), *The Distribution of Income in China*, London: Macmillan, 173–215.

—— —— (1999). *The Rural–Urban Divide. Economic Disparities and Interactions in China*, Oxford: Oxford University Press.

—— —— and Jia Huaibin (1999). 'Chinese rural migrants in urban enterprises: three perspectives', *Journal of Development Studies*, 35, 3: 73–104.

—— —— (2003). 'Chinese peasant choices: migration, rural industry or farming', *Oxford Development Studies*, 31, 2:123–47.

—— and Shi Li (1997). 'Cumulative causation and inequality among villages in China', *Oxford Development Studies*, 25, 2: 149–72.

Magnac, T. (1991). 'Segmented or competitive labor markets?', *Econometrica*, 59, 1: 165–87.

Poirier, Dale J. (1980). 'Partial observability in bivariate probit models', *Journal of Econometrics*, 12: 209–17.

Wu, Quhui, Wang Hansheng and Xu Xinxin (1990). 'Non-economic determinants of workers' incomes', in William A. Byrd and Lin Qingsong (eds), *China's Rural Industry. Structure, Development and Reform*, New York: Oxford University Press, 323–37.

Yao, Yang (1997). 'Rural industry and labor market integration in eastern China', *Journal of Development Economics*, 59: 463–96.

Zhao, Yaohui (1996). 'Labor migration and education in rural Sichuan Province: a special pattern', paper presented at the International Conference on the Flow of Rural Labor in China, Beijing, 25–27 June, typescript.

PART IV

THE IMPERFECT LABOUR MARKET

9

Information, Social Networks, and the Labour Market

9.1 INTRODUCTION

In a perfectly competitive labour market in which all agents have perfect information, entry to the market ensures employment at the going wage. Only limited general information is required for a worker to participate in the labour market. All that is needed is knowledge of the market wage. Job-specific information is unnecessary and irrelevant. Transaction costs of market participation are negligible. The process of job search would have little intrinsic interest in such a market.

If the labour market is imperfect or market information is imperfect, transaction costs become positive and can be important. These transaction costs include the monetary and time costs of acquiring information, much of which comes under the heading of job search. In imperfectly competitive labour markets and with imperfect information, the existence of wage differences involves searching for preferred jobs. It is no longer sufficient to have general market information: Job-specific information becomes relevant. The availability of information is then an important determinant of the transaction costs involved in urban labour market participation.

The conditions facing labour market participants in China are very different from those of a perfectly competitive market with perfect information. It is therefore worth examining the likely response of economic agents to the need for information possessing economic value.

The term 'social capital' has recently attracted the attention of social scientists (Granovetter 1995 [1974] being a pioneer, and Dasgupta and Serageldin (2000)). It can operate through social networks, providing mutual benefits, or through social norms, relating to trust, reciprocity, and cooperation. Social networks and social norms represent social capital insofar as they are economically valuable assets. An important and pervasive aspect of Chinese society, both traditional and modern, is the Chinese variant of social capital known as *guanxi*, that is, the relationships that an individual maintains in social networks. Oi (1989: 132) regards *guanxi* as the 'operational code' for how best to get things done in China. The social relationships that constitute *guanxi* are potentially no less important in the labour market than in other aspects of Chinese life.

There are various reasons why social capital may be important in China's urban labour market. In the case of urban residents, the predominant form of job sorting until recent years was bureaucratic allocation. Labour turnover among urban residents has been extremely low (Chapter 7) and the allocated employer generally remains the current employer. The main changes in recent years have been the development of a non-state sector in which more conventional labour market recruitment practices apply, and the growing number of young people and redundant workers who can no longer rely on being allocated jobs and must look to this non-state sector for employment. It is possible that *guanxi* secured advantages in placement and promotion within the administered labour system. It is also possible that *guanxi* continues to serve the same purposes in the embryonic and imperfect labour market that has emerged both within and beyond the administered labour system. Because earnings are not based solely on productive economic characteristics, *guanxi* can be valuable in providing access to economic rents.

Rural residents can join the wage labour market either locally or through migration. Information about the township or village labour market is likely to be good, although access to employment may depend on social networks or on township- or village-owned enterprise policy and practice rather than on market forces. It is in the case of rural–urban migration, however, that information plays a crucial role. Entry to urban employment poses a great problem of imperfect information and transaction costs. A little recruitment takes place through official channels, that is, the local labour bureaux in sending areas which serve as recruitment agents for urban enterprises. For the rest, the would-be migrant is on his own in an alien world. It is natural for him to turn to his social network for information and support. Except for those well endowed with human capital, few are willing to enter 'blindly' into the cities.

This chapter contains two main pieces of analysis, both related to informational and operational imperfections in the labour market. Sections 9.2–9.4 are concerned with rural–urban migrants. Recognizing that their information needs and problems are acute, we decided to conduct empirical research on this topic. The results cannot be generalized to other labour market participants—urban residents and rural residents employed locally. Nevertheless, they reveal something important about the most dynamic part of the urban labour market in China. Section 9.2 examines the types and sources of information to which the migrants had access prior to their migration. In Section 9.3 we analyse the costs of migration and their relationship to different types of information and to possession of social networks. Section 9.4, throws light on the relationship between information and migrants' actual and expected wages. In Section 9.5 we turn to urban residents, using specially designed survey questions to examine the role that social networks play in their labour market outcomes. Section 9.6 concludes.

9.2 TYPES AND SOURCES OF MIGRANT INFORMATION

Information about jobs can be of two types: Generalized information and specific information. The former is information about the general situation in a labour market, and the latter is information about specific jobs in that labour market. This distinction, attributed to Nelson (1959), has been widely applied in empirical research on migration. In the Chinese context, both types of information may be lacking for would-be migrants. General information about a prospective urban centre is scarce because of the imperfect working of the urban labour market for migrants, the isolated nature of rural life, and the weakness of urban–rural information flows through the media. Specific information about particular jobs in that centre is scarce insofar as it relies on urban contacts.

Would-be migrants with neither general nor specific information must incur the highest costs and risks of urban-based job search, and this may deter their migration. Those with only general information may also be deterred by the costs and risks of urban-based job search. Would-be migrants with only specific information are able to compare their current situation with the option or options about which they have knowledge, but they cannot compare it with better options that are in principle available. Only those with both general and specific information are in a good position to take rational decisions. Both general and specific information have an economic value. Information has greater value, the more accurate it is, the more it reduces the cost of job search, and the more it helps to raise income. Specific information is likely to be more valuable on each score.

Chinese society still relies heavily on *guanxi*, based on kinship and personal contacts. If would-be migrants possess social networks in urban areas—whether kin, friends, or fellow-villagers—these sources can transmit general and specific information to them. The closer the contact, the more efficient the information is liable to be. Such contacts can be helpful not only in providing information about jobs but also in lining up jobs for the migrants.

A second source of information is official organizations. Most cities have job centres, established initially to help urban workers to find employment, but recently their services have been extended to rural workers. Nevertheless, their first priority when jobs are scarce is towards their own citizens. Rural job centres are intended to serve their own residents. They tend to form links with urban job centres or enterprises, and they provide information on urban jobs and, at a price, organize group migration to the jobs.

Reflecting the inadequacy of the labour market for migrants, a labour contractor system has developed, emerging at an early stage in the reform process. Urban enterprises, especially in construction, sign contracts with intermediaries who then take responsibility for providing the labour and paying the wages. Labour contractors commonly recruit in their own villages or local areas, and are most active in poor and remote rural locations. The contractors hold exploitative power on account of their informational advantage and the nature of the contracts. The wage is set high enough to recruit migrants but less than even migrant wages in the destination area. Workers are not paid monthly (apart from pocket money) but at the end of the contract (normally lasting one year). The migrants work long hours and live in poor conditions.

Local job market fairs have become common in the cities in recent years. Fairs are held at particular venues and attract those looking for work and those looking for workers. The fair managers (normally city neighbourhood committees) charge fees for entry and benefit from other sales. Such fairs are likely to attract migrants without specific labour market information.

We propose to analyse the value of different types and sources of information. For migrant i before migrating, we have data on j types of information (T_j):

T_1 = both general and specific information
T_2 = only specific information
T_3 = only general information
T_4 = neither general nor specific information

and on six sources of specific information (S_k):

S_1 = from an official organization
S_2 = from family or relatives
S_3 = from friends or fellow-villagers
S_4 = from the media
S_5 = by chance
S_6 = from non-specified sources.

We hypothesize that, where $V(T_j)$ is the value of the j types of information,

$$V(T_1) > V(T_2) > V(T_3) > V(T_4).$$

We also hypothesize that there are differences in the value of the k different sources of information $V(S_k)$.

9.2.1   The survey and the data

The survey of rural–urban migrants was conducted in Handan, a city of nearly a million people in the southern part of Hebei Province, over 400 km from Beijing. Handan city and its surrounding counties are fairly typical of a large part of central China. The city had a good deal of heavy industry and the surrounding rural counties have average density of population and medium agricultural resources.

The Handan survey of rural–urban migrants (hereafter HRUM 1992) was planned and supervised, and the questionnaires and sampling procedures designed, by the authors. They are analysed more fully in Knight and Song (1999: ch. 9). Here we concentrate on the light that they throw on the role of information in rural–urban migration. Over 700 migrants with rural *hukous* were sampled from thirteen enterprises known to employ temporary workers. They were well representative of migrant workers employed in urban enterprises. This rich data set on household and individual characteristics contains evidence on the process of migration, the costs of migration, the income from migration, and the information

TABLE 9.1 *The characteristics of the migrants, their households, and their villages*

Variable	Mean value or percentage	Standard deviation
Characteristics of migrant		
Age (years)	24.9	7.7
Education (years)	7.6	2.6
Male (%)	75.6	
Married (%)	42.3	
Hukou in rural village (%)	82.5	
Communist Party member (%)	5.3	
Previously worked as peasant (%)	66.1	
Currently employed as migrant worker (%)	74.9	
Characteristics of rural household		
No. of household members	4.9	2.1
No. of household labourers	2.8	1.5
Total household farming land (mu)	4.5	4.1
Household per capita income previous year (yuan)	442	406
Characteristics of village		
Distance to Handan (km)	189	481
Bus station in township (%)	61	
Trading centre in township (%)	23	
Rural industry enterprises in village	3	

Note: There are 737 observations.

Source: Of this table, and of Tables 9.2–9.7, the Handan survey of rural–urban migrants (HRUM 1992).

that had been available to the migrants. It is therefore possible to throw light on the role that information plays in migration.

Table 9.1 describes the basic characteristics of the sampled migrants: 75 per cent are currently employed and 25 per cent are still waiting for job assignments by the official job centre, 76 per cent are male, and 58 per cent are unmarried. Their average educational attainment is 7.6 years (a little beyond primary school), and their mean age 25 years. The great majority (83 per cent) retain *hukou* registration in a village, the others being registered in county towns or rural townships. Two-thirds (66 per cent) worked as peasants prior to migration. Their average household—in their rural homestead—contains 4.9 members and 2.8 labourers, and is located 189 km from Handan.

9.2.2 *What information did the migrants possess?*

Table 9.2 shows that 46 per cent of the migrants had possessed general information about jobs in the city before arriving there, the predominant source (77 per cent) of

TABLE 9.2 *Information about the labour market: type, source, and relation to migration behaviour*

	Percentage of respondents
General information	
Received general information about jobs in this city before coming?	
Yes	46
No	54
If yes, source of information?*	
Social network	77
Family, relatives	43
Friends, fellow-villagers	34
Media	9
Official organizations	8
Chance	6
Specific information	
Do you have any contacts in this city?	
Family	22
Relatives	31
Friends, fellow-villagers	17
None	30
Why did you come to look for job in this city?	
Have social network	65
Family, relatives	43
Friends, fellow-villagers	22
Easy to find jobs	7
Higher income	8
Closer to home	14
How did you first hear of this job?**	
Social network	70
Family, relatives	46
Friends, fellow-villagers	24
Media	13
Official organizations	7
Chance	10

Notes: * Expressed as a percentage of those responding to this question; ** expressed as a percentage of those currently employed and responding. Otherwise the figures are percentages of total respondents (737 cases).

this information being their social network. However, 70 per cent claimed to have contacts in the city, and 65 per cent said that they had come to look for a job in the city because of their social network. No less than 70 per cent of these currently employed had first heard of their job through their social network.

TABLE 9.3 *Types of information received by migrants*

	Type of information recipients (%)
General and specific (T_1)	44
Specific only (T_2)	33
General only (T_3)	2
Received no information prior to migration (T_4)	21
Number of observations	737

Table 9.3 shows that nearly half (44 per cent) of the migrants had received both general and specific information and another 33 per cent had received specific information, whereas hardly any had migrated on the basis of general information only. A multinominal logit regression is estimated to discover the determinants of the type of information that migrants received prior to migration. The dependent variable T_j is valued as follows:[1]

$T_1 =$ the migrant received general and specific information
$T_2 =$ the migrant received only specific information
$T_4 =$ the migrant did not receive any type of information.

A full set of personal, household, and village characteristics is included as explanatory variables. Only those deserving comment are shown in Table 9.4 (the others being listed in the notes). Three sets of independent variables are presented in the table: Human capital including the migrant's age and education and the highest educational level of the household, social capital including political status and service in the army, and rural locality characteristics that proxy the degree of local development, such as the presence of a bus station or a trading centre in the township.

Reliance on only specific information decreases sharply with age, the standardized probability declining from 45 per cent at age 20 to 18 per cent at age 55. The same result is obtained for the migrant's level of education, the probability declining from 53 per cent at 3 years of schooling to 31 per cent at 12 years. Moreover, the probability of having both general and specific information rises with both age and education. The reverse is true for the highest educational level of members of the migrant's household: The probability of relying only on specific information rises sharply with this education. As rural workers become older and as they acquire education, they are likely to become informed about the world outside the village. It is thus to be expected that reliance on specific information alone will decline. The reverse result for the most educated member of the household is also plausible: Education increases the likelihood of migration and so enhances the scope for the respondent to receive specific information from his migrant kin. A rural person does not need education in order to receive specific information

TABLE 9.4 *Determinants of the types of information received: probability values generated from multinomial logit coefficients*

Variable	Probability (%)		
	General and Specific	Specific only	No information
Constant***			
Age of migrant (years)**			
20	44	45	13
30	49	36	11
40	53	28	19
55	56	18	26
Schooling (years)***			
0	31	60	9
3	37	53	10
6	44	45	11
9	50	37	13
12	56	31	13
15	61	24	15
Communist Party member	27	64	9
Not Communist Party member**	48	39	13
Served in the army	35	58	7
Never served in the army*	48	40	12
Highest educational level of a household member			
Professional high school and above	34	47	19
Upper middle school	39	54	7
Lower middle school***	51	34	15
Completed primary school**	60	36	4
Dropped out from primary school*	67	20*	13
No schooling	30	21	49
Bus station in township	52	38	10
No bus station in township***	39	44	17
Trading centre in village	44	51	5
No trading centre in village*	47	37	16
Income per capita of village (yuan) (00)			
200	47	40	13
800	47	43	10
1,500	47	47	6
Distance from village to destination***			
0	44	42	14
50	44	42	14
100	45	41	14

TABLE 9.4 (*continued*)

Variable	Probability (%)		
	General and Specific	Specific only	No information
300	46	40	14
500+	48	40	12
Number of observations	737		
Log likelihood function	−677.93		
Restricted log likelihood	−766.74		
Pseudo-R^2	0.116		

Notes: Explanatory variables included but not reported (the coefficients either being not significant or not having a substantial effect) are female, married, years worked as a migrant, number of other out-migrants in household, distance from home to the city, village with local industry. The omitted categories in the dummy variable analysis are Communist Party member, served in the army, highest educational level of a family member is professional high school or above, bus station in township, trading centre in village. The mean probability values of the three levels of the dependent variable are 0.44 (T_1), 0.38 (T_2), and 0.18 (T_3). The probabilities are calculated by setting all continuous variables at their mean values and dummy variables at their omitted category values (zero). Coefficients are not reported. However, the significance levels of coefficients are reported on the reported independent variables. *** Denotes a significance at the 1%, ** at the 5%, and * at the 10% level.

(the crucial information for access to urban jobs) but education helps him to receive general information (which is less important for access).

When the urban labour market is highly imperfect, news about jobs tend to flow through agents, such as personal or social relations, contractors, or social organizations. Specific information is spread within networks and not through an impersonal market. Those with better opportunities to build up their networks also have better chances of being recruited. Being a Communist Party member, or having served in the People's Liberation Army, strikingly changes the probabilities of the types of information received. Party membership raises reliance on only specific information from 35 to 64 per cent, and army service raises it from 40 to 58 per cent. One might expect both party members and ex-soldiers (less than half of whom are party members) to have wider experience of the world than other rural-dwellers. However, the results can be understood in terms of the advantages that such people acquire. From the networks that they have built up—often outside their rural origins—they are able to get specific information about jobs and introductions to jobs without general knowledge of the labour market in the destination city.

The location of the household is important in determining the type of information received. The presence of a bus station in the migrant's township raises the probability of receiving general information by 13 percentage points. The presence of a trading centre in the village increases the probability of migrating with only specific information by 14 percentage points. It is understandable that buses carry the news in a talk-and-listen way whereas trading between people can build up networks. When a village becomes more developed it will attract more people to visit for different reasons and will stimulate more relations between villagers and outsiders who are normally the carriers of specific information. The importance of specific information does indeed rise with village income per capita although the effect is not statistically significant.

Those who claim to have possessed no information before coming to the city fall into the group officially described as 'blind floaters'. These risk-takers tend to have more human capital and poorer opportunities for receiving information than the others (Table 9.4).

9.3 INFORMATION AND THE COSTS OF MIGRATION

We noted that very few migrants came to the city without specific information on jobs. This is understandable: It is common for city governments to try to ensure that jobs available to migrants are residual and rationed. Random searching is extremely difficult in the absence of an efficiently operating labour market. Accommodation—often provided to migrants by their employer—presents a problem for the period of job search. Recall that, when asked why they chose to work in that particular city, almost two-thirds of the migrants said that they already had a social network in the Handan (Table 9.2). These networks have the potential to help with both search and accommodation. However, few migrants acquired their urban jobs after urban-based job hunting: They were generally informed about the jobs before they moved to the city. The survey showed that the average waiting time they had expected between arrival and recruitment was short (seventeen days). This implies that they would either get a job quickly or return to their origins quickly.

Table 9.5 shows the benefits and costs of migration by source of information. The costs include the direct cost of migration and subsistence while searching and also any initial charge made by the employer for providing the job. This deposit can be understood as a 'cost of trust', refundable on good behaviour or continued employment. The average total cost of migration is not high: Less than one month's salary irrespective of information source.

Migrants informed by official organizations paid no deposit, and migrants informed through the media paid the highest deposit. In their case the employer would not know the migrant and therefore there could be no initial trust. The deposit would help to avoid losing the worker after training and would make the worker more liable for his behaviour. Such pecuniary bonds are less necessary if social bonds already exist. For instance, if the migrant has a contact known to the employer, the contact can be held responsible for the migrant's conduct. Trust based on social connections is a widespread norm in Chinese society. Social connections differ according to the closeness of the relationships involved—close family, other kin, friends, or fellow-villagers. The closeness determines the extent of liability of the 'guarantor' for their 'guarantee'.

T A B L E 9.5 *The economic benefits and costs of migration, by source of specific information*

	Source		
	Media	Network	Official organization
Direct cost	70	52	93
Deposit paid to employer	129	48	0
Total cost of migration	199	100	93
Monthly wage	265	254	333
Total cost of migration as percentage of monthly wage	75	39	28
Number of observations	43	356	37

Notes: The total number of observations (including 'other sources') is 464. In the case of official organizations, the direct cost of migration is the amount of money taken from the household and may exclude the charge made by the official organization.

On the one hand, closeness reduces the deposit required. On the other hand, some managers during our interviews complained that workers who are introduced through social connections feel more protected and less vulnerable, and therefore tend not to work so hard. This may help to explain the fact that migrants informed by their social networks on average received the lowest wage (Table 9.5).

It appears from the table that official organizations offer the highest wage benefits and involve the lowest job-search costs. However, a multivariate analysis of the cost of migration is needed to isolate the true values of information sources, controlling for other explanatory variables. We therefore estimate an OLS regression model of the initial cost of the migration which brought them to the city (Table 9.6). This cost consists of the travel expenses and expenditure on food and accommodation while waiting for the job.[2] Personal characteristics (such as age, gender, marital status, and education), distance between the rural origin and destination, whether the migrant is from the local area, from a village or a township, and whether he is currently employed are all included as explanatory variables. We also have information on the migrant's income in the year prior to migration at both the household and the village level, which are included so as to standardize for the income effects of migration cost, for example, influencing the chosen mode of transport.[3] These are all control variables. It is the types of information, and the sources of specific information, that are the key variables to be tested.

Possession of general information has no significant impact on the cost of migration, *ceteris paribus*. Possession of specific information from non-official sources—either from a social network or from the market—raises migration costs significantly. Compared with receiving specific job information from official agents, if a migrant received such information from his family or relatives the cost of his migration would be 87 per cent higher, if from friend or fellow-villagers 127 per cent higher, if from the media 205 per cent higher, and if by chance

TABLE 9.6 *Determinants of the cost of migration: OLS regression*

Variable	Coefficient	T-ratio
Control variables		
Intercept	0.8991	0.91
Age	0.0950	1.72*
Age squared	−0.0014	−1.73*
Female	−0.5113	−3.01***
Married	−0.1668	−0.92
Education (years)	−0.0931	−3.34***
From rural village	−0.1803	−1.05
Distance from village to the city (km)	0.0018	1.91
Currently employed	1.5784	9.11
From surrounding area	−1.6516	−9.15
Logged per capita income in village in the previous year	0.0445	0.55
Logged household per capita income in the previous year	−0.0965	−1.14
Information variables		
Received general information	−0.1036	−0.76
Received specific information of this current job		
From family or relatives	0.6247	3.31***
From friends or fellow-villagers	0.8197	3.6***
From the media	1.1138	5.05***
By chance	1.3240	4.53***
By other non-specified means	2.4083	1.59
Number of observations	543	
Adj. R^2	0.4007	
F-value	22.35	
Dependent mean	2.4984	

Notes: The dependent variable is the logged initial cost in yuan of migration prior to the current job. Omitted dummy variables in this model are: male, not married, from suburban county town or small rural town, did not receive general information about the city prior to migration, received the specific information about this job from official agency, still waiting for job assignment, not from surrounding area. *** Denotes statistical significance at the 1%, ** at the 5%, and * at the 10% level.

276 per cent higher.[4] Why, then, do so few migrants rely on official organizations? Unlike social networks, official organizations may be as remote from the peasants as the urban jobs themselves: Most peasants do not know of their existence. If official organizations were better known and more widespread, the number of urban jobs that they are allocated for migrant employment by city governments would be insufficient.

9.4 INFORMATION AND MIGRANT WAGES

Prior to migration, migrants differ in the amount of information they possess about urban labour markets, the less-well informed being at a disadvantage in the market. After migration, the less well-informed might be able to catch up as a result of their urban experience. We therefore expect differences in pre-migration information to have more effect on income in the current job than in the next job. Initial informational disadvantages would not disappear immediately, both because it takes time to learn and because of contractual restrictions. For instance, some migrants in the survey had obtained work from job contractors. Compared to others in urban areas, they tended to work hard in poor conditions for low pay. During their period of contract—normally a year—they would realize that their contracts were unfavourable but they could not breach their contracts without losing heavily. Nevertheless, comparing those with much and those with little to learn, the former should expect their incomes to increase more as they move to their next jobs.

This section estimates the determinants of three variables: The migrant's actual income, the expected income in his next migration job, and the difference between actual and expected future income, all expressed in logarithms. This third equation is partially redundant since it can be inferred from a comparison of the coefficients of the first and second equations, but it provides tests of significance of the differences between the other two.

We focus on the role of information in explaining the three dependent variables. One explanatory variable is the type of information that the migrant had before migrating: Those who had information about a specific job were at a potential advantage. We expect those with family, relatives, friends, or acquaintances in the city to be better informed. A third variable is distance from the rural origin to the urban destination: On average people should be better informed about nearer places. The way in which the migrant obtained his job is also relevant. In addition to these informational variables, we include various personal and employment characteristics that are likely to affect wages.

Our hypotheses are twofold: First, that those who started at an informational disadvantage have a lower current wage, secondly, that they expect a larger increase in the future as their informational disadvantage declines. A difficulty in testing these hypotheses is that informational disadvantage may be correlated with other determinants of pay, such as compensating differences and human capital acquisition.

The results are presented in Table 9.7. Consider first the determinants of the current wage. By comparison with those who received both general and specific information, the few who received only general information are at a substantial and significant disadvantage in pay (receiving 32 per cent less): Specific information has value. Those with family members in the city were less well paid than those with other relatives (who received 12 per cent more), those with friends or acquaintances (28 per cent more), and those without any social network (24 per cent more). It appears that the differences in pay required to compensate those who lacked a social network exceeded any effect on pay arising from their informational disadvantage. The same explanation might apply to those who were recruited from outside the province (receiving 20 per cent more than those recruited from nearby). Migrants who were recruited by official organizations were better paid than those recruited through their social networks, through the media, or by chance, but the differences were not statistically significant. Consistent with the

TABLE 9.7 *Estimates of migrants' current income, expected income, and the difference between them: OLS analysis*

	Current income	Expected income	Expected minus actual income
Intercept	4.704 (16.0)***	5.070 (15.6)***	0.366 (0.9)
Informational effects			
Information received			
General	−0.384 (2.2)**	−0.360 (1.8)*	0.024 (0.1)
Specific	0.020 (0.4)	0.004 (0.1)	−0.016 (0.2)
Source of current job			
Family or relatives	−0.139 (1.5)	−0.294 (3.0)*	−0.156 (1.2)*
Friends or fellow-villagers	−0.112 (1.2)	−0.209 (1.9)*	−0.097 (0.7)
Media	−0.147 (1.4)	−0.482 (4.2)***	−0.335 (2.3)**
Chance	−0.177 (1.6)	−0.057 (0.4)	0.119 (0.7)
Network in city			
Relatives	0.118 (2.2)**	0.006 (0.1)	−0.125 (1.5)
Friends or fellow-villagers	0.248 (3.5)***	−0.145 (1.9)*	−0.393 (3.8)***
None	0.215 (3.2)***	−0.078 (1.1)	−0.293 (3.0)***
Rural origin			
Outside municipality, inside province	0.088 (1.0)	−0.228 (2.5)***	−0.315 (2.6)***
Outside province	0.185 (2.6)***	0.018 (0.2)	−0.167 (1.7)*
Personal characteristics			
Age (years)	0.002 (0.1)	0.038 (2.1)**	0.036 (1.4)*
Age squared	0.000 (0.2)	−0.001 (2.1)**	−0.001 (1.8)**
Education (years)	0.002 (0.2)	−0.002 (0.2)	−0.004 (0.3)
Female	−0.258 (4.2)***	−0.394 (5.9)***	−0.137 (1.6)*
Number of observations	347	347	347
Mean of dependent variable	5.036	5.401	0.365
Adj. R^2	0.264	0.172	0.097
F-value	4.894***	3.258***	2.166**

Notes: The dependent variables are expressed in natural logarithms. Other explanatory variables included in the equation but not reported (generally insignificant) are industry of migration job, occupation of migration job, months in current job, months in current job squared. The omitted categories in the dummy variable analyses are both general and specific information received, current job received from official organization, family in city, rural origin in the municipality, male. *T*-ratios are in brackets; *** denotes statistical significance at the 1%, ** at the 5%, and * at the 10% level.

generally low, unskilled nature of migrant jobs, the returns to human capital are relatively low and not significant. Women are paid a good deal less (23 per cent less) than men in this labour market dominated by non-state employers.

The evidence for our first hypothesis is rather weak. It is clear that specific information and its equivalent—recruitment through an official organization—raise the current wage. However, other potential informational effects appear to be overridden by the need for compensatory income to induce peasants to come to the city without social networks, or from a distance, and to remain there.

The sample of migrants expect a substantial average increase in their wages between the current and the next job. Contrary to our second hypothesis, those who received only general information expect to remain at a substantial wage disadvantage. Those with weak or no social networks expect to do worse in the future than those with strong social networks. It is possible that people are prepared to migrate to a low-paying initial job provided that they have strong social networks to help them find something better in the future. It is also possible that the need for a compensating difference is expected to diminish as new networks are formed in the city. The same interpretation can be given to the disappearance of the expected wage premium of those who migrated from another province.

The expected advantage of those recruited through official organizations exceeds their current advantage, and this increase is significant. The fact that they are under the wings of official organizations may affect the sorts of jobs to which they are recruited. They are more likely to work in large state enterprises, in which migrants are paid by reference to the permanent urban employees—albeit less than them—and have some expectation of gaining skills. The evidence generally goes against our second hypothesis, but this may be because other factors, such as compensating differences and human capital acquisition, override the effects that we are looking for.

9.5 SOCIAL NETWORKS AMONG URBAN WORKERS

In this section we turn to urban residents, examining the effect of social capital on their wages. Social capital might play a role either in the administered labour system of the past or in the emerging market of today. It is relevant to ask: Is *guanxi* more, or less, important in the more competitive parts of the labour market for urban workers? Bian (1994) finds that *guanxi* was a determinant of employment success in the system of allocated jobs. Lee (1998) concludes that managers use referrals from existing employees to generate goodwill and to reduce the chances of hiring undesirable workers. Both Bian (1994) and Lee (1998) argue that promotions in jobs and in pay can depend on connections. Only Knight and Yueh (2003), however, have attempted to quantify the effect of social capital on the wages of urban workers. We summarize their research methods and findings.

9.5.1 *Does social capital raise wages?*

Knight and Yueh (2003) hypothesize that *guanxi* generates returns in the urban labour market. They use two main measures of social capital: The size of the worker's social network and the worker's associational membership of the

Communist Party. They analyse IE, CASS 1999, which contained a module specifically designed to examine the role of social capital. Their measure of social network is the reported number of close contacts, based on the question: 'In the past year, how many relatives, friends, colleagues, or acquaintances did you exchange gifts with or often maintain contact with?' For the working-age population the mean size of social network was 6.4 persons.

Given the importance of the Communist Party in China's society and its power structure, the access to influence which it provides makes membership the most promising indicator of associational social capital. The survey contains information on whether the individual is currently a member of the Communist Party, but not on the date joined. Some 23 per cent of the working-age sample are members of the party.

Knight and Yueh (2003) estimated the determinants of both social network and party membership. The estimates suggest that they are distinct phenomena. The size of social network can be explained only by education, employment experience, and gender, whereas Communist Party membership is well explained by numerous characteristics; neither variable is a determinant of the other. The authors proceeded to estimate earnings functions which included the two social capital measures among the explanatory variables. They did so by means of ordinary least squares (OLS), selection-corrected maximum likelihood (MLE), and two-stage least squares (2SLS). The MLE estimates are preferred to OLS on account of sample selection into employment. The 2SLS estimates are preferred whenever the social capital variables are endogenous and need to be instrumented.

A recurring issue in the estimations is the possibility that social capital is endogenous. The authors used appropriate tests of endogeneity and, where endogeneity was established, of the validity of the instruments being used. The instruments were found to pass the tests comfortably, suggesting that the reverse causal relationship from income to social capital was eliminated and that the causal relationship from social capital to income could be measured.

Table 9.8 shows the determinants of income for the sample of employed individuals, the dependent variable being the logarithm of earned income. A comparison of equations (1) and (2) shows the effect of introducing the social network variable. In equation (2) there is a 4.9 per cent return to each year of education, a 2.1 per cent return to each year of employment experience at the mean value of employment experience, and a large gender gap: Women are paid 18 per cent less than men. In equation (2) social network generates a positive premium of 10 per cent and is significant at the 10 per cent level. However, the returns to education and to employment experience, and the gender gap, all fall somewhat. There appears to be a positive correlation between social network and these variables. For instance, part of the gender gap can be attributed to differences in social networks.

In equation (3) there is a 14 per cent income premium associated with Communist Party membership, which is significant at the 1 per cent level.

TABLE 9.8 *The determinants of income for employed individuals aged 19–55: urban resident sample*

Dependent variable: log of annual income	Coefficient (*t*-statistic)			
Equation	(1) MLE	(2) 2SLS with SN	(3) MLE with Communist Party	(4) 2SLS with SN and Communist Party
Intercept	7.3349	6.9102	7.3796	6.9458
	(112.982)***	(30.088)***	(113.547)***	(30.130)***
Guanxi				
Social network	—	0.1021	—	0.0981
		(1.924)*		(1.877)*
Communist Party member	—	—	0.1331	0.0980
			(7.585)***	(2.059)**
Personal characteristics				
Female	−0.195	−0.1326	−0.1809	−0.1267
	(−13.984)***	(−2.574)***	(−12.708)***	(−2.605)***
Years of education	0.0490	0.0245	0.0455	0.0231
	(15.101)***	(1.995)**	(14.039)***	(2.008)**
Years of employment	0.0345	0.0262	0.033	0.0265
	(9.469)***	(2.342)**	(9.047)***	(2.414)**
Employment years squared	−0.0005	−0.0004	−0.0005	−0.0004
	(−5.769)***	(−1.463)	(−5.816)***	(−1.607)
Occupation				
Nonmanual worker	0.2885	0.2799	0.2608	0.2610
	(11.147)***	(3.213)***	(10.018)***	(3.227)***
Production worker	0.0797	0.1279	0.0792	0.1260
	(2.886)***	(1.815)*	(2.882)***	(1.836)*

TABLE 9.8 (continued)

Dependent variable: log of annual income	Coefficient (t-statistic)			
Equation	(1) MLE	(2) 2SLS with SN	(3) MLE with Communist Party	(4) 2SLS with SN and Communist Party
Self-employed	0.3658	0.5338	0.3548	0.5315
	(3.717)***	(3.802)***	(3.593)***	(3.851)***
Other occupation	0.1085	0.1664	0.1	0.1628
	(2.957)***	(1.952)*	(2.729)***	(1.945)*
Sector of employer				
State sector	0.2492	0.2819	0.2416	0.2740
	(10.699)***	(4.382)***	(10.403)***	(4.446)***
Private sector	0.2751	0.3465	0.2788	0.3426
	(8.050)***	(4.570)***	(8.170)***	(4.648)***

Notes: Omitted dummy variables are: Non-Communist Party member, urban collective sector, and unskilled worker, *** denotes statistical significance at the 1%, ** at the 5%, and * at the 10%. City dummy variables—mostly with significant coefficients—are estimated but the results are not reported in the table. Heteroskedasticity-consistent robust standard errors adjusted for clustering at the household level are computed.

The exclusion restriction for equations (1) and (3) is whether childcare is available in the home. It is a dummy variable that equals one if there are grandparents and a child under the age of 17 who are living in the household and zero otherwise. The exclusion restrictions are significant at the 5% level and used for all equations unless otherwise indicated. The instrument for social network in equations (2) and (4) is an attitudinal question that asked: 'Has the importance of political status, which influences household income, changed compared with before?' Answers were (1) decreased, (2) unchanged, (3) increased. The identifying instruments were jointly significant at the 1% level ($F = 7.51$) in equation (2). The instrument for Communist Party membership in equation (4) is a dummy variable that equals zero if an individual's father is/was an unskilled worker and equals one otherwise. The identifying instruments were jointly significant at the 1% level ($F = 3.82$ and $F = 6.46$, respectively) in equation (4). Social network is endogenous while Communist Party membership is not endogenous in these estimations.

Source: Drawn from Knight and Yueh (2003: table 3).

When both social network and Communist Party membership are introduced, in equation (4), we find an income premium of approximately 10 per cent associated with each variable. Thus, the basic hypothesis is supported. Moreover, the social network variable and other personal variables are correlated. Insofar as the correlation between education and social network is non-causal, one more reported member of a social network is worth more than one more year of education; insofar as education expands a social network, the latter coefficient indicates the mechanism by which education raises pay.

9.5.2 Does labour market competition reduce the return on social capital?

Knight and Yueh (2003) re-estimated their equations for the sample divided into three age cohorts. The oldest cohort (aged 42–55) is the group most likely to have been allocated jobs during the period of central planning, and many were in the same job in 1999. Social network does not benefit this group, whereas parental party membership does. Parental party membership was apparently important in securing a favourable job allocation under central planning. The coefficient on own party membership is positive, significant, and more or less the same for all three cohorts. Social network is significant for the youngest (aged 19–30) and middle (aged 31–41) cohorts, but the coefficient is lower for the former. For labour market entrants, parental social network (not measured in the survey) may be more important.

Three ownership sectors are distinguished in Table 9.9. The most important category, accounting for 78 per cent of employees, is the state sector, followed by urban collectives (15 per cent) and private firms (7 per cent). Although it is the case that by 1999, the state-owned enterprises (SOEs) had considerable freedom to manage workers, the state sector is the one least affected by labour market forces. The differences between SOEs and urban collective enterprises (UCEs) is not large, except that collectives are more likely to face 'hard' budgets. Labour market competition is most likely to be experienced in the private sector.

The social network variable has a positive and significant effect on pay in all three sectors, as does the party membership variable. The coefficient on social network is considerably lower for each subsample than for the sample as a whole, but is on a par with the MLE estimates for the sample. There is an explanation for this pattern. Whereas social network proved to be endogenous in the sample and its instrumenting raised the coefficient substantially, it proved to be exogenous in each of the subsamples and was therefore not instrumented: The MLE estimates are reported. It is in the private sector that both social network and Communist Party membership contribute most to pay, their coefficients being respectively 2.1 and 1.3 times larger than in the state sector. It appears from Table 9.9 that social capital plays a role in both the administered and the market-oriented segments of employment. However, its greater importance in the private sector implies that social capital is by no means just a dwindling relic of central planning.

TABLE 9.9 *The determinants of income for employed individuals, by ownership sector of employer: urban resident sample*

Dependent variable: log of annual income	Coefficient (*t*-statistic)					
	SOEs		Urban collectives		Private firms	
	(1) MLE	(2) MLE with SN and CP	(3) MLE	(4) MLE with SN and CP	(5) MLE	(6) MLE with SN and CP
Intercept	8.0445 (103.186)***	8.0459 (96.621)***	7.9159 (29.321)***	7.9755 (26.756)***	7.7155 (16.250)***	8.0948 (9.628)***
Guanxi						
Social network	—	0.0066 (3.041)***	—	0.011 (2.570)***	—	0.0140 (3.030)***
Communist Party member	—	0.1362 (6.743)***	—	0.1232 (1.765)*	—	0.1823 (2.481)**
Personal characteristics						
Female	−0.154 (−10.084)***	−0.137 (−8.211)***	−0.2532 (−5.606)***	−0.2624 (−5.409)***	−0.2601 (−4.665)***	−0.2146 (−3.442)***
Years of education	0.05 (14.433)***	0.0448 (12.247)***	0.0474 (4.492)***	0.0396 (3.562)***	0.0227 (−1.474)	0.0025 (−0.142)
Years of employment	0.0314 (7.200)***	0.0276 (6.077)***	0.0323 (2.938)***	0.0315 (2.660)***	0.0558 (4.218)***	0.0638 (4.349)***
Employment years squared	−0.0004 (−4.035)***	−0.0004 (−3.726)***	−0.0006 (−2.313)**	−0.0006 (−2.172)**	−0.0012 (−3.247)***	−0.0015 (−3.616)***
Inverse Mills ratio	−0.5155 (−18.435)***	−0.5102 (−17.053)***	−0.5821 (−10.054)***	−0.5325 (−6.161)***	−0.6842 (−18.009)***	−0.6742 (−15.438)***

Wald X^2 (7)	1644.13***	—	—	—	—	—
Wald X^2 (9)	—	—	—	—	—	—
Wald X^2 (11)	—	—	—	—	—	—
Wald X^2 (15)	—	—	—	—	97.50***	127.82***
Wald X^2 (17)	—	—	250.30***	—	—	—
Wald X^2 (18)	—	1491.71***	—	—	—	—
Wald X^2 (19)	—	—	—	274.14***	—	—
Number of observations	5,585	4,883	1,039	916	523	437

Notes: The omitted dummy variable is non-Communist Party member. Dummy variables for occupations and cities are estimated but their coefficients are not reported in the table. *** Denotes statistical significance at the 1% level, ** at the 5% level, and * at the 10% level. Heteroskedasticity-consistent robust adjusted for clustering at the household level are computed.

For the state sector, the exclusion restriction is a dummy variable that is equal to 1 if the individual is in poor health and zero otherwise. For urban collectives and private firms, the exclusion restriction is a dummy variable that is equal to 1 if the individual has no drive and zero otherwise, based on the question: 'Do you agree or disagree with the following statement in order to secure a stable household standard of living in the long run? Don't want to do much apart from following the crowd.' Answers: (1) agree, (2) disagree. The instrument for social network is an attitudinal question that asked: 'Has the importance of political status, which influences household income, changed compared with before?' Answers were (1) decreased, (2) unchanged, (3) increased. The instrument for Communist Party membership is a dummy variable that equals zero if an individual's father is/was an unskilled worker and equals one otherwise. Social network and Communist Party membership are both exogenous. We accordingly report maximum likelihood estimates for all estimations.

Source: Drawn from Knight and Yueh (2003: table 5).

9.6 CONCLUSIONS

The very imperfect labour market that still exists in urban China places an economic value on information. Better-informed workers are better able to seek out and secure the higher-paying jobs. In this chapter we have shown that general information about the urban labour market—which might be adequate in conditions approaching perfect competition—is not as important as specific information about particular jobs. Specific information is valuable but difficult to come by. Hence the importance of social networks—contacts and *guanxi*—for success in the labour market.

In the case of migrants, even general information about distant urban centres is very limited and there is need for local support during the difficult process of job search in an alien environment. Rural–urban migrants must place heavy reliance on their social networks in the transition to urban life and work. We examined the role of information and social networks in the employment and pay of rural–urban migrants in a particular city, Handan, using a specially designed survey. We posed four questions. First, what are the types and sources of migrant information? Secondly, what are the determinants of the types of information that migrants received? Thirdly, how do the various types of information affect the cost of migration and job search? Fourthly, how does an initial informational disadvantage affect the migrant wage, both the actual wage and the future expected wage?

The majority of the migrants had come without any general information about the labour market in Handan. By contrast, three-quarters had received specific information about jobs. The preponderant source of this information was the migrant's social network, comprising family, relatives, friends, and fellow-villagers. Two-thirds of the migrants cited the presence of a social network in Handan as the reason for coming to work there. Information is mainly spread through personal contacts rather than through an impersonal market: Those with good networks have better chances of being recruited, making them more likely not only to migrate but also to migrate successfully. Relatively few rural-dwellers are willing to be 'blind floaters'.

Our proxies for possession of good social networks—membership of the Communist Party and previous service in the army—increases the probability of receiving specific information. Our proxies for local economic development and contact with outsiders also generate specific information. By contrast, having more education contributes to general rather than to specific information.

The different sources of specific information had very different effects on the cost of migration. The cheapest source was specific information (and job placement) by official agencies. By comparison, specific information obtained from social networks raised migration cost substantially, and from broader market sources even more so. Although few of the migrants in this case study had access to them, these results suggest that rural employment bureaux can play an efficient and important role in rural–urban migration.

We expected that the less well-informed migrants would obtain lower wages, but that they might be able to catch up later as a result of their urban experience. We found that migrants who had come without specific information received lower wages: Specific information does indeed have economic value. However, our other hypotheses about the effect of information on wages were not borne out by the evidence, probably because the possession of kith and kin in the city induces people to move with low supply prices.

The earnings function analysis based on IE, CASS 1999 indicated that social capital is important in the labour market for urban workers in China. Both measures of social capital—social network and Communist Party membership—substantially raise the incomes of employed persons. Even if these measures are correlated with unobserved personal attributes, such as sociability, it is likely that such personal characteristics enhance income through their effects in expanding social networks and encouraging associational membership.

Social capital is rewarded both in the administered labour system, where jobs were allocated and wages institutionally determined, and in the market-oriented system, especially an underdeveloped one in which information is poor and transaction costs are high. The evidence is consistent with *guanxi* both providing access to economic rents and also reducing informational and transaction costs. Social networks appear to be more beneficial in the private sector than in the state or collective sectors. Since the private sector is the rapidly expanding sector, this suggests that *guanxi* will continue to play an important role in the urban labour market. That role is likely to diminish only when the market becomes less imperfect, so reducing the scope for workers to seek rents and increasing the importance of general, rather than specific, labour market information.

NOTES

1. Since only fifteen migrants received general information alone, we exclude them from this exercise.
2. If the migrant lived with his social network without payment, hours of housework for the host's family are valued at the opportunity cost (the reported hourly wage in the migrant's village). If the migrant was still waiting for a job, his estimate of the most likely length of wait for employment is used to calculate expenditure on food and accommodation.
3. As the income was received prior to migration, it is not endogenous to migration cost.
4. The percentage change is calculated as $100[\exp(\beta) - 1]$ where β is the estimated coefficient.

REFERENCES

Bian, Y. (1994). '*Guanxi* and the allocation of jobs in urban China', *The China Quarterly*, 140: 971–99.

Dasgupta, Partha and I. Serageldin (eds) (2000). *Social Capital: A Multifaceted Perspective*, Washington DC: The World Bank.

Granovetter, Mark (1995 [1974]). *Getting a Job: A Study of Contacts and Careers*, Chicago: University of Chicago Press.

Knight, John and Lina Song (1999). *The Rural–Urban Divide. Economic Disparities and Interactions in China,* Oxford: Oxford University Press.

—— and Linda Yueh (2003). 'The role of social capital in the labour market in China', Department of Economics, University of Oxford, mimeo.

Lee, C.K. (1998). *Gender and the South China Miracle: Two Worlds of Factory Women,* Berkeley: University of California Press.

Nelson, Phillip (1959). 'Migration, real income and information', *Journal of Regional Science*, 1, 2: 43–74.

Oi, Jean C. (1989). *State and Peasant in Contemporary China: The Political Economy of Village Government*, Berkeley: University of California Press.

10

Conclusion

10.1 INTRODUCTION

There are two ways of describing a glass and its contents, each as accurate as the other: the glass is half full; the glass is half empty. The choice of description may well depend on the context. Judged from the perspective of the administered labour system that prevailed under central planning, China has come a long way towards a labour market. From the perspective of labour markets in various countries including the United States and the United Kingdom, China still has a long way to go.

Our standard is not the theoretical models of perfect competition found in textbooks. Labour markets are rarely characterized by large numbers of price-taking buyers and sellers possessing perfect information. There are elements of market imperfection in all real labour markets. They arise from imperfect information, non-market wage determination, product market imperfections, the long-term nature of the employment relationship, the importance of non-marketable skills, lack of labour mobility, and the interaction among these characteristics. Labour markets are commonly rule-based and custom-based institutions that provide the incentives and information required for their smooth operation, and their actors are often embodied in systems of personal relations and social networks that help to generate information, trust, and cooperation. Nevertheless, the labour market in China remains particularly imperfect and incomplete.

In this chapter we summarize the conclusions of each previous substantive chapter and combine them into an argument, so as to make the whole greater than the sum of the parts. Our concern is to understand the forces that underlie the results obtained from our detailed data analyses. In Section 10.2 we consider how the process of labour market reform, by removing controls and lifting restrictions on economic agents, has changed the allocation and remuneration of labour and contributed to the creation of a functioning labour market. China is indeed on the path from labour system to labour market. We go on, in Section 10.3, to consider the various characteristics of the Chinese labour market which make that journey still incomplete. We examine both the progress and the lack of progress with two concepts in mind: Wages as incentives, and responses to wage incentives. To what extent do wages provide efficient signals for labour allocation, and to what extent does labour allocation respond to the signals? In Section 10.4 we peer into the future and pose the question: Whither the Chinese labour market? We do so in both positive and, in Section 10.5, normative terms.

10.2 PROGRESS TOWARDS A LABOUR MARKET

Under central planning there was no labour market at all in China. The labour system was heavily directed, providing very little scope for preferences or responses to economic incentives on the part of either workers or their employers. It was the plan, and not market wages, that governed labour supply and demand. Labour mobility was tightly controlled and restricted, both from place to place and from employer to employer. Rural workers had no choice but to work in the communes where they were born and where they lived. Urban workers were allocated to work units in which they would remain throughout their working lives. Wages were determined administratively, with scant regard for worker productivity. The centralized control of enterprises provided no inducement for their efficient use of labour, and indeed surplus labour was imposed on enterprises. Workers had few incentives to acquire human capital, to work efficiently, or to improve work methods. By these means the Chinese government was able to pursue its objectives of egalitarianism, ideology, and social control. The labour system ensured that everyone was employed and provided worker security, and it avoided the socio-economic problems that unfettered rural–urban migration has created in many poor countries. However, it scored badly in terms of the mobility, flexibility, incentives, and efficiency of labour.

Reform of the urban labour system began in the early 1980s, when the state monopoly of labour allocation was replaced by a somewhat more decentralized one. Labour exchanges were set up for the registration of job vacancies, most job placements, and training. In the 1990s, the planning quota for recruitment by state enterprises was abolished, and enterprises were allowed to choose their own employees. The state no longer took responsibility for matching the supply of and demand for labour. An unemployment insurance scheme was gradually introduced during the first decade of urban reform, so entertaining the possibility of urban workers becoming unemployed. Enterprise reform gained pace in the mid-1980s, and the greater managerial autonomy included some say on wage and employment matters. Bonus and piecework systems were introduced, over which the firm had restricted but growing powers. The Labour Law of 1994 further increased managerial discretion over wage determination. In the mid-1990s, the government decided to steer the state enterprises into the market, holding them responsible for their losses. Although a system of labour contracts of limited duration for new recruits had been introduced in 1984, it was only in the mid-1990s, when the government introduced its radical retrenchment programme, that the distinction between permanent and contract workers became important. Each of these institutional and policy changes, although incremental in nature, helped to provide the conditions for an urban labour market to emerge.

Market forces cannot influence wages unless labour is mobile or potentially mobile. Starting from almost complete immobility—lifetime employment in the *danwei*—under central planning, the urban labour force has become somewhat more mobile. We showed that, standardizing for length of time in employment, there was a monotonic rise in the percentage of first job separations over the reform period. For instance, in the case of those who had entered employment a decade before, the first job separation rate was 3.9 per cent in 1985–9, 5.7 per cent in 1990–4, and 10.5 per cent in 1995–9. The voluntary mobility rate rose over time, and the involuntary mobility rate was far higher during the period of the government's retrenchment programme, 1995–9, than in previous five-year periods. Most of the mobility, especially if it was voluntary, took place within the, preferred, state sector. As expected, voluntary mobility appeared to involve a rise in wages. We also showed that the mobility rate was higher for workers who owned their own homes (lowering the cost of moving) and for those with human capital and social capital (raising the benefit of moving).

In Chapter 3, we were able to show how the urban labour reforms changed the distribution and structure of urban wages. The Gini coefficient of urban wage inequality rose by 8 percentage points over the seven years 1988–95, for which we have comparable nationally representative data. Whereas the mean wage increased by 52 per cent, the pay of the 10th percentile rose by only 6 per cent, and that of the 90th percentile rose by as much as 75 per cent. Moreover, various employee characteristics that are likely to represent human capital became better rewarded. The returns to education rose sharply, as did the returns to occupation-specific skills. The initially slight inverse U-shape of the age–earnings profile became more pronounced—a change consistent with human capital theory. Thus the productive characteristics of workers were increasingly rewarded in the labour market. However, there were also signs of greater wage discrimination—against women and minorities and in favour of Communist Party members. This might reflect the greater scope for employers to exercise a taste for discrimination as managerial autonomy waxed and government directives waned. In particular, market forces operated more freely in the growing private sector.

Decomposition analyses were conducted in order to illuminate the processes of wage differentiation in China. Our decomposition of the rapid increase in mean earnings showed that, whereas the unskilled market wage rose only a little in real terms, the impetus came especially from the rising returns to education and the growing gap between the low-paying local private sector and other ownership sectors. We also decomposed the contribution of particular characteristics to the rise of the Gini coefficient for urban wages. Only a third of urban wages could be explained, and 55 per cent of its increase: The unobserved determinants are clearly important to the increase in earnings dispersion. Some but not all components of human capital were disequalizing. The disequalizing components—education beyond secondary school, the professional, technical, and administrative occupations, and age below 26 or above 60—together account for 65 per cent of the explained increase in the Gini coefficient. These particular changes are likely to represent the stirring of labour market forces.

By definition, we cannot know the unobserved determinants of earnings. Nevertheless, quantile regressions were estimated in order to shed light on the relationships between the observable and unobservable determinants. Clear patterns emerged. For each of the four characteristics considered, it was possible to provide an explanation in terms of either varying payments to employees for their unobserved abilities or varying willingness of employers to pay wages above market rates. In the case of education and age, however, the explanation in terms of employers was more plausible than that in terms of employees. Those employers that, by virtue of their low conditional pay, appeared more subject to market discipline, were also more prone to reward these human capital variables. The locally- or foreign-owned private sector, and the most reformed province, were the most sensitive to the unobservables, suggesting that marketization increases the importance of the unobserved influences on wages, whether they be employee or employer characteristics.

Did the rise in wage inequality involve a trade-off between efficiency and equity objectives? Our data and methodology could not provide a reliable answer but they could provide pointers. Some of the new inequalities appear justifiable in terms of the greater incentives or efficiency to which they give rise. In particular, it is likely that initially the returns to education and occupational skills were too low, and that the pattern of returns to age did not adequately reflect the age–productivity relationship. Other emerging disparities are more difficult to justify in terms of output objectives.

Our analysis in Chapter 4 of spatial trends in urban wages provided some evidence of the role of market forces. One finding was that wage inequality rose in all provinces but that the extent of wage inequality converged across provinces. We explained this convergence in terms of the process and timing of market reforms in different cities and provinces. The reform leaders had higher initial inequality but a lower increase in inequality over the period 1988–95. Turning to mean wages, we found powerful divergence among provinces. The widening of the difference in mean wages between the coastal and the interior provinces over the seven years was due partly to the relative pay of unskilled labour and partly to the sharper rise in the premium on education in the coastal provinces. This last result suggests that market pressures for scarce labour were a driving force. Another indication that market forces were at work is the finding that mean earnings converged among the cities of a province but diverged among provinces: Mobility being higher within than among provinces, the movement of workers is seen to assist convergence and limit divergence of wages.

Our analysis of the panel element in the 1999 urban household survey revealed how the returns to human capital had changed over the period 1995–9. In the case of workers who had never been retrenched, education became more highly rewarded over the period—at 6 per cent per year of schooling in 1999, it was 1 per cent higher than in 1995. This finding is consistent with the greater rewarding of productive characteristics, and thus with the hypothesis of an increasingly competitive labour market. By contrast, the returns to experience fell over the four-year period. Under central planning, seniority was a core aspect of China's administered wage system. We showed that in 1988 the earnings of workers peaked only in their fifties, *ceteris paribus*. Given the extreme weakness of labour market forces at that time, it is unlikely that these payments reflected on-the-job skill formation. Indeed, seniority was probably overpaid prior to reform.

An important landmark on the road towards a labour market was the remarkable change in government policies that took place in the mid-1990s: A reform of the state sector that had as its centrepiece a programme of mass redundancies which was intended to eliminate or reduce surplus labour in the state sector. This policy was forced on the government by the falling profits and rising losses of the state-owned enterprises (SOEs), which threatened to curb economic growth and government revenues. The 1999 urban survey, analysed in Chapter 6, showed that the incidence of job loss was widespread: 19 per cent of households and 11 per cent of workers had experienced a retrenchment. This remarkable shake-up meant that suddenly there were millions of unemployed urban-*hukou* workers searching for jobs in competitive conditions. As though in a deliberate experiment, a labour market had been created by decree!

How did this labour market perform? Personal productivity—proxied by education, occupational skills, and good health—provided some protection against retrenchment, and also improved the chances of finding another job. Those eligible for government financial assistance received government assistance in job search, so raising the probability of re-employment. However, almost all the displaced workers faced a tough labour market. The majority (63 per cent) had not yet found re-employment. The application of survival analysis suggested that the average expected duration of unemployment was almost four years. Those who found employment suffered a 'scarring' effect: Their re-employment wages were lower than the wage they could be earning if they had never been retrenched. The longer the duration of unemployment, the lower the subsequent wage—probably reflecting a fall in the wage they would be prepared to accept as they became more desperate. Moreover, they had to enter jobs which did not reward productive characteristics such as education and experience.

We now turn to the market for rural–urban migrants. In the 1950s, the state became concerned about the tide of migrants entering the cities, and made various attempts to stem it. These included the introduction of the residence registration (*hukou*) system, the enactment of a series of laws to restrict movement, centralized hiring of peasants, and its method of rationing basic necessities. Accordingly, net migration was negligible from the end of the Great Leap Forward until after the Cultural Revolution, 1960–78 (Knight and Song 1999: 256–7). Migration commenced again as a result of the rural reforms: The disbanding of the communes and the introduction of the household responsibility system reduced official intervention in the lives of the peasants. Rural industrialization created new towns populated by former peasants, and after 1983 rural people were able to enter the urban informal sector as temporary migrants. With free markets for food, peasants could buy grain to meet their production quotas, that is, to pay their taxes in the form of compulsory grain sales to state agencies, so they could more easily leave their farms. When the economic reforms were extended to urban China in the mid-1980s, the accelerated growth of the urban economy, the relaxation of

rules on peasant settlement in towns and small cities, and the general loosening of
social controls reduced the constraints on migration. The development of urban
food markets made it easier for rural people to live in the cities.

Most of this movement was temporary, non-*hukou* migration, referred to as
'floating' (*liudong*). The term 'migration' (*qianyi*) is used of *hukou* migration,
which is permanent. The *hukou* system, especially in the pre-reform era, functioned
as a de facto internal passport system. In recent years the *hukou* system has been
preserved but its effectiveness has declined. After the ration coupon system was
abolished in the mid-1990s, urban governments—no longer needing to provide
subsidized food—were somewhat less concerned to restrict *hukou* migration.
It became possible to buy an urban *hukou* in most of the towns and small cities at
a high, revenue-raising price.

Rural people had a powerful economic incentive to go to work in the urban
areas, and urban employers had a profit incentive to employ migrants from the
countryside. The government at various levels permitted the orderly inflow of
migrants to fill the increasing number of residual jobs as the growing urban demand
for labour outstripped the slow natural increase in the urban-*hukou* labour force.
Rural–urban migration is estimated at no less than 83 million over the decade
1984–93. There are difficult conceptual and measurement problems in counting the
number of rural–urban migrants. However, according to an estimate of absentees
reported in a national rural household survey for 1993, the number of rural people
working in the urban areas in that year was 39 million (Knight and Song 1999:
256–8, 270–4). An estimate of rural–urban migrants based on a sample of the
2000 national population census indicates that there were 88 million rural–urban
migrants in that year (Cai 2003: 32). China's rural–urban migration of recent
years has been referred to as the greatest migration in human history! Be that
as it may, a vast labour market for migrant workers now exists in urban China.
Moreover, the migrants are likely to be more subject to market forces than are their
urban-based counterparts.

10.3 OBSTACLES TO THE FORMATION OF
A LABOUR MARKET

Reform of the labour market in China has lagged behind other market reforms.
For example, in 2003 researchers in the State Council conducted a national survey
of local protectionism in China. Of all the various forms of local protection,
interventions in the labour market were reported to be the most severe—more
important than interventions in production, pricing, sales, subsidies, finance, etc.
(Li, Liu, and Chen 2003).

The processes of economic reform in rural and urban China were very different.
At the end of the Cultural Revolution rural China was ripe for reform. Once
they were given a signal, the peasants, acting in an uncoordinated way, took
the initiative. There were few losers, and thus there was little opposition from

vested interests. By a process of cumulative causation, reform begat further reform, and so on. The major elements of rural reform were complete within six years. It was at this time—in the mid-1980s—that urban economic reform commenced. By comparison, urban reform was slow and gradualist—well described by the saying 'crossing the river by feeling the stones'. There were two main obstacles to progress. One was the vested interests of the SOEs and their privileged urban employees. The other was the need for coordination of various interrelated reforms, giving rise to problems of sequencing. Both obstacles were relevant to the tardy process of moving from a labour system to a labour market.

Central to this issue is the *danwei*, a social institution very different from an employer in the Western sense. It was not going to be possible to create an urban labour market while the *danwei* continued to perform its functions of lifetime employer, mini welfare state, and—after wage-setting became decentralized—profit-sharer. In Section 10.2 we explained the extent to which these functions have been eroded. Nevertheless, the continuing influence of the *danwei* is apparent in the remaining and even growing extent of labour market segmentation that we document in this section.

Our analysis, in Chapter 3, of the evolving urban wage structure suggested that the market forces operating in the growing private sector and the relative immunity of the state sector from those forces generated greater wage segmentation among types of ownership. Moreover, provincial differences in the pace of reform and in economic growth created spatial segmentation in wages that could not be removed by the equilibrating movement of labour. These segmentation variables made the most important contribution in the decomposition of the rise in the Gini coefficient of wage inequality.

The sharper wage segmentation by ownership type and by province suggest that labour market reform has brought about not only greater efficiency in some respects but also new sources of economic inefficiency. The move of some but not all types of firm towards the payment of competitive market wages is liable to generate inefficiency of the sort associated with the 'theory of the second best'. Insofar as the widening province coefficients represent diverging marginal products, they provide efficient market signals. These signals are, however, not acted upon because labour is insufficiently mobile.

We examined the growing spatial segmentation of wages in more detail in Chapter 4. Mean wages across provinces, and across cities, were subject to divergence over the period 1988–95. In the first decade of enterprise reform bonuses—the component of wages over which the enterprise probably had the greatest autonomy—were subject to the strongest divergence. Being dependent on the profitability and negotiating power (over soft budgets) of enterprises, bonuses tended to segment the labour market by enterprise. Walder (1987) argued that bonuses were fairly equally distributed within the enterprise, reflecting worker pressures and preferences. However, there may be as many work units as households in our urban sample. We found bonuses to be the most disequalizing component of earnings. Bonuses were more unequally distributed among workers, and among provinces, in 1995 than in 1988. They may well have been the driving force behind the growth in real earnings over that period.

The policy of permitting SOEs to pay bonuses was intended to improve incentives for efficiency, at least at the level of the enterprise. However, the continuing weakness of both product market and labour market forces made possible large differences in enterprise profitability and thus in enterprise pay. Convergence of mean incomes among economies is consistent with models of technological diffusion and with neo-classical growth models of closed economies. It is also consistent with increased factor mobility across economies. There is much evidence of conditional economic convergence around the world. However, we found economic divergence among the regions of urban China. The most plausible explanation is the relative lack of factor mobility and the weakness of market forces. The former permitted very different income generation functions to exist, and the latter permitted wages in general, and bonuses in particular, to be influenced by rent-sharing behaviour as well as by local supply and demand conditions.

In Chapter 7, we explored in greater detail the remarkable and growing wage segmentation by firm that the process of labour market reform has generated. Enterprise reform had involved greater managerial autonomy, including more decentralized wage-setting. In principle, this should have produced a more competitive labour market, in which the 'law of one price' increasingly prevailed. However, the process was hampered by several factors. One was the lack of labour mobility of urban-*hukou* workers from one employer to another. Had employees in jobs with low wages been willing to move to jobs with high wages, the resultant adjustments in labour supply should have generated market forces bringing wages closer together. Another factor was the structure of managerial incentives. Even in the late 1990s, it was not necessary for firms to be profit maximizing, and they were apparently willing to hand over some of their profits to their workers. This profit-sharing, associated with the nature of the *danwei*, contributed to growing wage segmentation among firms.

The extreme immobility of most urban workers is an outstanding feature of the Chinese labour market: Job mobility among urban residents is remarkably low by international standards. The high returns to seniority, that is, length of tenure in the job, and the threat of losing housing or pension provided by the firm are among the factors that have deterred job search. Using the 1999 urban household survey, we found that the average job duration of urban-*hukou* workers was 19.9 years and that as many as 78 per cent of them had had only one job. This lack of mobility presents an obstacle to the achievement of a functioning labour market. Job stickiness begets wage stickiness. The extent of job mobility, or of expected job mobility, from one employer to another has not been sufficient to iron out wage differences among firms or sectors of the economy. By contrast, the relatively high inter-firm mobility observed among rural–urban migrants suggests that market forces can function in this segment of the urban labour market.

The combination of low labour mobility and profit-sharing may explain why we found a considerable difference in (standardized) mean wages between profit-making and loss-making firms. Despite the loosening of labour market policies and the redundancy programme of the late 1990s, it is evident that labour market segmentation among firms became stronger during that period. The relationship between profits and wages also contributed to a widening of wage inequalities over the late 1990s. Not only were employees of loss-making firms paid less than those of profit-making firms in 1995 but also their wages grew less rapidly over the subsequent four years, and among them it was particularly the unskilled with low-paying characteristics who fell behind.

Our interpretation of the wage–profit nexus is that managers, if they have profits, are willing to share them with their workers, and that some loss-making firms are unable to pay even contracted wages. We favour the rent-sharing, rather than the conventional efficiency wage, explanation for two reasons. First, we were unable to reject the exogeneity of profits in the wage equation. Second, the lay-offs of the late 1990s should have acted as a disciplinary device for employees, so reducing the equilibrium efficiency wage, whereas the sensitivity of wages to profits actually rose. In any case, it is plausible in Chinese conditions that failure to share profits can lead to the withdrawal of cooperation by workers. Given this threat, the efficiency wage is a positive function of profits: Profit-sharing and efficiency wage effects are intertwined, and their separation would be artificial. This intertwining reflects the distinctive characteristics of the Chinese *danwei*. To some extent it remains a social institution with a set of managerial objectives and worker attitudes that set it apart from a textbook enterprise.

The relatively privileged position of urban workers in China was challenged in the 1990s first by a great wave of migrants from the rural areas and then by a programme of mass lay-offs within the state sector. Both developments might be expected to act as restraining forces on wages for urban workers and possibly to usher in an era of labour market competition. However, the evidence adduced from the 1999 urban household survey and reported in Chapter 7 was more consistent with the creation of a 'three-tier' labour market. The highest-paid tier—corresponding to the economist's concept of a 'primary' labour market—consists of those urban workers who were not made redundant during the 1990s. Even after standardizing for their personal characteristics, the group are paid more than rural–urban migrants or urban workers who have been re-employed after having been made redundant.

The wage structures of migrants and of retrenched urban workers differ from that of the non-retrenched urban workers and from each other. For instance, in contrast to the non-retrenched group, the other two do not obtain wage premia for Communist Party membership or for employment in central SOEs. One might be tempted to ascribe this to the effect of greater competition in eroding wage differentials not related to productivity. However, exposure to greater competition has not prevented the emergence of increased gender discrimination. Where the migrants and the retrenched workers differ, however, is in wage structure by education and occupation. For the re-employed there appear to be no returns to education and limited occupational differentials, suggesting that the market they face is a tough one that is not working well for them. Their different wage structures make it unlikely that migrants and retrenched workers can be regarded as forming a single 'secondary' labour market. The evidence suggests that the urban labour market in 1999 comprised three tiers, created because the three groups of workers differ in the institutional arrangements that they face and thus in the extent to which they are open to market forces.

Recall-evidence from the 1999 survey enabled us to examine the wages of urban workers over time, in a panel. The real wage growth of non-retrenched urban workers was no less than 8 per cent per annum. Only a part of this wage growth can be regarded as compensation for the phasing out of subsidies, associated with the marketization of in-kind services such as housing, pensions, and health-care. For wages to rise at a time of retrenchment and high unemployment suggests a weakness of competition. In a competitive labour market one would expect a fall in the demand for labour to depress wages. The fact that real wages rose is more consistent with rent-sharing theory, whereby the retrench-ment of excess labour raises the surplus available to firms and some of this rise is shared with the remaining workers through higher pay. These results are in sharp contrast with those for retrenched workers. Soon-to-be retrenched workers did not receive the wage increases enjoyed by their never-retrenched colleagues, probably because the enterprises in which they worked were in financial diffi-culties and thus unable to fund wage increases. Moreover, the 1999 wage of re-employed workers was no higher than in 1995. Thus the re-employed workers—like the retrenched in their old jobs—did not experience real wage growth over this period. Wage segmentation between retrenched and non-retrenched urban workers grew over time, with only the former feeling the forces of labour market competition.

The very imperfect labour market that still exists in urban China places an economic value on information. Better-informed workers are better able to seek out and secure higher-paying jobs. In Chapter 9, we showed that general informa-tion about the urban labour market—which might be adequate in conditions approaching perfect competition—is not as important as specific information about particular jobs. The high degree of wage segmentation in the labour market means that specific information is valuable. However, it is also difficult to come by: Hence the importance of social networks—contacts and *guanxi*—for success in the labour market. The earnings function analysis based on the 1999 household survey indicated that social capital is important in the labour market for urban-*hukou* workers. Both measures of social capital—social network and Communist Party membership—substantially raise the incomes of employed persons. Even if these measures are correlated with unobserved personal attributes, such as soci-ability, it is likely that such personal characteristics enhance income through their effects in expanding social networks and encouraging associational memberships.

The urban labour market for migrants was very different from that for urban residents. Our 1995 study of rural migrants employed in urban enterprises pre-sented a picture of restricted opportunities (Chapter 5). The human capital of the migrants was not well rewarded. This reflects the low-potential jobs in which they were mostly employed, and the disincentive for employers to give more than rudimentary training to these temporary workers. Migrants were less well-paid than urban residents: On average the migrant wage was 80 per cent of the non-migrant wage (and employers' provision for housing, healthcare, and retirement further favoured urban workers). The large disparity that remained after standardization for differences in characteristics is likely to reflect labour market segmentation and lack of competition between migrants and non-migrants. The former were more subject to market forces. Moreover, their lack of information, contacts, and alternatives served to depress their supply prices. The latter were protected by differential access to urban employment, institutional determination of wages and benefits-in-kind, and iron rice bowls. It is notable, however, that the 1999 urban survey—although not precisely comparable—showed the standardized wage disadvantage of migrants to be somewhat smaller than in 1995 and their returns to education to have risen (Chapter 7).

Government successfully implemented its general policies of severely restricting permanent urban settlement of rural people and ensuring preferential access to urban jobs for urban residents. Our evidence also indicates that that government at various levels also restricted the employment of 'floating' migrants by imposing controls on enterprises, and by erecting a labyrinthine system of permissions and fees through which migrants had to pass. These impositions served to segment the labour market and place migrants at a clear disadvantage in competition with urban residents.

Migrant and non-migrant workers are highly imperfect substitutes or even complements: Migrants do the jobs that non-migrants shun. The majority of enterprises nevertheless reported that the training of migrants required them to remain in employment for some time. We found that the average duration of completed tenure with the enterprise was almost five years. Our enterprise production functions imply that the marginal product of migrants was double their wage whereas that of non-migrants was below their wage. Urban enterprises were therefore constrained in the number of migrants and non-migrants they were permitted to employ: Too few migrants and too many non-migrants. Although many enterprises had surplus urban workers, they found it beneficial to hire migrant workers as well, and were prevented from employing as many migrants as they would have chosen. Managerial attitudes might also have been relevant: Whereas urban-*hukou* employees were members of the *danwei*, the employment of migrants was a commercial transaction.

Probably because their reference groups were rural, despite their disadvantage many migrants were fairly pleased with their migration experience. A high proportion wanted to stay with the enterprise as long as possible, and this attitude was amenable to economic incentives. The apparent inconsistency that few migrants wanted to settle in the city reflects the hazardous nature of city life without an urban *hukou* and a secure job. The extent of remittances and contacts indicates that most migrants remained part of their rural households.

In Chapter 8 we approached migrant labour from a rural perspective, using a nationally representative rural household survey of 1994. The object was to discover how Chinese peasant households allocate their labour among migration, rural industry, and farming, the hypothesis being that many households are rationed in their non-farm activities. There were a number of pieces of supporting evidence. Attitudinal responses suggest that many rural people wish to diversify their economic activities but feel prevented in various ways. Rural workers work for less than a full working year, and the estimated marginal product of labour in farming is extremely low. The average and marginal returns to labour are far higher in non-farm than in farm activities. Additional days worked off the farm appear to increase the total number of days worked by households. Some of the determinants of workers' economic activities, and of the time spent in them, suggest demand-side explanations.

Our most striking evidence was the large differences in marginal returns among activities. These differences can represent non-price rationing but other explanations are possible. They might at least partly reflect compensating differentials for the risks, the psychic costs and the financial costs of migration. In the case of local non-farm activities, the difference in marginal returns might result from market imperfections in the supply of capital and skills. Differential returns might also reflect the inertia of economic agents when information is poor. Nevertheless, taken as a whole our evidence suggests that many Chinese peasant households have limited opportunities to expand their non-farm activities, and that an important reason for this is the rationing of employment that results from labour market segmentation.

Migration opportunities can be limited for two main reasons. One stems from the institutional protection which urban and village 'insiders' are accorded against rural 'outsiders'. Rural migrants can aspire only to the residual jobs not wanted by incumbents or insider entrants. The other reason concerns the risks and costs involved in migration. The latter source of segmentation between farming and migrant employment was further explored in our study, in Chapter 9, of the problems facing migrants and would-be migrants to Handan in 1993. This revealed their heavy reliance on social networks during the difficult process of job search in an alien environment. Most had come to the city with specific information about jobs, derived from family, relatives, friends, and fellow-villagers, and most cited the presence of a social network as their reason for coming to work there. Those with good social networks have better chances of being recruited, making them not only more likely to migrate but also to migrate successfully. Relatively few rural-dwellers are willing to be 'blind floaters'. We found that the minority of migrants who had come without specific information about jobs received lower wages. Although the possession of kith and kin in the city may induce people to move with low supply prices, specific information does indeed have economic value. Migration opportunities appear to be rationed, at least in part, by high informational and transaction costs. The importance of social networks in the migration process suggests that, as more and more migrants come to work in the towns and cities, migrant networks will multiply, so spreading opportunities for migration among rural people. Accordingly, migration may accelerate by a process of cumulative causation. Although few of the migrants in this case study had access to them, the evidence suggests that rural employment bureaux could play an efficient and important role in rural–urban migration.

To summarize this section: What has held back progress towards a functioning labour market? At the conceptual level, the underlying problem is that market-equilibrating wage movements have been impeded. Where there is excess supply, the undercutting of wages does not generally happen. Subject to a profit constraint, enterprises support their (generally long-standing) urban employees. Indeed, arrangements and incentives within the *danwei* encourage managers to share profits with their urban workers. Real wages rose rapidly during the period of retrenchment policy and high urban unemployment, and only the urban workers who lost their jobs, and rural–urban migrant workers, felt the forces of competition. In the case of excess demand, there is too little voluntary mobility of urban-*hukou* labour for employers generally to use wage policy as a recruitment device. A reason for the lack of voluntary mobility is the high private cost of changing jobs, associated with the social welfare provision—such as housing, healthcare, and pensions—that has been tied to the employer. Thus a fully functioning labour market waits on continuing enterprise and social welfare reforms.

10.4 WHITHER THE CHINESE LABOUR MARKET?

Finally, we shall attempt to answer the question 'Whither the Chinese labour market?'. To a considerable extent labour market reform has been driven by other economic reforms, such as the incentivization of the SOEs and the development of the private sector. Similarly, labour market reform has required and induced other reforms, such as the policies on self-employment, unemployment insurance, housing, and pensions. The future of the labour market is therefore intertwined with the reform programme in general. Progress will necessarily continue to be incremental and sequential: It is no easier to plan the economic transition from plan to market than it was to plan the economy.

Our point of departure is to consider the objectives of the major players, beginning with the Chinese Government. Its two main priorities are the achievement of rapid economic growth and the avoidance of political instability. These objectives are closely related in a circular process of causation, in that economic stagnation can generate political instability and political instability can generate economic stagnation. It is because urban workers are more likely to cause political instability than the peasantry that government has accorded them preferential treatment, and has displayed powerful 'urban bias' in many of its policies. There are two superficially apparent exceptions to this favouring of urban workers. First, being concerned about any non-state institution that can organize protest, government has controlled and subordinated the trade unions. Secondly, when the inefficiency of the state sector threatened the continued growth of the economy and of government revenue, the state embarked on a draconian policy of SOE reform, including the dismissal of many urban employees. However, in both cases the advantages of the policy—judged against the two main priorities—exceeded the disadvantages.

With regard to the labour market, the government has gradually withdrawn from its initial position of extreme intervention. Although the *danwei* retains some of its traditional custom and practice, the government is moving towards a market-based system of wage determination, in which there is little room for institutionalized collective bargaining involving trade unions in the Western sense. Except in the matter of protecting urban workers from a deluge of rural–urban migrants, the role of government in the labour market may eventually be confined to minimum standards protection. Even in the case of the legal minimum wage introduced in the Labour Law of 1994, enforcement appears to be limited. Labour market policies will be whatever is conducive to rapid economic growth and political stability.

The move towards a labour market benefits those people who are well able to compete in it and has the potential to harm people with limited abilities to do so. In developed economies, characterized by democratic processes and governance, market capitalism is tempered by a 'social contract': The government plays a substantial role based on a recognition of market failures and a consideration of social justice. Democracy has given rise to a welfare state or at least has prevented income distribution from becoming very unequal. In a transition economy such as China's, there is a danger that the marketization of labour will proceed too far or too fast, so either destroying non-market institutions or not allowing time or opportunity for new non-market institutions to develop—institutions which would temper unbridled market forces. There is a tendency in China's political system for the rising economic inequality resultant on the rapid growth and marketization of the economy to be a matter of policy concern only insofar as it threatens continued growth and stability. China's 'retreat from equality'[1] that has been taking place as a result of the economic reforms may well be permitted to continue.

What are the implications of this assessment for government support of poor and disadvantaged people who lose from the move towards a labour market? Government revenue as a proportion of GDP fell over the reform period (from 26 per cent in 1980 to 11 per cent in 1995, rising with fiscal reform to 15 per cent in 2000). The mini welfare state previously provided by the *danwei* to its members is more likely to be marketized piecemeal than to be generalized and publicly provided and subsidized from general revenues.

Several provinces have recently introduced means-tested social assistance— the 'minimum living level' programme—in response to rising unemployment and in anticipation of the phasing out of *xia gang* payments. This programme is normally only, or more generously, found in urban areas. In 2000, 4.0 million urban people were supported by the scheme but the Ministry of Labour and Social Security estimated that a further 10 million urban people were eligible for support but did not receive it (OECD 2002: 563). In that year 3.0 million rural people

(0.4 per cent of the rural population) benefited under the minimum living level programme, and relief funds reached 16.7 million rural people (PRC, NBS 2002: 806). In rural China the family is normally expected to be the principal provider of social protection for its members. Being wealthy, Zhejiang province has recently introduced a universal minimum living standard programme covering both urban and rural areas, but few other provinces will be able to afford universal welfare provision. China's model for social security is unlikely to be the Western welfare state. Its social protection system remains ill-prepared to deal with the creation of a labour market and the risks and inequalities that necessarily accompany it.

Turning from the objectives of the government to those of the employers, the future of the *danwei* will depend very much on changes in corporate governance. Most of the large and medium-sized SOEs are moving towards 51 per cent ownership, and thus continued control, by the state, although the central government may continue its policy of owning 100 per cent of the few hundred largest SOEs. The small SOEs have generally been pushed into the market, privatized, and expected to sink or swim. The *danwei* has some of the characteristics of an internal labour market. These characteristics were imposed, and are not necessarily the choice of employers. It is nevertheless possible that many firms—especially the larger ones—will choose to retain or adapt some internal labour market characteristics. This is more likely to happen if they are found to be functional for efficient training, retention, and motivation of employees—as in other economies, of which Japan is an extreme example. However, in addition the Chinese tradition of egalitarianism, patronage, and a sense of fairness within the work group may well live on.

Thirdly, consider urban workers. Except in the case of the minority who in recent years have been retrenched as a result of government policy, they have benefited from the many forms of 'urban bias' observable in the policies of the Communist Party and the state. This disproportionate weight in the government's objective function reflects the potential for causing social and political instability that residential concentration, greater awareness and articulateness, and latent capacity for organization confer on urban people. An important threat to urban workers is the labour market competition that unrestricted rural–urban migration could generate. It will be in the continuing interests of government to avoid policies on labour market competition which urban residents perceive as undermining their interests. Trade unions are not important to urban workers for as long as the real wages of the majority continue to rise rapidly—as they did in the 1990s—but official and unofficial trade unions could become a vehicle for expressing discontent if workers were in the future to feel threatened.

Is the labour market segmentation that we documented particularly in Chapters 4 and 7 likely to prove a transitional phenomenon? Consider first whether labour mobility can be expected to continue to rise. A reason for the lack of voluntary mobility has been the high private cost of changing jobs, associated with the social welfare services that have remained tied to the employer. Services provided by the *danwei*—such as housing, healthcare, and pensions—are in the process of being privatized or of being provided and funded separately from the employer.

This process is likely to facilitate voluntary labour mobility and thus to promote labour market competition.

Secondly, consider wage segmentation among firms. We saw that wage differences, based on profitability, increased over the period 1995–9. Insofar as wages continue to be linked to profits, the variability of wages is influenced by the variability of profits. The rapid structural change associated with economic transition to a market economy gives rise to supernormal and subnormal profits in different industries and firms. Profits will become more standardized as the pace of structural change slows down, as supernormal profits are competed away, as unprofitable industries contract, and as unprofitable firms are allowed to merge with profitable firms, wither or die. The state and urban collective sectors have been contracting rapidly in recent years, giving way to the privatization of existing enterprises and the establishment of new private enterprises. With the change in ownership comes a change in managerial incentives, which should erode the traditional custom and practice of the *danwei*. Provided that labour mobility is sufficient to generate market-determined wages, the current influence of profits on wages should wane.

Blecher (2002: 286–93) conducted interviews with Chinese workers and found them to be well aware that their wages depend on the economic health of their employer. Workers generally felt that this was unfair, but they tended to accept the unfairness as inevitable or to blame their enterprise managers rather than the system or the government. If profit-related wages do not generate resentment and discontent, this stumbling block on China's path to a functioning labour market is unlikely to have political consequences that would create pressures for remedying the phenomenon.

Thirdly, consider the three labour market tiers based on segmentation among workers. Retrenched workers have not enjoyed the substantial wage increases paid to non-retrenched workers. As in other countries, retrenchment in China marks the worker with a 'scar'. Although the scarring may be long-lasting—as has been proved elsewhere—some of the scars will no doubt heal and disappear as voluntary labour mobility increases, as re-employed workers and their jobs become better matched, and as new and relevant specific human capital is acquired. Similarly, the disadvantages experienced by the urban-based rural migrants may wither as institutional discrimination based on *hukou* status diminishes, and as migrants acquire more skills relevant to urban work. Moreover, the privileges enjoyed by non-retrenched urban workers can be expected to erode as product market competition stiffens and as the profit motive becomes more prevalent. The current three tiers may in these ways become closer to each other.

The analysis of Chapter 4 suggests that economic reform may have a once-for-all and finite effect on wage inequality. The late reforming provinces tended to catch up with the early reformers: The growth of wage inequality is limited by the processes that produced cross-province convergence in this inequality. Although the divergence in mean earnings and incomes may continue across provinces, further reform of the labour market—assisting labour mobility, and giving more rein to market forces in the slower reforming provinces—can slow it down and may eventually reverse it. Nevertheless, forces of cumulative causation appear to be at work in the Chinese economy—making some regions and provinces more prosperous and more profitable than others—and this may keep wage divergence going for some years yet.

In Chapter 9, we found that social capital is rewarded both in the administered labour system, where jobs were allocated and wages were institutionally determined, and in the market-oriented system that is emerging. The latter finding may reflect the underdeveloped state of that market, in which information is poor and transaction costs are high. The evidence is consistent with *guanxi* both providing access to rents and also reducing informational and transaction costs. Social networks appear to be more beneficial in the private sector than in the state or collective sectors. Since the private sector is the rapidly expanding sector, this suggests that *guanxi* will continue to play an important role in the urban labour market. That role is likely to diminish only when the market becomes less imperfect, so reducing the scope for workers to seek rents and increasing the importance of general, rather than specific, labour market information.

Consider the various forces that will determine the future of rural–urban migration in China. Its main determinant will be the rate and structure of economic growth in China but it will also be influenced by the incentives and behaviour of the three main players: The migrants themselves, the urban employers, and the government. Migrant employment will grow in quantity and quality if all three parties are in favour: Any one could hinder such a development. We examine migration from these distinct perspectives.

First, the migrants: The model underlying our description of the Chinese peasant labour allocation in Chapter 8 is a modified version of the probabilistic model of rural–urban migration. This posits a rural–urban income differential and rationed urban employment opportunities, and predicts open or disguised search unemployment. So far the process of rural–urban migration in China has been sufficiently orderly to avoid serious urban unemployment of migrants, owing partly to government controls and restrictions and partly to the relative lack of migrant networks for what is only a recent phenomenon. Nevertheless, the incentives to seek non-farm employment are powerful. They will increase if inequalities between rural and urban China, or within rural China, continue to grow.

There are two potential sources of non-farm work. In this book we have had little to say about local non-farm activities. Most of these involve employment in township, village and private enterprises, which grew by 12.1 per cent per annum from 30 million in 1980 to 94 million in 1990, and by 4.1 per cent per annum to 140 million in 2000 (PRC, SSB 1994: 85; PRC, NBS 2002: 117). Of crucial concern to a peasant household is whether the village, or the township, has developed industrial enterprises. This is a matter of having a good agricultural or natural resource base, a favourable location or transport facilities, funds for investment, and relevant business and technical skills, partly acquired through learning-by-doing. Mechanisms of cumulative causation can launch some villages into rapid local industrialization. Capital market imperfections and the favouring of village members then makes it possible for villages that are geographically close together to be economically far apart. Such processes give rise to unequal opportunities for local non-farm employment: In many villages people have little option but to migrate.

Rural industry grew much less rapidly in the 1990s than in the 1980s. As urban restrictions on non-state activity have been relaxed and as the reform or privatization of the SOEs has proceeded, so rural industry has faced tougher competition from the urban sector. This process is likely to continue. The predictable depressing effect of entry to the World Trade Organization on the land-intensive sectors of Chinese agriculture is also likely to spur migration. Since migration is a cumulative process, facilitated by networks, these pressures could in time even lead to great and potentially excessive movements of labour. The peasants should not constitute an impediment to rural–urban migration.

Second, consider the employers. Urban enterprises have a profit incentive to employ more migrants, and appear to be constrained in the number of migrants they recruit. This constraint is to a considerable extent the result of government interventions to protect urban workers, particularly in the light of the recent redundancy programme. However, the culture and motives of *danwei* managers may also serve to protect their *danwei* insiders against outsiders. Insofar as this is the case, then a strengthening of the profit motive would bring rural- and urban-*hukou* holders into closer labour market competition. The continuing reform or privatization of the SOEs, and increasing competition in the product market, could thus have this consequence.

Third, government at different levels—central, province, city, and county—has been the key player on migration. It has effectively implemented policies that severely restricted the permanent urban settlement of rural-*hukou* people and ensured preferential access to urban jobs for urban-*hukou* people. Other objectives have included organizing the 'orderly' movement of temporary migrant labour so as to avoid both too much and too little supply in relation to urban residual demand for labour; assisting potential migrants from poor areas, for instance through setting up local employment bureaux; and ensuring satisfactory conditions of service for migrants employed in urban areas. The degree of official control and influence in these matters is looser, reflecting the government's limited information, resources, leverage, and powers of enforcement. The decentralized nature of government, both among ministries and at different tiers within the Ministry of Labour and Social Security, means that there is a lack of coherence and cohesion in government policies on migration. Nevertheless, we can be confident that the government will not prevent the orderly flow of migrants into the towns and cities to meet the excess demand for labour that cannot be met by urban residents. It is therefore relevant to estimate how that excess demand will evolve.

Because China has had a surplus labour economy, it was helpful to adopt the theoretical framework of the Lewis model. The model proved to be appropriate for the period of central planning, except in one respect: Surplus labour, in the form of over-manning, was found in the urban as well as the rural sector. The model proved to be less appropriate for the period of economic reform. The growth of rural industry and the growing differentiation among urban workers did not fit the simple distinction between the rural, agricultural sector and the urban, industrial sector. Moreover, the rapid urban real wage growth was inconsistent with the predictions of the model. The evidence for claiming that urban wages rose in response to labour market forces is weak. Nevertheless, provided that the Chinese economy continues to grow rapidly, the prospects for China reaching the second, neoclassical, stage of the Lewis model are good and deserve examination.

Huang et al. (2002) analysed a survey of 1,200 households in six provinces to examine changes in economic activities over time. The proportion of the rural labour force engaged in at least some non-farm activities rose from 16 per cent in 1981 to 22 per cent in 1990, and to 41 per cent in 2000; the corresponding proportions for the migration component were 5, 7, and 20 per cent, respectively (their figure 2). Despite the retrenchment programme within the state sector, non-farm employment grew rapidly over the latter decade—particularly non-local employment, particularly for young people, and particularly for women. Of workers aged under 30 years, 29 per cent were engaged in some non-farm activities in 1990, but 65 per cent in 2000; the proportion of this group who worked outside their county of residence rose from 63 to 74 per cent between those years (their tables 2 and 3). The process had gone furthest in the most developed of the six surveyed provinces, Zhejiang. A projection of these trends into the future would suggest that the rural population will shift rapidly out of the agricultural sector and out of the rural areas.

Two variables enter into the equation for the urban demand for rural labour: The rate of growth of the urban-born labour force and the rate of growth of urban employment. Consider these in turn. We project the urban-born labour force over the period 1990–2010 using the *1990 Census of Population*.[2] We estimate the number of entries to and retirements from the labour force in each year from 1990 onwards. People are assumed to enter at age 16 and to retire at age 60. The urban age-specific mortality rates of 1989 are used to estimate deaths of 16–59 year-olds in each year, and the urban age-specific participation rates of 1990 are used to convert from population of working age to labour force.[3] The ensuing projections of the urban-born labour force are shown as *Urban-born supply* in Figure 10.1. The projections imply an average growth rate of only 0.8 per cent per annum over the period 1990–2010. This extremely low rate of natural increase primarily reflects the lagged consequences of the draconian one-child family policy, adopted in the late 1970s and applied particularly harshly to urban China. It had the effect of reducing urban-born entry to the labour force from the mid-1990s onwards.

We have data on urban employment for the period of urban economic reform, from 1985 up to 2001.[4] We project the growth trend of urban employment over that period (4.0 per cent per annum) onwards from 2001 to 2010, so generating the series labelled *Urban demand* in Figure 10.1. The growth of urban employment depends not only on the growth of the urban economy but also on the extent of labour shedding by urban enterprises if, as a result of reform, they eliminate

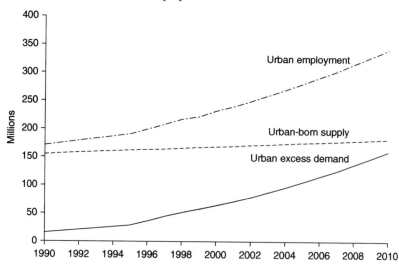

F I G. 10.1 *Urban labour demand and supply, 1990–2010*

their surplus labour. We know from the rise in official unemployment and in *xia gang* employment that there was much labour shedding by the state enterprises and the urban collective enterprises from the mid-1990s onwards (Chapter 6). Nevertheless, such was the pace of China's non-agricultural development that urban employment as a whole—including private sector and individual employment—continued to grow (by 3.7 per cent per annum) over the five years 1996–2001.

Although it is clear from Chapter 5 that urban and rural workers are not close substitutes, we assume that the increased demand for urban labour generally enables urban-*hukou* workers to move up the occupational ladder in order to fill vacancies, and rural-*hukou* workers to enter the less-skilled, residual jobs left vacant. The result of the projected faster growth of employment than of the urban-born labour force is growing excess demand for labour, representing potential demand for rural–urban migrants. This is shown by the curve *Urban excess demand* in the figure. Although the estimates of demand and supply are obtained from different sources, it is notable that the estimate of excess demand in 1995 (29 million) is double the recorded number of rural employees of urban work units, that is, in formal sector employment (14 million) in that year (PRC, MOL 1997: 39). In 1995, *Urban excess demand* is 15 per cent of urban employment, but by 2002 it is 31 per cent and in 2010 no less than 47 per cent. On the heroic assumption that something like the past rate of economic growth can be maintained, rural migrants are likely to become increasingly important in the urban economy.

These projections affect the prospects both for rural development and for registration of residence (*hukou*) policy. The rural population of China peaked at 859 million in 1995 and thereafter fell monotonically, by 1.3 per cent per annum, to 796 million in 2001. Rural employment was reportedly stagnant over that period, being 490 million in 1995 and 491 million in 2001 (PRC, NBS 2002: 93, 121). The source of the discrepancy in the two series is not clear, as the growing number of migrants should have reduced the recorded numbers of both people and workers. However, what is important for our purpose is that the numbers of rural residents and of rural workers, which had increased consistently up to 1995, did not grow beyond that year: Pressure on rural resources was no longer increasing. The second, neoclassical, stage of the Lewis model may well have been reached some years previously in large tracts of the rural areas of the most developed provinces, such as Zhejiang and Jiangsu; that stage may still be far off in the least developed or most over-populated provinces, such as Gansu or Sichuan. Nevertheless, it is a landmark that the pressure on rural resources in China taken as a whole has begun to decline and that the prospects for the continuation of this trend are good.

The future of *hukou* policy is tied up with the amount of rural–urban migration and the skills required of the migrants, as well as with the extent of privilege that urban-*hukou* status offers, the size of urban settlements to which migration occurs, and the objectives of the migrants. The *hukou* system has ceased to be an instrument of political control but it remains an instrument of economic privilege. Rural people are often able to settle in the towns and small cities, and to live even in large cities provided that they can find work and accommodation. However, they are at a serious disadvantage in securing access to urban employment, housing, and public services. By the end of 2000, only 540,000 people had applied for a *hukou* in towns and small cities (Brooks and Tao 2003: 20). An urban *hukou* possesses an economic value—highest in the major cities—because it provides access, or privileged or subsidized access, to such facilities as housing, schooling, and healthcare.

The impetus for ending the *hukou* system may come from the de facto urban settlement of rural people. If enterprise demand for migrants increases in the way we expect, it will necessitate adjustments by employers and government. In those dynamic parts of China where the growth of employment has far exceeded the growth of the urban-born population, migrants have moved up the ladder into more skilled jobs. We saw the beginnings of this process in our comparison of cities in Chapter 5: Migrants have become more important, and have more human capital and better opportunities, in the rapidly growing Shenzhen and Beijing than in the more traditional Wuhan and Suzhou.

Skill and its associated training bring the need for more permanent employment: Why should employers train migrants and provide them with the skills they need in their city jobs if they subsequently return to their villages? As migrant workers move up the job ladder, so the Chinese system of 'floating'—temporary migration—will become economically inefficient. The solution to this problem which employers around the world have adopted is to try to stabilize migrant labour by improving the rewards for staying, for example Knight and Sabot (1982). If employers have an incentive to reward long service, migrants have an incentive to acquire it. Long service encourages a worker to settle with his or her family in the city. However, some of the relatively unskilled may continue to float, especially if short contracts are seen to give employers more flexibility over employment levels and rural households more security through the spreading of risks across economic activities.

In summary, the economic imperative will be to allow more and more migrants to settle with their families and to become urbanized. Living long in the city encourages the adoption of urban attitudes, and the transfer of the migrant's social reference group from the village to the city. This process may well give rise to feelings of relative deprivation in relation to urban-*hukou* residents. As more and more former peasants make the transition from migrant to proletarian, so the pressures on government to treat them on par with urban-born residents is likely to grow, and *hukou* privilege accordingly to be eroded.

10.5 OUR VISION

Our approach in this chapter has so far been analytical and positive. We end on an evaluative and normative note. Our vision is of China with a functioning labour market, more competitive in many respects than it is at present. Such a labour market will provide socially efficient incentives for the allocation, use and improvement of labour. It will contain a job search service which ensures that workers are well-informed. It will permit and encourage the mobility of workers from low-income to high-income activities, at no greater cost than the social cost of such movement and in cognizance of the public good element of mobility, that is, the externalities involved in creating efficient market signals. It will reward education and vocational skills sufficiently highly as fully to reflect the social returns on human capital accumulation. It will eliminate wage differences among workers that cannot be justified by differences in individual productivity. It will not contain a discriminatory *hukou* system, and will make no distinction between workers simply on the basis of whether they were born in an urban or a rural place.

All this implies the creation of a functioning labour market. Yet at the same time there will be an effective social safety net: The labour market will be qualified, and competition within it will be tempered, by a form of social contract of the sort that has evolved in most Western democracies. We have in mind the retention and development of redistributive mechanisms which—without their having to resort to protest and threat—will ensure that the people who lose from the arrival of the competitive labour market receive fair and equitable treatment.

If and when our vision becomes a reality, this book will be an economic history. It will nevertheless be an economic history of a remarkable and fascinating process. That is the transformation of a socialist labour system into a functioning labour market in a poor country undergoing rapid economic development, with powerful implications for the lives, livelihoods and living standards of a fifth of humanity.

NOTES

1. We take the term from the title of Riskin et al. (2001).
2. PRC, SSB (1993: Vol. 2, 20–4, 282–90, Vol. 4, 32–55), provides detailed information for both cities and towns on population by age, on age-specific mortality rates, and on age-specific labour force participation.
3. We make the plausible assumption here that involuntary unemployment among urban residents was then very low: The non-participants were in education (many urban children continue beyond 15), in retirement (women normally retire at 55), housewives, etc.
4. The data are based on reports by enterprises (although they include registered self-employed workers). It can be inferred from the notes to the tables that migrant workers are included.

REFERENCES

Blecher, Mark J. (2002). 'Hegemony and workers' politics in China', *The China Quarterly*, 170 (June): 283–303.

Brooks, Ray and Ran Tao (2003). 'China's labor market performance and challenges', IMF Working Paper WP/03/210, Washington DC: IMF.

Cai, Fang (2003). 'Reform of labour policy in China: a perspective of political economy', *China and World Economy*, 11, 4: 30–7.

Huang, Jikun, Scott Rozelle, Linxiu Zhang, and Yigang Zhang (2002). 'The evolution of China's rural labor markets during the reforms', *Journal of Comparative Economics*, 30: 329–53.

Knight, J.B and R.H Sabot (1982). 'From migrants to proletarians: employment experience, mobility and wages in Tanzania', *Oxford Bulletin of Economics and Statistics*, 44, 3: 199–226.

Knight, John and Lina Song (1999). *The Rural–Urban Divide. Economic Disparities and Interactions in China*, Oxford: Oxford University Press.

Li, Shantong, Yunzhong Liu, and Bo Chen (2003). 'Research on measures—objects and degrees of local protection in the Chinese domestic market. An analysis based on a sample survey', paper presented at the Conference on the Efficiency of China's Economic Policy, IDREC, Clermont-Ferrand, France, October.

People's Republic of China, Ministry of Labour (PRC, MOL) (1997). *China Labour Statistical Yearbook 1997*, Beijing: China Statistical Publishing House.

People's Republic of China, National Bureau of Statistics (PRC, NBS) (2002). *China Statistical Yearbook 2002*, Beijing: China Statistics Press.

People's Republic of China, State Statistical Bureau (PRC, SSB) (1993). *Tabulation of the 1990 Population Census of the People's Republic of China*, 4 volumes, Beijing: China Statistical Publishing House.

—— (PRC, SSB) (1994). *Statistical Yearbook of China 1994*, Beijing: China Statistical Publishing House.

Riskin, Carl, Renwei Zhao, and Shi Li (eds) (2001). *China's Retreat from Equality. Income Distribution and Economic Transition*, Armonk, NY: M.E. Sharpe.

Walder, Andrew (1987). 'Wage reform and the web of factory interests', *China Quarterly*, 109: 21–41.

Index of Subjects

Index of Names